»» Peacocks,

«» Chameleons,

»« Centaurs

»» Peacocks,
«» Chameleons,
»« Centaurs

Gay Suburbia and the
Grammar of Social Identity

Wayne Brekhus

The University of Chicago Press
Chicago and London

The University of Chicago Press, Chicago 60637
The University of Chicago Press, Ltd., London
© 2003 by The University of Chicago
All rights reserved. Published 2003
Printed in the United States of America

16 15 14 13 12 11 10 09 08 07   2 3 4 5 6

ISBN-13: 978-0-226-07291-3 (cloth)
ISBN-13: 978-0-226-07292-0 (paper)
ISBN-10: 0-226-07291-6 (cloth)
ISBN-10: 0-226-07292-4 (paper)

Library of Congress Cataloging-in-Publication Data

Brekhus, Wayne.
    Peacocks, chameleons, centaurs : gay suburbia and the grammar of social
identity / Wayne Brekhus.
        p. cm.
Based on the author's Ph.D. thesis, Rutgers University.
    ISBN 0-226-07291-6 (cloth : alk. paper) — ISBN 0-226-07292-4 (pbk.)
    1. Gay men—New York Suburban Area—Case studies.   2. Gay men—
Identity—Case studies.   3. Group identity—New York Suburban Area—
Case studies.   4. Suburban life—New York Suburban Area—Case studies.
5. Lifestyles—New York Suburban Area—Case studies.   I. Title: Gay
suburbia and the grammar of social identity.   II. Title.
    HQ76.2.N4852 N493 2003
    305.38'9664'09747—dc21

                                                          2003001356

Contents

Acknowledgments

I am indebted to a number of people who helped make this book possible. My first debt is to the generous men who entertained my questions in public space, welcomed me into their homes, and gave willingly of their time. While I cannot mention them by name, I owe all of them a great debt of gratitude. I owe a special thanks to "Jerry," my first key informant, who provided a wealth of interesting conversation and who enthusiastically introduced me to other gay men in the suburbs. Elaine, my hair stylist, took an active interest in my project, suggested new avenues for finding suburban gay men, and introduced me to several of her clients. Nitsat Hadas tirelessly transcribed several of my interviews.

A Rutgers University dissertation completion fellowship from the graduate school provided financial support during part of the writing of this project. At Rutgers I benefited from conversations about my ideas or comments on portions of my writing from Karen Cerulo, Lee Clarke, Ira Cohen, Sharon Cook, Karen Danielsen, Leslie Fishbein, Roberto Franzosi, Shawna Hudson, Robert Lang, Justin Levinson, John Martin, Jamie Mullaney, Richard Phillips, Kristen Purcell, and Richard Williams. Judith Gerson and John Gagnon served on my dissertation committee and provided very helpful comments that aided the writing of this book. I am especially grateful to my mentors Cathy Greenblat and Eviatar Zerubavel. Both of them encouraged me to aim high, take intellectual risks, and follow my passion. Cathy turned me on to ethnography and to the thrill of studying social life as a participant as well as an observer. She encouraged me to talk to gay men in my own community, to overcome shyness, to constantly step outside my comfort zone to make new friends. Her inspiration, support, advice, and friendship have been invaluable. Eviatar inspired my passion for doing theory and for dreaming big. Several years ago, when this project was in its infancy, he encouraged me to envision it as a future University of Chicago book. Eviatar has been a first-rate intellectual guide and friend.

I was fortunate to be the recipient of a doctoral fellowship from the Sexuality Research Fellowship Program sponsored by the Social Science Research Council, with funds provided by the Ford Foundation during the research phase of this project. The Sexuality Research Fellowship Program not only provided financial resources but connected me to a network of exciting and interesting scholars. The conversations I had with fellow SRFP fellows Sharon Abbott, Elizabeth Armstrong, the late Lionel Cantu, Pat Pugliani, and David Valentine were helpful in advancing my thinking.

At national conferences I have benefited from presenting my research and talking with a number of scholars. Dan Chambliss, Murray Davis, Mary Rogers, and Dan Ryan have all provided good conversation and helpful advice.

My colleagues and friends at the University of Missouri have provided an excellent supportive environment and intellectual climate in which to write this book. I have benefited from astute observations by my sociological theory undergraduate students and social control graduate students in class discussions on parts of the manuscript. John Galliher read an entire draft in its late stages and provided helpful comments. Ian Watson and Natalie Feibish helped me translate my concepts into graphic form for the in-text diagrams. Several years ago I met with Doug Mitchell for the first time to discuss my book idea. He has been the source of stimulating conversation and helpful advice ever since. Elizabeth Armstrong, Christena Nippert-Eng, and an anonymous reviewer gave me extraordinarily detailed feedback on my manuscript and offered a number of excellent suggestions. Michael Koplow, my copyeditor, provided helpful advice on both style and substance when my manuscript was in its final stages.

Finally, I thank my brother Keith and my wife Rachel. Keith helped with the bibliography and locating stray sources despite a hectic schedule running for political office. Rachel read and edited countless drafts and helped track down examples of peacocks, chameleons, and centaurs in a variety of identity contexts. Her intellectual advice and moral support have been tremendous every step of the way.

»1«

Gay Suburbanites

A Case Study in the Grammar and Microecology of Social Identity

I hate the stereotypical flaming fag image because then people who I come out to say, "How could you be gay? You're not like them." I get so sick of that. No, I do not wear a dress. No, I don't like RuPaul. The last time I came out to a really conservative friend it took me an hour to convince him I was gay! "No, I really am gay." And then once I did convince him, he went through the whole thing again: "But you don't do this and you don't look like this." God, I'm so sick of that. I totally blame the media for that. I'm sick of them. I want them to make just an Average Joe Gay Guy Show, but they won't do it because it's not interesting.

Mark[1] (a suburban gay man)

Mark defines himself as an Average Joe Gay Guy. From his point of view, "Average Joe" describes him just as much as "gay man." His frustration with both his conservative friend and the media results from their assumptions that "gay people" or "gays" necessarily have a set of easily identifiable auxiliary characteristics that emanate from their being "gay." (*Auxiliary characteristics* are the expected characteristics that go along with a status role.) Mark objects to his gay identity being treated as a

---

1. All interview informants are identified with pseudonyms.

master status that shapes everything else about how he acts and lives his life, since he believes that other facets of his life are equally relevant to who he is. (See Hughes [1945] for further discussion of auxiliary characteristics and master status.) He is frustrated that others assume they know *everything* about him if they know he is gay. In an interesting reversal to the "closeted gay," who tries to pull off a convincing performance that he is not gay, Mark's problem was that he could not immediately make a convincing case that he was gay. Mark is in most ways typical of the men I met during the course of my research among gay male suburbanites. He is white, male, middle-class, socially and politically moderate, and in his twenties. All of these facets are important to his self-identity, and he rejects the idea that his many socially ordinary attributes make him any less authentically gay than the more visible urban gays that he refers to unfavorably as "gay subculture–oriented gays." Moreover, like almost all of the men I talked to, Mark used New York's visible gay subculture as a reference point to define himself against. In the typical view of my suburban informants[2] New York was extraordinary and so were its gays, and suburban Northgate, New Jersey,[3] was ordinary and so were its gay men. Whether suburban gay men gravitated to New York or avoided it, it served as an important referent point to what the "other gay America"—the one that is highly publicized in the media and the popular culture—was like.

When I started my ethnographic research, I expected to tell a primarily descriptive story about people like Mark, who experience gay life in the suburbs rather than the city. From 1992 to 1998 I interviewed, hung out with, and interacted with a number of gay men in a suburban community located about one hour away from New York City (for more on methods, see the appendix). Since most studies of gay life and most popular images of

---

2. Ethnographers refer to the people whom they interview and hang out with as "informants" because they provide insider knowledge on their subculture.
3. "Northgate" is the pseudonym for the suburban area where this study took place.

gay culture come from the "gay ghettos" of large urban centers, I was interested in seeing how gay life in the suburbs might be different. It did differ, at least from the most visible facets of urban gay communities, in significant ways. Most gay life in the suburbs was mundane, uneventful, and at times indistinguishable from more general suburban living. One could see gay men mowing lawns, holding barbecues, attending church, driving their cars or SUVs to work early in the morning, coming home to their partners after work, supporting Republicans nearly as often as Democrats, watching baseball and football, and doing a host of other things that strike one as closer to public perceptions of what it means to be "suburban" than what it means to be "gay."

The ordinariness of their lives was not lost on the men I talked to, many of whom considered it odd that I wanted to study gay life in the suburbs when the more interesting setting of New York City was so close at hand. As one informant said with a laugh, "You're going to have a one-page thesis! There isn't anything to write about!" Expressing a sentiment shared by several other informants, he added, "You should go to New York City instead, then you'll have something to write about." For him, there was nothing especially definitively gay about the suburbs and thus nothing "interesting" for me to write about. In a similar story with an academic twist, a colleague of mine who proposed studying lesbian life in the Midwest had her funding proposal rejected by one reviewer who argued that the Midwest wasn't a good location for studying homosexuality; the reviewer suggested my colleague study lesbians on one of the coasts instead. Implicit in the reviewer's suggestion was the idea that the lives of Midwestern lesbians would be less interesting than those of coastal lesbians and even that Midwestern gay life was somehow less authentically gay. But the assumption that mundane, ordinary suburban gay men or Midwestern lesbians are somehow less authentically gay than visible urban coastal gays and lesbians is problematic.

By itself, the ordinariness of gay suburban living would have made an interesting enough story, but as I continued to spend time with these men an intriguing theory began to emerge along with the empirical story. I noticed that different "types" of gay men had conflicting ideas about how to organize their "gayness" in relation to their overall "presentation of self"[4] and that this conflict seemed to have important implications for a more general theory of social identity. For some informants, being gay was a more important and salient facet of their lives than being suburban, while for others being suburban seemed to play a bigger role in their overall cultural tastes, politics, worldview, and lifestyle than being gay. I became especially aware of the role a *suburban identity* might play in their lives upon reading Baumgartner's (1988:1) ethnography of conflict management in a New Jersey suburb; I found that the initial comments of her suburban informants (who were not gay) sounded oddly familiar. They, too, suggested to their interlocutor that she shouldn't study the suburbs because "nothing ever happens" and it's "a boring place to look at conflict." Like my gay suburban informants, her nongay suburban informants also suggested that she should go to the city, as she "could find some good conflicts there." What I had initially assumed to be only a gay suburban reaction to studying gay life in the suburbs now appeared to be a more general suburban reaction toward selecting their communities for study when there were far more "interesting" things to study in the cities.

In one sense my informants' suggestions that New York would be more interesting were correct; the gay cultural milieu of New York's Greenwich Village provides an esoteric, colorful setting with a rich and inspiring cultural history. Gay men are visible, proud, and socially active in what is clearly one of the great centers of gay culture. But however interesting Village gay life is culturally, politically, and empirically, suburban gay life actually may have more to offer theoretically and analytically. By looking at gay men in the more socially mundane environment of suburbia rather than the gay-friendly enclaves of New York one can wit-

4. Goffman (1959) uses the phrase "presentation of self" to describe the ways social actors present an impression and an identity to others.

ness the multiple ways in which individuals manage a "marked" identity attribute like gayness in a culturally "unmarked" identity space like the suburbs. Gay suburbanites are an interesting case not only because they must manage a potentially stigmatizing gay identity but because they also balance it with a privileging suburban identity. As gay suburbanites have competing membership claims to both stigmatized gayness and privileging suburbanness, their identity strategies illustrate how one balances competing positions of stigma and privilege. Since most individuals have a combination of devalued and valued attributes with regard to the larger society, this has important implications beyond gay identity for how all individuals organize and balance competing ingredients of the self.

Despite the analytic advantages of studying the organization of the extraordinary where the ordinary is privileged, many studies of minority identities go to the spaces where the extraordinary is facilitated rather than negatively sanctioned, discouraged, or even oppressed. This is an analytic mistake because studying the most open environments selects against more covert and nuanced strategies of dealing with minority or extraordinary identities. Giving our theoretical attention to gay activists, leathermen, and drag queens in the city, for instance, misses the analytic importance of rank-and-file gays who may have the most to offer to our understanding of how identity is organized by the social averages rather than the social extremes (or outliers) in everyday social life. While it is certainly valid to study the most visible and dramatic tip of the iceberg, researchers should not ignore the rest of the iceberg just because it is less obvious and appears less dramatic when observed from the surface (see Brekhus, 2000).

Expressive, difference-tolerant spaces such as the gay ghettos of San Francisco and New York are very specialized places that tell us little about how identity is organized in the mundane, difference-submerging spaces where most people live. In gay ghettos (see Levine, 1979), as in other ghettos or enclaves, the everyday, the leisure, the political, and the work worlds are heavily concentrated in such a way that it is difficult to separate them out spatially and temporally, as one must if one is trying to measure changes of identity across different domains of social and cultural space. Since many identity strategies make use of spatial boundaries and separations, such ghettos provide an analytically truncated site from which to look at one of the most important facets of social identity: how people incorporate spatial and temporal variables into their socially constructed identity. Most studies of gay life choose the most visibly gay environments such as gay neighborhoods, pride parades, and bars,[5] and thus systematically exclude from their analysis instances where individuals, perhaps even the very same individuals, are highlighting a side of themselves other than "gayness" or playing up the *un*marked facets of their self (such as being middle-class, suburban, masculine, or white). The suburbs, by contrast, with their spread-out spaces and their often rigidly segregated commercial and residential areas, provide an ideal site from which to observe identity changes across social space. Moreover, with their location between urban centers and rural areas, they provide a view into the middle rather than the ends of the urban/rural continuum. Finally, they provide an ideal site from which to observe individuals playing up their "averageness" and their unmarkedness rather than highlighting their most distinctive facets of self. The suburbs of New York City proved an especially instructive research site because some individuals used New York regularly as an environment to travel to in order to play out a dramatic part-time "satellite self," while others deliberately avoided the city and even defined much of their identity and worldview against what they saw as the excesses of the big city.

As a sociological theorist I have found it disappointing that mainstream social theory has often seemed to ghettoize queer theory, feminist theory, and multicultural theory into special enclaves of knowledge about specific groups rather than more

---

5. See, e.g., Levine (1979, 1998) on gay ghettos, Herrell (1992) on pride parades, and Weightman (1980) on gay bars.

broadly integral to general theory development. In much the same way as people often see gay life as belonging to the specialized spaces of New York and San Francisco, we too often see the study of gay life as belonging to the identity-specific analytic spaces of queer theory and gay studies. Yet just as the majority of gay men are integrated into the mundane fabric of ordinary social space and everyday life, it is high time that studies of gay life also be integrated into the routine non-group-specific dimensions of general social theory.[6] This book provides a general theory of social identity based on my ethnographic fieldwork in a suburban gay community. I use the fieldwork to build a theory; I then employ a variety of secondary data from a broad range of sources to expand the scope of the theory to all arenas of social identity. In doing so I make the claim that gay life is not analytically unique and that the conclusions of this book apply to all social actors.

Theory-Based Ethnography:
A Note on the Use of Ideal Types and Analytic Highlight Reels

The reader should be aware up front that my use of ethnographic data emphasizes highlighting theoretical possibilities and developing a broad general theoretical framework for analyzing social identity. The ethnographic approach I use borrows more from the tradition of Erving Goffman than from that of Elliot Liebow. Thus, it differs from the more standard "thick description" approach employed by many anthropologists and sociologists. In thick description the emphasis is on describing a community in full detail and on interpreting subcultural meanings only within the context of the local subculture from which the quotes or actions came (see Geertz, 1973); this approach tends to be descriptively detailed but at the cost of theoretical richness and analytic generalizability. My approach, by contrast, limits ethnographic thickness

---

6. See Brekhus (1998) on the importance of making generic observations from the marked.

for the purposes of developing analytic richness, conceptual clarity, and theoretical generalizability. This is reflected in the way I present the ethnographic data. In contrast to the traditional ethnographic practice of carefully describing in naturalistic detail all relationships among the individuals in a study, I have chosen to present "analytic highlight reels" rather than full "play-by-play commentary" on the social lives and interactions of my informants. I have also chosen to leave out biographical details except in cases where they are directly relevant to the concepts they illuminate. This both maintains my emphasis on conceptual patterns that illuminate the general features of social identity grammar rather than on individual personalities and protects the anonymity of my informants.[7]

Key to my "analytic highlight reels" approach is the use of *ideal types* (Weber, [1925] 1978) to construct a general typology of identity management strategies and to clarify the relationship among different identity strategies. Ideal types are examples that reflect a category in its most pure, prototypical, and analytically sharp form for the purposes of heuristic and conceptual clarity.

In studying leadership, Max Weber developed the ideal types of "traditional," "charismatic," and "legal-rational" authority to show the different ways in which authority can be manifested. While no individuals fit any of Weber's categories in their ideal form, the categories are useful for understanding the basic components of authority in society.[8] In a similar vein, I provide examples from my informants' quotes that best represent when people treat an identity attribute more like a "noun," a "verb," or an "adjective" to show the different ways in which identity can be

---

7. It should be noted that a small number of informants wanted their real names to appear in print without pseudonyms. Honoring their requests, however, would have jeopardized the anonymity of some of their close acquaintances who wanted their identity protected.

8. Flanagan (2002:148) refers to ideal types as "useful fictions" to point out that the term is neither meant to convey a value judgment (such as ideal = good) nor meant to convey reality exactly as it is.

managed and organized. Although real life individuals do not always fit cleanly and rigidly into a single category of the typology, the categories I developed came from noticeable patterns in the behavior and the quotes of gay men, and these categories represent three distinct forms that help to conceptually illustrate the ways in which individuals organize an identity. I use these ideal types to formulate an array of concepts useful to the general study of identity in the social sciences and humanities. Just as Erving Goffman used his ethnographic study of Shetland Islanders (1959) to develop a general theory of social interaction rather than a Shetlander theory of social interaction, I have chosen to develop a general theory rather than a gay suburban male–specific theory of social identity.

The Empirical Case: Gay Identity in a Northeast Suburb

Although the main story driving this book is theoretical, I believe that the empirical story I have provided will still be of interest to readers who are interested in gay identity and gay male life in the suburbs. While some ethnographic detail was sacrificed, there is still a compelling empirical story that runs with the analytic story. In short, the reader will be able to follow along with two main branches of gay life in suburbia. On one branch are *gay commuters*, who work ordinary jobs and who live otherwise conventional suburban lives but who use the personal privacy of the suburbs to pursue segmented gay social and sexual lives apart from their "ordinary suburban selves." On the other branch are *gay integrators*, who combine regular jobs, suburban homes, and gay social and sexual activities into one comfortable hyphenated suburban-gay self that is neither discretely suburban nor uniquely gay. Both of these branches I contrast with *gay lifestylers*, who represent the vibrant and expressive core of New York's gay subculture. These gay lifestylers often served as the reference point and negative role model against which suburban gay men defined themselves.

The setting of the ethnographic study in Northgate, a medium-

sized (population between forty and fifty thousand) outer suburb, and several surrounding suburbs approximately an hour
from New York City provides a location between the urban and
rural geographic extremes. Between the two ends of the continuum we are likely to see a range of identity management strategies that may not be captured well at the urban and rural poles.
In the gay subcultures of New York and San Francisco strategies
that minimize one's gay visibility or that adapt to a dominantly
heterosexual society are underrepresented because of the gay-
friendly nature of the space that gay people have worked so hard
to carve out of the larger city. Similarly, in the most rural areas
some strategies may be difficult to find because the space is too
restrictive of individual agency in identity management for such
strategies. The suburbs provide an analytic window between the
most polar strategies of living openly as an enclave minority and
living invisibly as an oppressed and silent minority.[9]

Northgate possessed a few moderately visible sources of gay
life but no residential or commercial concentrations of gay men.
There was a gay bar in a neighboring suburb, a college campus
nearby, and a few scattered, small gay social organizations, but
most of the suburban lives of most gay men were conducted in
private homes and in predominantly heterosexual public space.
The proximity to a college campus and relative closeness to New
York meant that some predominantly heterosexual space was gay
friendly as well as generally friendly to diversity. Gay men who
did not care for the gay bar often interacted in these mixed spaces
such as coffee shops, theaters, and non–gay specific restaurants
and clubs. While the gay bar played an important community role
for many of the area's gay men, especially single men in the 21–
30 age range, and the campus provided connections for college
students, many gay social networks were established by informal
friendship networks without a clear public center. Some of the

---

9. This is not to suggest that all urban gays are openly visible members of a
gay enclave or that all rural gays are closeted and silent, only that these strategies tend to be more dominant and less contested in such areas.

gay men I met never attended gay bars or meetings of gay organizations. Others spent their publicly gay social lives entirely in the city and thus had no connection to the small number of gay institutions in their own suburbs. They used New York as a travel destination to manifest a gay identity that they kept submerged beneath an ensemble of suburbanness when outside of the city.

These gay men in the suburbs not only complicate our understanding of gay identity but illuminate challenges and modifications to the broader general concept of minority and marked identities as master statuses. Portrayers of marked and minority populations have often gone to concentrated urban subcultures and have thus captured those members of the community most likely to live their marked identity as a master status. In doing so they may have missed the strategies of category members who do not organize their lifestyle around that attribute. Master status is an important and well-established sociological concept, but treating a marked attribute as a master status may not be the only or even the main organizing principle for such an attribute as gayness. Contrary to the public perception of a unitary, easily identifiable, and coherent way to be gay (or to be any other identity), there are multiple ways to present and organize a marked identity. Moreover there is considerable conflict within identity categories about how to perform one's identity.

One thing the empirical case will show in later chapters, and that I will develop in conjunction with the theoretical argument, is that the assumption that visible urban gays are necessarily more representative of what it means to be gay than suburban ones, rather than just gay in a different way, is problematic. We as a culture in general, as well as social researchers in particular, have come to accept too readily that gay is necessarily a master status and that all gay individuals experience their gay identity as such. We have generally come to accept gay identity as something that can be measured from less to more and from closeted to out. In this model, one is more authentically gay if he is out, highly visible, and shares the many auxiliary characteristics expected to derive from a gay sexual identity. And one is "less authentically gay" or even a "self-denying gay" if he is closeted, invisible, or shows few auxiliary characteristics associated with gayness. The closeted-to-out and the less gay–to–more gay continua obscure the diverse ways in which gay identity is managed.

To be sure, some gay men do in fact carve out specialized enclaves to live their identity visibly and openly as a master status all of the time. They accept society's imposition of a master identity, but they invert its negative value into a positive value that entails pride and produces supportive and sustaining social networks. Like peacocks, they display their master colors with pride, making them available for all to see. Other men move in and out of gayness as a momentary master status and experience it as their primary status only in specifically gay environments. Elsewhere they effectively mask this identity and promote alternative selves that others may accept as their only or primary self. Like chameleons, they wear different master colors to match the varying social environments in which they move. Still others keep the power of their socially imposed master status in check by allowing multiple attributes to share control of the self. Like centaurs, they combine more than one attribute into a composite self that has no single master role. These same strategies extend beyond gay life to other areas of identity. It is these strategies employed by the identity peacock, the identity chameleon, and the identity centaur that I will examine first in the context of gay identity (chapters 2–6) and then in the context of general social identity (chapters 7–11). Before applying my analytic lens to the data it is necessary to introduce the orienting concepts of marked and unmarked identity attributes, to clarify my approach to identity, and to discuss what I mean by the grammar and microecology of social identity.

Orienting Concepts: Marked and Unmarked Identity Attributes

When I told people that I was writing a book on the sociology of identity, using suburban gays as a case study, I was often asked if I am gay. No one ever asked, however, if I was suburban. Yet, if matching the social location or standpoint of my informants is an issue, both questions should have been relevant. In theory, gay suburbanites are just as much members of the category "suburban" as they are of the category "gay." It is a *social logic* and not a *natural logic* that allows people to see "gay" as necessarily a central feature of one's standpoint while ignoring "suburban" as though it were irrelevant. This discrepancy between the attention paid to my relationship to a gay identity and my relationship to a suburban identity underlies an important distinction between socially marked and socially unmarked identity attributes.

All individuals possess a combination of identity attributes that define who they are. Some attributes are socially salient and perceived as highly relevant, while others are socially taken-for-granted, treated as generic and typically ignored as relevant to who one is. In the contemporary United States gay is a salient identity attribute while suburban is not.[10] To refine the kind of salience I am referring to, I borrow the terms "marked" and "unmarked" from their original use in linguistics (see Trubetzkoy, 1975:162). In the orthographic representation of phonetic contrasts one item of a pair of values may be given a written mark such as an accent or cedilla while the other is passively defined by the absence of a mark. The linguistic contrast between the marked and the unmarked parallels visual psychology's distinction between figure and ground. Gestalt psychologists have demonstrated that we focus on the figure of visual contrasts without actively perceiving its background (see Koffka, 1935:184–86; Kohler, 1947:202–3). The same principles are also useful in analyzing the ways people perceive identity distinctions. Just as we visually highlight some physical contours and ignore others, we socially and psychologically foreground some identity attributes

---

10. There are exceptions such as political pollsters, marketers, and urban sociologists who do recognize suburbanness as an important facet of self and see regional variables as no less important than the more widely regarded variables of race, class, gender, and sexual orientation.

while ignoring others. The marked represents attributes that are actively defined as *socially specialized,* while the unmarked represents the vast expanse of social attributes that are passively defined as unremarkable, average, and *socially generic* (Brekhus, 1998:35; 1996:502).

The basic properties of markedness can be translated from linguistics to identity as follows: (1) the marked is accented and socially highlighted (and often stigmatized) while the unmarked remains unarticulated and taken for granted; (2) the marked is treated as a *specialized* subset of the larger set while the unmarked is treated as a *generic* representative of the set; and (3) distinctions within the marked are neutralized making it appear more homogeneous, while distinctions among the unmarked are accented, thus reflecting heterogeneity (see also Brekhus, 1996:508, 1998:36; Greenberg, 1966:26–27; Waugh, 1982). Key to the marking process is a fundamental asymmetry between the ways in which social actors regard marked and unmarked items as "generalizable attributes" (see Brekhus, 1996:519). A marked item or trait is perceived as conveying more information than an unmarked one. Thus socially marked identities such as "gay," "woman," "black," and "immigrant" receive far more attention as coherent social categories than unmarked identities such as "heterosexual," "man," "white," and "native." For instance, the generalization that homosexuals are promiscuous receives currency in the popular culture because noteworthy individual homosexuals are often seen as representative of all homosexuals as a category. Few would generalize, however, that heterosexuals are prone to divorce and are inclined toward prostitution, since they would treat such things as characteristic of only some noteworthy heterosexuals and not characteristic of heterosexuals as a category. Heterosexuals, unlike homosexuals, are regarded as too heterogeneous to merit category-wide generalizations.

There is also an asymmetry in the way people present their marked and unmarked attributes. Since an unmarked identity is the *default assumption,* absent any clear signifiers of a marked status, one often does not have to actively do anything to be perceived as a member of the unmarked category. Most heterosexuals, for instance, need not exert any effort to get others to assume they are heterosexual. Similarly, most natives of a country need not highlight that they are natives to be treated as such. Their identity will be assumed and taken for granted and they will not need to consciously perform their identity. In fact, people who play up unmarked attributes such as heterosexuality or native status are sometimes regarded with suspicion, as though they are overcompensating for some insecurity with their identity or hiding a secret identity (one may ask, Why is he trying so hard to demonstrate what most people take for granted? What is he hiding?).

I should note, of course, that there are contexts where a culture's general marking patterns are reversed. Reversals of markedness occur where the dominant cultural patterns of markedness are inverted within a given subculture (see Waugh, 1982:310; Brekhus, 1998:37). For example, whereas the default human is usually assumed to be male, among nurses it is men who are marked and women who are the default assumption. Similarly, in a gay bar, homosexuality becomes the default value and heterosexuality is marked.

These reversals of markedness are important to keep in mind when one looks at the ecology of identity. Since some social spaces and time periods offer alternative default settings, many individuals alter their identity presentations across time and space. It is this contextual nature of default identities that makes suburban gays an interesting case study. Given that suburban unmarked space encourages very different presentations than the group-specific environments of gay ghettos, how do gay men in the suburbs manage their identities? Do they play up a gay self at all times, even when it amounts to high-risk activism?[11] Do they

---

11. See McAdam (1986) for development of the term "high-risk activism." See Taylor and Raeburn (1995) for its expansion to the context of identity and identity politics and for its application to gay and lesbian identities.

live a double life, presenting a straight self in the suburbs and traveling to gay ghettos to present a gay self? Or do they present a self with a dash of gayness, but many other bland elements that wash out some of the gay flavor? What combination of these factors do they use? And how do these factors relate to stigma and privilege? How do these same principles apply to identity in other contexts? These are some of the questions that this book explores.

Identity Settings: The Microecology of Identity

Claude Fischer (1975) suggests that urbanism is a causal variable with independent social effects just like class, race, gender, and other more commonly used variables. Despite Fischer's claim, the effects of place have not played as prominently in identity theories as those variables that can be directly attached to physical bodies. Even though much sociological writing discusses identity as socially constructed and context dependent, there is still a tendency to look at identity as something that is relatively static in individuals, rather than as something that varies depending on the specific social settings in which individuals are located.

Moreover, characteristics of place have often been conflated with the personal qualities of individuals residing in the places (Knopp, 1992:652; Forest, 1995:134). When place does figure in, it is often presupposed that individuals influence the identity of places, rather than places shaping the identity of individuals. For instance, within geographies of sexuality most work has concerned the effects gays have had on particular ghettoized and recreational spaces (Forest, 1995:137). Such work implicitly assumes a static, constant, and unproblematic quality to the identity of individuals. The underlying assumption is that gay individuals make a space more gay, but not necessarily that gay spaces might also make the individual more gay. This notion misses the importance of varying concentrations and saliencies of identity within an individual depending on his or her environmental setting. Individuals may shift their overall concentration of a marked identity trait (such as "gayness") to match their environmental surroundings. That is, *who* one is depends, in part, on *where* one is and *when* one is. Identity resides not in the individual alone, but in the interaction between the individual and his or her social environment.

Sites and times are *identity settings* for how to feel, how to act, and even for who to "be." Individuals have a package of multiple identity characteristics and they may foreground different parts of that package depending on the site or time in which they are situated. They may engage in microtemporal shifts of identity from one setting to the next, playing up different facets of their self to match different temporal and spatial contexts. I refer to this identity variability across time and space as *the microecology of identity*.

Spatial and temporal settings elicit independent effects on human behavior. Context has the power to drive conduct. Barker and Wright ([1955] 1971:7–8) demonstrate, for instance, that there are "behavior settings" that elicit standing behavior patterns with a supraindividual quality. In the same way we can think of "identity settings" that elicit standing patterns of identity. Sexuality, gender, age, race, class, and identity itself are social properties of sites and times as well as individuals. They are "social facts" (Durkheim, 1982) that exist independently of the sum of individuals constituting a site at any one time. For example, singles bars are sexier than the sum of their individuals,[12] the Marine Corps is more macho than the sum of its individuals, and bachelors' parties are more sexist than the sum of individual males present. And the night is more deviant (Melbin, 1987; Black, 1976:110–11) and sexier (Davis, 1983:15) than the day even though all individuals inhabit both day and night. It is the interaction between the night and its inhabitants, not simply the sum of individuals present, that contributes to the more sexualized identity of the night. It is not so much that *deviants* and *sexual beings* are nocturnal but rather that *deviance* and *sexuality*

---

12. Lecture by John Gagnon, spring 1992.

themselves are nocturnal and occupy a greater territory of the night. Deviance, sexuality, and marked elements, in general, are diluted in the day, but they become ever more concentrated and amplified as the night progresses and ages.

Most social space and time is unmarked and treated as *generic public space*. A few spaces (such as youth centers, gay bars, ethnic neighborhoods, and red light districts) and select times (such as the night, weekends, and holidays) are marked off as *marked identity spaces* and *marked identity times,* where identity communities are allowed to congregate to openly display their brightest colors. Within "generic public space" the full range of identity expressions is restricted, policed, and homogenized through a variety of means including social disapproval, harassment, discrimination, and even legal controls. As such, most generic space is really a "false generic" (Minnich, 1990), something that appears neutral but is actually stacked in favor of those who are endowed with invisible privilege. Studies have documented, for instance, that racial minorities (Feagin, 1991), gay men, lesbians, and heterosexual women (Gardner, 1994), teenagers (Gaines, 1990), the homeless (Davis, 1998:384–85), and other socially marked groups are subjected to various forms of harassment and discrimination that limit their full access to generic public spaces.

The range of public gendered, sexualized, and other presentations is closely monitored in generic public space in order to limit social extremes and encourage social cohesion. Such sites encourage homogenizing performances of genericness rather than conspicuous displays of social markedness. The most extreme examples of homogenizing presentations occur in the public facework done in settings such as elevators (see Goffman, 1963a) and bureaucracies. Generic public space allows only a restricted range of presentations. Social extremes in identity and presentation are discouraged. Individuals are encouraged to blend in with the majority and not stand out as extreme or unique. Those who have socially extreme characteristics generally mask or downplay their markedness or migrate to marked identity spaces, where they are allowed to openly display it. To put it bluntly, those who are at the social extremes also get pushed to the spatial and temporal extremes. Note, for instance, that crime rates, rates of alcoholism, extremes of wealth and poverty, and other measures of social deviation are highest at both the urban and rural extremes. Likewise, deviance tends to be pushed further into the temporal extremes of the late night (see Melbin, 1987); the greater the deviation, the further into the night one must travel.

A society's spatial organization also reflects its social and mental organization (see Davis, 1983; Zerubavel, 1991:34, 1996:429). Our society's spatial ghettos reflect the "mental ghettos" with which we classify social identities. Marked identities are highly concentrated in specialized ghettos while unmarked ones are distributed across most social space without heavy concentrations in a limited number of areas. Sites that encourage highly specialized group-specific displays of identity are marked identity spaces. In such spaces individuals often foreground their socially specialized (or marked) attributes and submerge their socially unmarked ones. Identity enclaves such as ethnic enclaves, gay ghettos, and gender- and age-segregated spaces elicit conspicuous (or "peacock") displays of markedness. Generic public space, by contrast, elicits submerged displays of marked attributes and either default or intentional displays of unmarked ones.

There is a mathematical quality to the use of social settings. If we assign a negative $(-)$ sign to an attribute that's marked in socially generic settings and a positive $(+)$ sign to the absence of that attribute, in any situation in which the identity of the setting and the identity of the individual have the same sign, the individual will be unmarked. If the signs differ, the individual will be marked. Thus, whereas being gay will be marked in unmarked space, it will not be marked in gay-specific marked spaces. Instead, being straight will be marked. The effect of having a conventionally marked identity in a marked social space is akin to multiplying two negative numbers. The end result is an unmarked identity in that space. By contrast, being heterosexual $(+)$ in gay settings $(-)$ is just as marked as being gay $(-)$ in socially generic time and space $(+)$. In marked identity settings conventional patterns of markedness are reversed so that what is usually marked becomes unmarked and what is typically unmarked becomes marked.

This property of social space informs an understanding of how social actors use space to construct, present, and negotiate their social identities. Most commonly, individuals will attempt to match their spatial and temporal surroundings. And the surroundings themselves will elicit individual responses of submerging or foregrounding certain characteristics. Suburbs, for instance, have a sanitizing effect on public displays, while commercial and red light districts of large cities encourage more conspicuous identity displays. Although individuals generally attempt to match the sign of their environments, some individuals deliberately display the opposite sign as a strategy of confrontation and political resistance. Members of Queer Nation, for instance, deliberately invade generic "heterosexualized" public spaces such as shopping centers and sports bars and pretend they are queer spaces. They thus kiss, cuddle, and grope one another while feigning offense at similar displays of heterosexual intimacy (see Knopp, 1992:665). They in effect pretend that they are in marked social space and that heterosexuality (the unmarked) is therefore deviant and inappropriate.

Managing Identity and Doing Identity Work: Identity as Accomplishment

Recognizing the microtemporal and spatial variability of identity requires that we see identity as mutable and fluid rather than static and permanent. Identity is enacted, accomplished, and managed in our daily interactions. Some theorists and researchers of identity have treated identity as something that is "essential" and fixed in the individual.[13] They have treated identity as a "noun," and as we will see, some individuals do experience their

---

13. See Jenkins (1996: chap. 1) for a critique of this view.

identity this way. This treatment, however, ignores the ways in which identity is accomplished in everyday interactions. Identity is not simply something one *has*, it is something one *works on* (see Schwalbe and Mason-Shrock, 1996; Jenkins, 1996). Here I follow the tradition of researchers who have located identity as an interactional accomplishment rather than as a fixed entity. Garfinkel (1967:134–37), for instance, uses the case study of "Agnes," a male-to-female transsexual, to demonstrate that gender identity cannot simply be taken for granted; it must be enacted in everyday practices. Goffman (1959) shows that social actors often present themselves in a manner designed to impress others around them; their presentation of self changes depending on the audience and the social context. Anderson (1978) demonstrates, in his study of African-American street corner men, that individuals had to keep "doing" things within their primary group to maintain and reaffirm their identity. Jones similarly shows, in a study of English national identity in the United States, that individuals do considerable work to construct their identities and that the salience of a given identity waxes and wanes across different situations (Jones, 2001:7). West and Zimmerman (1987) write explicitly about "doing gender" and West and Fenstermaker (1995) later expand this notion to "doing difference" such as race, class, and gender in general. Butler (1990) develops a "performative theory" of gender suggesting that gender and identities are "performed" rather than "essentially there."

Following in the interactionist tradition, I see the self, self-identity, and identity attributes as potentially flexible. Contrary to the commonly held popular notion of identity and self as fixed, unchanging inner essences, I conceive of the self as changing and shifting across time and across social contexts. Often changes in the self are slow and gradual, while at other times they can be swift and abrupt. These changes can be linear or cyclical, relatively permanent or temporary. Sometimes the individual can perceive a "core self" that appears to be stable, with changes in presentation and self-perception occurring only at the minor fringes of a more important idealized inner core. At other times the individual may perceive a "core self" to be in a state of flux and lacking consistency. The concept of "born again" implies such a change. Similarly a sudden serious change in health or a major disaster can cause people to feel as if their perceived "core self" has been uprooted and fundamentally altered. Moreover there can be changes in the salience of different attributes of both the presentational self and the perceived internal self. For instance, an individual can consider being "white" or "black" an important part of their internal "core self" at one moment and a minor facet on the peripheral and more insignificant fringes of their self-identity at another. Whites in the United States, for instance, generally see their "whiteness" as insignificant, but a white person who moves to an all-black neighborhood may eventually "discover" that "whiteness" is a much more central quality to their being than they anticipated. Whether "whiteness" was an always dormant unrecognized core ingredient of their internal self or whether it moved from the periphery to the core of the internal self over time because of the change in contexts is precisely the kind of question that one encounters when discussing self-identity.

The various facets of identity and self make it difficult for analysts to agree on a uniform definition of identity. Moreover, self-identity appears multilayered, with a combination of internal, socially shared, and performed dimensions. I have tried, for the most part, to present informants' conceptions of their identities with sensitivity toward the relationship between their internal and socially performed conceptions of self. While lifestylers often conceive of their selves as an internal single main-ingredient noun with little spatial and temporal variability, the permutations get more complicated with commuters and integrators. Some gay commuters, for instance, perceived their socially performed identities as very flexible and changing from one environment to the next, while still personally experiencing gayness as one stable component or even the main component in their "core self," while other gay commuters experienced both their socially performed selves and their "core sexual self" as fluid and shifting.

And gay integrators tended to view gayness as a small attribute in a relatively stable "core self," but not the main attribute.

Because these various layers of identity and self can be confusing, I offer some suggestions for understanding how I use different phrases related to identity and self. I use the term *identity* in three ways: (1) to refer to widely recognized collective group identities such as gay identity, female identity, Korean-American identity, and Muslim identity, (2) to refer to commonly recognized dimensions along which group identities are formed such as sexual identity, gender identity, ethnic identity, and religious identity, and (3) to refer to one's own *self-identity*—an individual's behavior, values, and worldview, and how that individual perceives and performs who they are, and what components of their self are important to them. In many cases the meaning of identity should be apparent from the context, but in some cases it may be ambiguous. Thus, when referring to self-identity I employ either *self-identity* or *self* to distinguish self-identity from the other forms. I use the term *identity attributes* to refer to specific components (such as race, class, gender, and occupation) of one's overall self and *overall self* to refer to the composite self produced from the combination of identity attributes. Finally, I use the terms *"core self"* and *"true self"* to refer to an identity attribute or an overall self that an individual believes is at the very core of who they are and reflects an inner, true, unchanging, context-independent essence of their being.

My analysis looks at identity within an environmental context to observe the ways we "do" identity differently depending on the ecological setting. To understand the interaction between time, space, and identity presentation it is worth concentrating on the performative dimensions of identity. I refer to these as *identity duration* (the time one spends presenting a particular identity attribute or facet of oneself), *identity density* or *identity volume* (the intensity with which one presents a particular facet of oneself), and *identity dominance* (the quantity of significant attributes allowed in the constitution of one's identity; dominance is a composite of duration and density).

Identity Duration: Full-Time and Part-Time Identity Work

The intersection of time and identity is *identity duration*—the length or percentage of time that one performs a certain facet of an identity. If one thinks of identity work one can draw a parallel between working an identity on either a *full-time* or a *part-time* basis and being either a full-time or a part-time employee in one's occupation. In some professions, such as medicine, military leadership, and the priesthood, one's professional identity must be nearly always accessible to others, or have the characteristic of "ever-availability" (Zerubavel, 1981: 146, 148–49). Some attributes of nonprofessional identities similarly have more ever-availability than others; race among minority members and age among children, for instance, tend to be more ever available as a central attribute than race among whites or age among thirty-five-year-olds or than more easily masked dimensions of identity such as class, occupation, and political affiliation. Some people do "sociologist," or "student," or "gay," or "drug dealer," or "parent," or "feminist," or "Christian" as full-time identities while others only enact or perform such facets of their identity on a part-time basis. Some individuals, for example, such as full-time street corner Christian evangelists or in-house fraternity members perform their "Christian" identity or their "fraternity" identity all of the time. Their specific identity is always available and omnipresent. Others, however, such as Christians who only "practice" on Sunday or fraternity members who only show up for weekend parties, manifest the identity only during specific times and in specific spaces. They are "part-timers" to these identities.

Identity Density: Concentrated and Diluted Identities

How concentrated or diluted an identity trait is relative to one's overall "presentation of self" is referred to as *identity density* (or *identity volume*). If one thinks of one's overall self-identity as possessing a variety of ingredients, the concentration of a particular ingredient represents its density. At one extreme, an individual may present oneself as 100 percent gay or 100 percent Christian or

100 percent black. Such individuals manifest one ingredient of self with a density of 100 percent. There is no mixture of other ingredients; some characteristic is simply 100 percent of one's self with no other facets of self to dilute that percentage. As an example of the high-density self-presentation strategy one can look at Garfinkel's (1967:128–29) study of Agnes—a male-to-female transsexual—who did her "female" identity with so much exaggeration that she suppressed all other identity characteristics. Garfinkel and his associates, in fact, came to refer to Agnes's presentation as 120 percent female (ibid.:129). She exaggerated all possible auxiliary characteristics associated with femininity and played down any evidences of other ingredients to her self. At the other extreme, people may possess attributes that they play down rather than play up. These attributes would have a very low volume. Thus, a black man who wants to minimize his association with the attribute black may play down the significance of race, treating it as a very minor percentage of his overall self. Rather than presenting himself as 100 percent black he will try to present himself, metaphorically, as a mere 8 percent or 12 percent black by playing down auxiliary characteristics associated with black culture and playing up attributes he shares with the larger "generic" culture. He will present his racial identity in a diluted, low-density form.

The notions of playing up or playing down facets of one's self also allow us to conceive of the volume metaphor in its other form (i.e., the noise level with which one presents oneself). When one is aggressively presenting a certain facet of oneself, one is turning up the volume of that facet. When one is downplaying that facet, one is turning down the volume. This use of the metaphor follows popular references to flamboyant displays of identity as "noisy" and other displays as more "quiet."

Identity-Potent (or High-Density) Settings

Both time and place are active agents in the constitution of social identity. Just as any given individual's identity is on a continuum of high to low duration and high to low volume, so too are the spaces and times in which individuals are located. Identity is as much a characteristic of settings as it is of the individuals who occupy settings.

Some spaces and times—*identity-potent* settings—elicit a greater concentration and higher visibility of marked identities. Such spatial and temporal enclaves serve as "amplifiers" for identity. Marked identity is amplified at night and in urban identity enclaves while it is muted in more generic spaces. The urban enclave, because it brings together a critical mass of people, is more potent in its overall concentration of identity than the sum of each of its individual inhabitants. Similarly, temporal settings such as weekends and holidays possess greater potency than unmarked days. The potency of such sites and spaces elicits active displays of identity among a broader range of people than other settings. Whereas some individuals possess such an intense identity that they are "on" even in nonpotent settings, others require a more interactive relationship with their spatial and temporal settings. They rely upon the added potency of the night and of urban enclaves to spread their feathers and turn their identity to "high visibility" and "high volume." Others avoid such settings because they do not wish to be "turned on at high volume" at any time.

Identity-Diluted (or Low-Density) Settings

Far more common and less analyzed are sites and times where identity and difference tend to be diluted rather than accentuated—*identity-diluted* settings. Most spaces have an overall muting effect on the volume of identity. Information control (Goffman, 1963b:41–104; Zerubavel, 1982:105) or concealment of identity (both forms of volume control) are the standard identity strategies within such settings. In suburbs and other identity-diluted settings with a dilution effect on identity there is a metaphorical noise ordinance against expressing too much markedness volume. Extravagant displays and other "disturbances of the peace" are less tolerated in such settings than in the high-volume spaces of large cities.

If this interaction between place and identity has been neglected, it is in part because studies of identity have tended to observe marked social groups in marked identity spaces. Often such
studies have presupposed that the marked identity of the individual rather than that of the space in which he or she resides accounts for the variance in the individual's behavior. Because
marked individuals are typically studied only in marked spaces, it
is difficult to separate the variance between effects of place and
effects of membership in a marked identity category. Everyday
unmarked spaces are often neglected in analyses of identity and
place. Geographers have, for instance, looked at how minority
groups constitute identity in social spaces,[14] but their focus has
been primarily on how minorities establish identity-exclusive enclaves rather than on how they organize identity across different
spaces and times, including nonghettoized ones. Chouinard and
Grant (1996:184) have argued, for instance, that most authors focus on lesbian, gay, and queer spaces, ignoring the fact that most
lesbians and gay men spend most of their time in "everyday
spaces" that are more heterosexualized and hostile to gay identity. In focusing on the interaction between gay men and their
environment in both marked and unmarked spaces, this study attempts to illuminate the ecological organization and temporal
variability of identity.

Lifestylers, Commuters, and Integrators: The Grammar of Identity

Given that society is divided between generic public space and
time on the one hand and marked identity spaces and times on
the other, how do individuals with marked identity characteristics
organize their markedness? I illustrate three ideal-typical identity

---

14. E.g., Adler and Brenner (1992); Bell (1991); Castells (1983:138–72); Crow
(1994); Gupta and Ferguson (1992); Peake (1993); Till (1993); Tuan (1984);
Valentine (1993).

management strategies around which individuals organize their markedness.

After demonstrating how they apply specifically to gay identity I will show, in chapters 7 through 11, that the three strategies are relevant to the organization of *all* marked social identities. The three identity management types are those of (1) lifestylers, (2) commuters, and (3) integrators. Underlying each of these identity types are different configurations of *identity duration* (the degree to which identity is distributed across various times and spaces of one's life), *identity density* (the degree to which identity is packaged and presented in a concentrated or diluted form), and *identity dominance* (the product of duration times density, or the degree to which an identity attribute occupies one's whole self).

The first type is the *identity lifestyler.* Gay lifestylers live openly in gay-specific ghettos and organize their life around their marked status. They keep their markedness on "high volume" and do it virtually all the time. They have a high-density, high-duration gay identity. Metaphorically, they are 100 percent gay, 100 percent of the time. Lifestylers take on the grammatical centrality of gayness as a *noun.*[15]

The second type is the *identity commuter.* Gay commuters treat their gay identity as a *verb.* They live other parts of themselves in heterosexual space and travel to identity-specific spaces to be their "gay self." They are weekend warriors and nighttime commuters to the gay community. In much the same way that work commuters travel from the suburbs to the city to do work on weekdays, identity commuters travel from the suburbs to the city to "do identity" on weekends. For them, gayness is a *temporary master status* that they turn on and off depending on their social environment—in gay spaces they often turn their marked identity

---

15. I wish to thank Eviatar Zerubavel for suggesting the idea of using noun, verb, and adjective metaphors to describe different identity strategies.

to high volume, but outside these spaces they turn it off completely. They commute to ghettos or bars and play up their markedness in marked social spaces. They submerge markedness and foreground their unmarked characteristics everywhere else. They limit open expression of their gay identity to very few spheres of their lives. Thus, it is a low-duration, high-density gay identity. Metaphorically, they may be something like 100 percent gay, 15 percent of the time. (These percentages are illustrative and not literal. I use 15 percent as the illustrative number for duration because it conveys a small but still significant portion of one's time. This also represents the kind of duration to an identity that is consistent with a weekend identity commitment. Time commitments as low as 1 percent or as high as 40 percent can also be seen as within the duration range of a real-life commuter.)

The third type is the *identity integrator*. The gay identity of gay integrators is an *adjective*. They live openly in heterosexual space and integrate their gay identity into living in a heterosexualized world. In fact, many integrators do not often travel to gay-specific spaces. While they are not closeted, they also do not play up their markedness as lifestylers or commuters do. Unlike commuters, their gay identity is turned on all of the time, but it is at a low volume. Their marked trait becomes just one of a number of facets by which they organize their life and identify themselves. Their gay identity is not entirely off, nor is it on high density. They do markedness on low volume and spread it across all spheres of their lives. They present a low-density, high-duration gay identity. Metaphorically, they might be 15 percent gay, 100 percent of the time. (Again both percentages are illustrative rather than literal. The 15 percent figure for density conveys an attribute that defines only a fraction of the self but a fraction that is still significant.)

In figure 1, the dominance of an identity is represented by the shaded area formed by the combination of duration (horizontal axis) and density (vertical axis). In the case of the lifestyler, values for both duration and density are high, so identity dominance is high. In the case of the commuter, duration is low and density

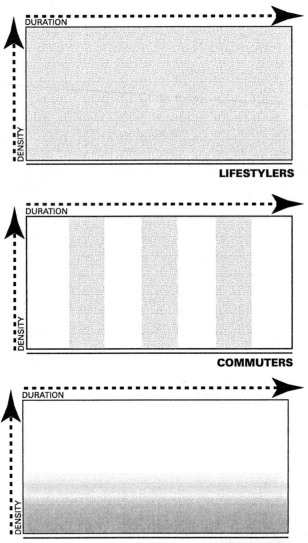

Figure 1: Density and duration strategies among lifestylers, commuters, and integrators (shaded portion = salience of marked attribute).

is high so identity dominance is moderate. In the integrator, duration is high and density is low so dominance is moderate.

Similarly, spaces themselves can have "lifestyler," "commuter," and "integrator" identities. The Castro, in San Francisco, possesses a high-volume, high-visibility, high-duration "gay identity." By contrast, many spaces are low-duration, high-volume "commuter" spaces, constantly changing their colors like a chameleon to adapt to different temporal settings over the course of a day or week. Some bars, for instance, occupy several identities in a single twenty-four-hour period, adopting a heterosexual atmosphere during the day and "coming out" as gay only late at night (Weightman, 1980:12) or hosting "gay nights" once a week. Similarly, many summer resort towns change their identity setting to match the season of the year. These, too, are commuter spaces. Most spaces, however, are low-volume, high-duration integrator spaces.

These identity types are formed through the people's interactions in social time and social space. Variations across time and space are captured by extending our analysis into the unmarked spaces and at the intersections between unmarked and marked space, where many individuals spend most of their time "doing identity." In the upcoming chapters, I will take a closer look at the ways in which individuals develop a lifestyling, commuting, or integrating strategy for organizing their "marked identity," beginning with my case study of gay male identity and then extending to other identity categories.

Chapter Overviews

In chapter 2, I begin by focusing on the ideal type of gay lifestylers (or peacocks), who treat their gay identity as an *essentializing noun* and experience their gay identity both politically and phenomenologically as a master status. This is the dominant narrative around gay identity in the United States; it is the cultural template of identity that the gay and lesbian movement has, for the most part, promoted as well as the way that most heterosexuals assume most gay people understand their gayness.[16] Although there were no "lifestylers" among my informants, I include the lifestyler as an important ideal type to start with because of its central role as a subcultural reference point. I use examples from others' research on urban gay subcultures and from gay movement representatives to show how the ideal-typical lifestyler presents gayness as both a high-duration and a high-density identity.

Chapter 3 draws on my ethnographic data to introduce the ideal type of gay commuters (or chameleons). These are gay men who treat their gay identity as a *mobile verb*, traveling across time and space to turn it now to high volume, now completely off, as though it were controlled by a toggle switch. Gay commuters present their gayness as being of low duration but high density, treating it as a temporary master status when they are in gay space and time but suppressing it and downplaying its significance in other times and spaces. I show how gay commuters play up an ordinary *diurnal self* and an extraordinary *nocturnal self*,[17] commuting to and from a publicly gay identity in order to fit into two distinct worlds. Gay commuters include both individuals who feel forced to commute and who perceive their satellite gay identity as their "real self," and individuals who consider their commute a choice and who see their "everyday self" and their "gay self" as equally real selves.

In chapter 4 I use more of my ethnographic data to introduce the ideal type of gay integrators (or centaurs), who treat their "gay identity as a *modifying adjective*. Gay integrators experience their gay identity as a *complementary status* that flavors, rather than a master status that saturates, the self.

In chapter 5 I focus on the interplay and conflict among

---

16. I thank Elizabeth Armstrong for pointing out that the lifestyler ideal type is the gay identity template even if the number of actual people who represent this template is low.

17. For the concept of nocturnal self, see Grazian (2000). I use the parallel concept of diurnal self to highlight the unmarked side of the contrast.

lifestylers, commuters, and integrators. I demonstrate, based on my interviews, that conflicts within the gay community can be understood as grammar disputes over whether to treat *gayness* as a noun, a verb, or an adjective. I analyze these disputes in relation to the dominance, duration, and density of identity. I show, for instance, that lifestylers value gay singularity (dominance) over the gay balance of commuters and integrators, that commuters value gay mobility over the gay stability of integrators and lifestylers (duration), and that integrators value gay moderation over the gay purity of lifestylers and commuters (density).

In chapter 6 I look at shifts in identity strategies over time and at the complex ways in which structural variables interacted to cause some gay men to favor certain identity strategies over others. I examine individual cases of shifting grammatical strategies and draw out factors that helped to bring about those changes.

In chapters 7 through 11 I apply the lifestyler, commuter, and integrator ideal types to identity generally, using examples from a broad range of identity dimensions such as ethnicity, religion, subcultural taste, race, political or ideological affiliation, age, region, occupation, and class to illustrate the theory's general applicability. The examples of types and disputes come from accounts in the sociological literature and the popular press.

In chapter 7 I present examples of social actors most closely approximating lifestylers (peacocks), commuters (chameleons), and integrators (centaurs) across a broad range of identity categories. In chapter 8 I examine disputes arising from opposing approaches to duration among lifestylers and integrators on the one hand, and commuters on the other, paralleling durational tensions found in my own data. In chapter 9 I examine density-based disagreements between lifestylers and commuters who favor identity purity and integrators who favor identity moderation. These conflicts too mirror the disputes within gay identity. In chapter 10, I examine identity dominance disputes between commuters and integrators (who both favor balancing competing identity attributes) on one side and lifestylers (who favor letting one attribute dominate the self) on the other. I conclude, in chapter 11, by complicating the portrait I have drawn on the three ideal-typical identity strategies. I discuss the ways structural variables influence these identity options, illustrate how individuals can employ different identity grammars for different contents of the self, and assess the practical relevance of these types for analyzing both collective and personal identity in one's own everyday life.

»2«

"Everything about Me Is Gay"

Identity Peacocks

Above all "gay" is a way of life; the gay world has its own vocabulary, customs, and rules for living. Gays are the high priests of trends, tastes, and tans. . . . Go into any gay man's home and chances are he'll have many of the same albums, books, and magazines as his counterparts elsewhere in the country. Most likely the home will be discerningly decorated and stylish clothes will be hanging in the closet. The man's dating habits, from cruising and meeting men to the mating ritual and nesting, will parallel those of his brother from coast to coast. And when he speaks of Judy, his friends will all know he means Garland.

Kevin Dilallo and Jack Krumholtz, *The Unofficial Gay Manual: Living the Lifestyle (or at Least Appearing To)*[1]

For the ideal type of the gay lifestyler (or peacock), gayness is more than a modifier of one's self or an expression of whom one is attracted to; it is the essential defining feature of who one is and how one lives. Every facet of his being, from what he eats to how he dresses to what he drives is consistent with and

---

1. Although Dilallo and Krumholtz (1994) is intended as a humorous how-to guide, its portrayal of a "gay lifestyle" with a set of auxiliary characteristics is still useful as a cultural artifact that illuminates the lifestyler template. Note that the parenthetical subtitle also hints that the guide can be of use to gay commuters who want to pass as gay lifestylers.

informed by his being gay. The gay lifestyler votes as a gay person, decorates his house as a gay person, goes to the gym as a gay person, listens to "gay" music, lives in a gay neighborhood, and has an exclusively gay social life. His self is dominated by one attribute: a master status, a virtual *identity monopoly*. Gayness is the undisputed ruler of his province of self. His lifestyle is all gay all of the time. Being gay includes not just his sexual tastes but also his social, cultural, and political tastes. He likes Judy Garland, stylish clothes, and disco music because it comes with the package of "being gay." Moreover "gay," from the lifestyler point of view, so saturates one's overall self that there is, or at least should be, a remarkable consistency across the board in the lives and cultural, social, and political values of gay men. In the peacock view there is an "authentically gay" package, and one's commitment to the identity can be measured by how well one matches that package.

Of all identity management types, the peacock is the most publicly visible and the most frequently represented template for gays in popular culture. The gay lifestyler is someone who everyone thinks of as gay first and other things second. Lifestylers capture public attention, often fascinating others with their conspicuous peacock displays of identity. Their subcultural world, while the most socially distant from the mainstream, is also the most culturally visible and analytically familiar "gay world" to the mainstream. Although the actual numbers of people representing this template may be low, it serves as the focal archetype by which both gays and straights define "the gay community." These peacocks are the dominant template of gay identity that has been promoted at gay pride parades and among the gay activist subculture, as well as in the news media. Their high-duration, high-density displays of gay identity are prominent in public and political perceptions of the gay community. Moreover, because their recipe of self consists of a one-ingredient identity monopoly, they are the most straightforward analytic category to begin with. It also makes sense to begin with lifestylers because they are the subcultural reference point according to which most gay men define and compare their own "gay identity." For the majority of gay people as well as straight people, the gay lifestyler is *the* ideal type of a person with a gay identity. In conventional wisdom, the lifestyler is the most authentically, most fully gay member of the category; he is at the far end of the closeted/out continuum and is thus widely perceived as having the most completely developed gay identity (see Troiden, 1979).

Although the gay lifestyler is the dominant ideal type by which gay people as a category are defined and measured, it is, like all ideal types, a useful fiction used to explain a more complicated reality. Even in the most heavily concentrated gay enclaves it is unlikely that the lifestyler in its purest caricature exists, though close approximations of the ideal type may be present. Although all three identity grammars presented in this book are useful heuristic fictions that some individuals approximate much more closely than others, the lifestyler may be even less realized in empirical reality than the others. If this is the case, it is all the more fascinating that the lifestyler represents the cultural model of what it means to be fully authentically gay.

In this chapter, I lay out the lifestyler template as a necessary foil against which gay people define themselves. Because the lifestyler is an analytic foil and because I encountered no one who closely matched the lifestyler ideal in the suburbs, I draw my lifestyler examples from an array of sources using what Black (1995:843) refers to as "naïve evidence"—that is, evidence that wasn't specifically gathered for one's own theory but that illustrates or validates the theory nonetheless. Black argues that one of the major advantages of naïve evidence is that it precludes the possibility of a favorable or unfavorable bias since the people who originally gathered the evidence had no desire to either support or contradict the theory being discussed by the secondary user of the evidence.[2] Using this naïve evidence, I develop and highlight the

---

2. It should be noted that this approach complements "grounded theory" since grounded theory involves initially gathering data without a theoretical focus. Many of my earlier interviews of "commuters" and "integrators" were

concepts of identity duration, density, and dominance as they appear in their ideal, purest forms to lay out the key dimensions of both gay identity and social identity that I will be using throughout this book.

I should add that the specific gay lifestyler template of the high-duration, high-density, high-dominance gay that I describe in this chapter is a relatively recent social type that came about as the result of political struggles and social forces in a particular historical era. Although I conceive of the generic identity strategies of lifestyler, commuter, and integrator as being broadly applicable across the human range of identities, I recognize that social, political, and historical forces mediate the degree to which the various identity strategies are available and that under conditions of extreme oppression and social invisibility the lifestyler template as a subcultural reference point may be rarely visible or nonexistent. Because there is already an excellent and well-developed literature on the larger issues surrounding the political struggle to carve out gay lifestyler spaces[3] and because my analysis is concerned with identity issues that transcend the given subculture, however, I do not cover these issues in depth here.

Omnirelevance: Gay Identity as Noun

The gay peacock's mantra is "everything about me is gay." For the lifestyler, gayness is always relevant, ever present, and consistently activated in a high-density manner. He doesn't simply "do gayness" once in a while or subtly; it is his life. He is metaphorically 100 percent gay, 100 percent of the time. He manifests a gay identity that is high in duration (the identity is on all the time),

---

conducted before I developed this theoretical focus and thus, in a way, these earliest interviews constitute naïve evidence from my own field notes and were also responsible for my recognizing and honing my theoretical focus.
3. See, e.g., Murray (1996); D'Emilio (1983); Adam (1987:75–101); LeVay and Nonas (1995); Chauncey (1994).

high in density (it is on in a pure and concentrated manner), and high in dominance (it dominates his self). Gay lifestylers act as the subcultural entrepreneurs and shapers of the "gay world." They carve out identity-specific spaces in "gay ghettos" that provide a safe haven for identity expression and resistance to the dominant culture.

The gay lifestyler experiences gayness as a *noun*, and his identity in its most extreme ideal-typical form is expressed in terms of duration, density, and dominance as follows: (1) he has a full-time commitment to the identity that encompasses both the diurnal and the nocturnal self *(duration)*; (2) he has an essentialist view of gayness and experiences it as his "true permanent self" from birth *(duration)*; (3) he emphasizes identity visibility and differentiation from the unmarked as a political strategy, accentuating his identity by playing up the expected auxiliary characteristics of "gayness" in their most "authentic" form *(density)*; and (4) he lives in a gay-specific space and has exclusively gay social networks *(dominance)*.

The key values around which the lifestyler organizes his gayness are *gay stability* (he experiences his gay "essence" as permanent and immutable), *gay authenticity* (he demonstrates his gay identity as "authentic" through the adoption of requisite "auxiliary characteristics" of gayness) and *gay dominance* (he places his gay attribute above other social attributes in his overall flavoring of self). He values stability in the duration of his gayness, purity in the density of his gayness, singularity in the dominance of his gayness.

Identity as a Full-Time Occupation: High-Duration Gayness

For the gay peacock, gayness is an *omnirelevant* social attribute. Its relevance pervades and is highly salient across all social contexts and at all times. He experiences his gay identity as a master status at the performative, phenomenological, and social psychological levels. His gayness cannot be and should not be turned off, for in his view it saturates his very essence.

> I seem to be surrounded at all times in all ways by who I
> am. . . . It goes with me wherever I go . . . and my life is
> gay and where I go I take my gay life with me. I don't con-
> sciously sit and think while I'm eating this soup that I'm
> eating this "gayly," but, you know, it surrounds me.
> (quoted in Epstein 1987:9)

Lifestyler narratives are essentialist, emphasizing their "nounness." They believe that a gay identity is an essential noun that
saturates their very being rather than a modifying adjective that
flavors it. From this perspective gayness is not something they *do*,
it is who they *are* and *always have been* (even if they didn't always recognize it). The commonly expressed view that "deep
down inside I always knew I was gay" reflects the narrative biog-
raphy typical of lifestylers. For lifestylers, a full-fledged gay identity has always been there on the inside; if the feelings and
behaviors associated with the gay identity did not appear until
later in life, it is only because he just recently discovered and
freed his "inner noun." The gay lifestyler not only experiences his
sexuality as essential and immutable,[4] but also sees related auxiliary characteristics as part of his immutable core as well. Statements like "I never liked sports" or "I was always the artsy type in
school" reflect the belief that being "born gay" also means being
born with such auxiliary characteristics as an aversion to sports
or a penchant for the arts.

Just as some professional identities have the characteristic
of ever-availability, there are some personal identities that individuals maintain on a permanent ever-available basis. A gay
lifestyler's gay identity is on call twenty-four hours a day, seven
days a week; whether at home, at work, on vacation, in the voting
booth, at a friend's, at a relative's, at a social gathering, or on a

---

4. Stein (1997:161) similarly found that some lesbian women experienced
their sexuality as involuntary and thus saw their sexuality as more "real" than
that of those who had chosen their sexuality.

public street, the lifestyler's gayness is readily available and omnipresent. It is a full-time social identity. His commitment to it is exclusive and undivided, constrained neither by time nor by space. As one individual says on his Web site, "My gayness permeates my being; I cannot compartmentalize it."[5] The stigmatization of an identity by others generally makes that identity more salient for the individual possessing it. Thus, marked identities like gayness are often greedier than unmarked ones in defining a person's overall self and demanding his conscious commitment to the identity.

One Hundred Percent Pure Concentrated Gayness: Identity on High Density

In addition to high duration, the gay peacock has a high-density (or high-volume) gay identity in his presentation of self. The degree to which gayness is concentrated and displayed to others through signifiers and auxiliary characteristics is its density or volume. A peacock will manifest his gay identity in its most potent, concentrated, and high-density form; there are no competing ingredients that water down or dilute his gayness. He is 100 percent pure unadulterated gay.

To have a high-density identity is to let one's colors shine, to turn it up to volume ten—to let everyone see and hear it. The notions of playing facets of one's self up or down allow us to conceive of the volume metaphor as the noise level at which an instrument of the self is played. When one is aggressively presenting a certain facet of the self, he is turning up the volume of that facet. For the gay lifestyler, for instance, gayness is always on lead guitar while the rest of his band of attributes plays quietly in the background as supporting cast. Those attributes are further supporting a self-definition of gayness rather than competing with it (e.g., "artistic" as a supporting instrument as opposed to

---

5. From www.uwec.edu/ranowlan/fever_birthday.html.

"Republican" as a competing one). This volume metaphor also follows popular uses of the terms loud and quiet to reflect high- and low-density identity presentations. Bawer (1996:3), for instance, uses this metaphor in referring to "the noisy [gay] ghetto barricades" and "the quiet closets" as the two extremes of gay identity. In addition to noise levels, volume and density metaphors can also relate to the concentration and potency of an identity. Walters (2001:13), for instance, uses a volume/density metaphor in this way when she argues that "the power of cultural visibility and memory is potent" in her discussion of the necessity of gay cultural visibility for social equality. In referring to the power of cultural visibility as "potent," Walters connects visibility with the concentrated volume/density or potency of an identity.

A high-density, high-volume, high-visibility identity is displayed through the use and accentuation of auxiliary characteristics. For the lifestyler, maintaining an "authentically gay" identity requires a great deal of work. Lifestylers establish authenticity by distancing themselves from mainstream culture as much as possible. From the lifestyler's perspective, auxiliary characteristics measure one's authenticity. Gay auxiliary characteristics, for example, can include such things as artisticness, creativity, progressiveness, activism in gay politics, having a cosmopolitan sensibility (see Bronski, 1984), and presenting a butch or queen appearance that differs from modal cultural presentations of gender. Forest (1995:145) suggests that "progressiveness seems to be at the very core of gay identity," thus effectively defining it as one of the requisite auxiliary characteristic of an authentically gay identity. The lifestyler uses an array of these auxiliary characteristics to *amplify* his identity, to maximize its density, and to differentiate his identity from other identities.

Like lifestylers in other minority categories, the gay peacock is committed to an identity politics strategy that emphasizes cultural visibility[6] and pride as important responses to oppression.

---

6. For an analysis of gay visibility in America see Walters (2001). See Bernstein (1997) on the competing strategies of difference and sameness in political movements.

He participates in and organizes social movements and promotes coming out as an important component of cultural liberation. The gay social movements of the lifestyler promote peacock visibility and "loud and proud" volume displays to assert a place in society and to accentuate a distinct subculture. Lifestylers amplify the divide between themselves and other social categories. They emphasize auxiliary characteristics and the most "concentrated" portrayals of their categories as a form of cultural differentiation. Thus gay activist groups like Queer Nation, the Sisters of Perpetual Indulgence, and BRATS (Big-Honkin' Radical Anti-Assimilationist Terrorist Super-Queers) celebrate and play up their differences from the staid and boring conventions of mainstream society. Their very labels imply both the 100 percent duration (e.g., "Perpetual") and 100 percent density (e.g., "Super-Queers") ideal of lifestylers. They are the proud peacocks of their identity category, displaying their "gay colors" at high intensity at all times and in all places. They refer to themselves as "queers" or "gays" (noun) and not merely "queer" or "gay" (adjective). The lifestyler's portrayal of gayness takes the outsiders' definition of gayness and plays it back in the mirror with an inverted value. The peacock, for instance, takes a negative label like "queer" and accepts its connotation of difference but inverts the negative value ascribed by outsiders and turns it into a positive value. Gay lifestylers play up their distinction from "mainstream society" by emphasizing different sexual norms, left-oriented politics, and an urban cosmopolitan sensibility.

For lifestylers, it is important to keep identity categories from overlapping or being ambiguous. This is done through a process of "splitting" oneself (both mentally and physically) from straight society and "lumping" oneself with an oppositional subculture.[7] The gay ghetto and other gay institutions become one's social reference points. They resocialize one into an oppositional culture and encourage subcultural norms that differentiate one from

---

7. See Zerubavel (1991:24–28) on the mental processes of "splitting" and "lumping."

mundane everyday society. The lifestyler demonstrates by active display that he is no ordinary bird; he is a proud peacock.

Gay Ghettos and Exclusively Gay Social Networks: Identity Dominance

The site where high gay duration and high gay density meet to form gay dominance is the gay ghetto.[8] This identity-specific enclave is important to lifestylers for durational reasons because it gives the lifestyler a space to safely manifest a gay identity at all times. It is important for density reasons because it concentrates gays in a high-volume, high-visibility manner that adds to the collective flavoring of gayness at the macro and spatial levels. This flavor is captured well in LeVay and Nonas's (1995:136) description of West Hollywood: "Style, sleaze, and all, West Hollywood exudes a civic pride, a togetherness, an exuberance, based on the conviction that gayness is the central attribute of gay people's nature, an attribute that reaches into every corner of their daily lives." Gay ghettos like the Castro, the Village, and West Hollywood have an amplifying effect on one's identity volume. They raise the volume level of gayness all around them. These identity-amplifying spaces encourage peacock displays of markedness and discourage the mundanities of unmarkedness. Urban spaces are "identity resources" (Davis, 2001:48) that display a smorgasbord of potential identities in their extremes so that the prospective identity consumer can clearly see the choices before him. Such spaces also allow one to adopt a unidimensional life of identity-specific social networks. One can associate with all gay networks to complement one's perception of a 100 percent gay core self.

The totality with which a lifestyler's self is dominated by his gayness can be witnessed in the following quotes from urban gay clones (clones are a particular gay social type that frequents gay

---

8. For a sociological description of the gay ghetto, see Levine (1979).

ghettos; their defining characteristics are a "butch," hypermasculine appearance and a youthful party- and sex-oriented lifestyle):

> I live in an all-clone world. All my friends are clones. I live in a clone building, in a clone neighborhood, and work in a clone bar. My family stopped talking to me and I stopped talking to my straight friends. (Levine, 1998:30)

> I live on the West Side with two gay men, work in a gay restaurant, and spend my summers on Fire Island. I never relate to straight people. Ibid., 41

This nicely captures the full-time, segregated character of a lifestyler identity. The gay lifestyler insulates himself from straight society by surrounding himself with others who share his marked identity. His social networks and social environment are identity specific and he has generally broken off social ties that are not directly related to his gay identity. His gay identity is a *greedy identity* that washes over other aspects of his self and pervades all his social networks. It requires exclusive and undivided identity work. Coser (1974:6) refers to institutions that pervade all facets of members' lives and demand an undivided commitment as "greedy institutions." The greedy identity is a parallel concept, an identity that commands an uncompromising commitment, undiluted by any attributes that could undermine it or by any time commitments that could divide it. A lifestyler is firmly committed to an identity, and he will put both time and intensity into maintaining and performing it. Greedy identities require both a full-time and maximum intensity commitment, and this combination of duration and density gives them their greedy quality of dominance.

Like the clone, other lifestylers create and depend on identity-specific enclaves to fully develop, express, and live their marked identities on a full-time basis. These enclaves or marked identity spaces are created primarily in large urban centers where a critical mass of a marked group can congregate and develop their own social institutions and residential neighborhoods. The concentration of members of an identity category in social space has a reinforcing effect on expressions of identity. Lifestylers carve out such social spaces segregated from more conventional public space. In doing so, they provide themselves, as well as others, with a social space where one's marked identity does not have to be muted and toned down to meet mainstream conventions for proper identity volume. Such enclaves, because of their high visibility, often come to represent various identities. For many, the Castro and the Village are symbolic of gay identity just as ethnic enclaves are symbolic of immigrant identities. Settings like these have an amplifying effect on the marked identities they house. In them one can live out an undivided (duration) and undiluted (density) gay self.

Outside of such identity-specific enclaves it is far more difficult to lead an all-marked lifestyle. Residential concentrations and identity-supporting institutions for marked categories are absent where the critical mass does not reach the levels present in large cities. Just as the population density of gays is lower, the identity density within individual gays is also lower. These problems present challenges that lead most individuals to either submerge their marked identities at some times (as commuters do) or to do their identities on low volume (as integrators do). Such spaces have a muting effect on markedness and identity. They divide its duration and dilute its density.

Conclusion

Lifestylers make up the most visible and publicly recognized members of any marked identity category. They exhibit an identity in its seemingly most pure and unadulterated form. They are the cultural vanguard of identity politics, and it is their aesthetics, values, and tastes that publicly define and trickle down to other members of the identity category. The lifestyler's values of identity authenticity, visibility, and commitment are the very issues insiders, outsiders, and scholars typically define as important to an identity. Present debates over gay identity that center on out/closeted, visible/invisible, and committed/uncommitted dualisms, for instance, are defined in lifestyler terms.

A rigid split between gay and straight culture characterizes the lifestyler mind-set. The gay lifestyler reinforces this rigid separation in physical space. He lives, works, and spends most, if not all, of his time in the gay ghettos of large urban areas, and his social networks are predominantly or exclusively gay. The lifestylers' identity-exclusive social networks encourage a full-time and heavily concentrated gay identity. As such, his aesthetic tastes, sexual values, and politics all have a heavy "gay flavor" to them. There is no blandness in his recipe of self, only spice.

The gay lifestyler lives and experiences his gayness as an omni-relevant social attribute. For him, it is a master status socially, politically, and phenomenologically. The lifestyler thus most clearly illustrates the consequences of social markedness and captures the concept of master status in its most ideal form.

»3«

You Have to Drive Somewhere Just to Be Gay

Identity Chameleons

Randy has lived all thirty-plus years of his life in the same small suburb about an hour from New York City. Employed as a real estate agent, he divorced his wife while in his late twenties and thus has entered the "gay world" later than most. Although Randy has never lived anywhere but suburbia, his "gay life" is distinctly urban. He commutes to the city to be gay. Not only does he travel to New York but he also goes to Provincetown, Fire Island, southern Florida, and California to participate in their gay subcultures. Indeed, his four recent trips to California exceed the number of trips he has taken to local suburban bars in the same time period. He may be more likely to meet a gay man who lives near him while he is in New York or Florida than when he is in his own neighborhood. The physical distance he puts between his straight suburban work life and his gay leisure life also reflects a cognitive distance between the two lives. In her book *Home and Work*, Nippert-Eng (1996:105–51) discusses how individuals who segment their home and work lives use their commute to and from work to mentally partition their "home selves" from their "work selves." In a parallel manner, identity commuters use travel to make a transition between different identities. Commuters use travel through space to mark off discrete chunks of their self.[1] At work and among his neighbors, for instance, Randy submerges his gay self and foregrounds other facets of his self. He commutes to New York to ensure separation between his "gay self" and his "everyday self." As he explains, "I really never go to the bars so close to home. That way I'm pretty safe from seeing someone I might know." Randy keeps his gay life and his everyday life separate largely to avoid detection as gay in his everyday life.

Like Randy, Allen also keeps his gay life and his everyday life separate. He frequently travels to New York City to partake in its vibrant gay culture but lives and works an hour away in the suburbs. He has separate suburban (and almost exclusively straight) and urban (exclusively gay) friendship networks. Although Allen enjoys traveling to New York City, he says he prefers to live most of his life in the suburbs. He explains:

> I like New York and the gay scene there is great, but I also like having an ordinary life here [in the suburbs]. I would not want to have to live that [New York] gay lifestyle every day. I see people who do and they seem burned out and jaded. I grew up in the suburbs and I'm comfortable here. But then as a gay person I also feel at home in the city. The

---

1. See Zerubavel (1991:7) on how spatial partitions are used to articulate passages through mental partitions.

great thing about living here is that you can have a normal middle-class lifestyle and still be a part of the New York scene without having to live there.

Both Randy and Allen represent a social type I refer to as an "identity commuter"[2] or "identity chameleon." They live in heterosexual space and commute to gay space to "turn on" their gay selves.

It is important to note that not all "gay commuters" experienced the same feelings about "commuting." While a small number, predictably, saw themselves as traveling between a passing façade in the heterosexual world and a "true self" in the gay world, others did not experience their suburban self as any less true than the gay self they commuted to. Far from the stereotypical closeted gay living a life of quiet desperation in the suburbs and sneaking off to the city in the cover of night to let out his "true self" for brief fleeting moments of liberation, for instance, Allen finds himself at home in the straight world of the suburbs as well as the gay world of New York. He prides himself on being able to live in and to negotiate both worlds equally well.

Although we normally think of commuting as work-related, one can also conceive of *leisure* or *reverse commutes* where an individual lives near his or her suburban workplace and commutes to the city for leisure at night and on the weekends. In Randy's case the reversal of business and leisure travel patterns goes a step further. Not only does he engage in short-term identity commutes, but his trips to California and southern Florida to participate in social activities with other gay men represent an extended version of *identity travel.* His identity-related travels to California have a similar frequency to the work-related trips to conferences of some business travelers. He himself hints that his gay identity is a significant reason for his travels: "Ever since I divorced and realized that I really was gay . . . I've never traveled so much in

---

2. Of my thirty informants, I classify thirteen as closest to the commuter type; four others who later became closer to the integrator type were closer to the commuter type when I first met them.

my life. I travel so much more now." While one could also attribute this travel to being single, it is significant to note that his travels are organized around his gay identity. He travels with other gay men to marked gay identity spaces. Moreover, he did not travel to similar spaces during or prior to his marriage. Only after deciding that he was gay, something he says he suspected earlier but did not admit, did he begin to map out new social spaces around which to organize his world. The mapping of his social world as a thirtysomething gay male appears very different from a similar mapping of his world just five years ago when he was still married and identifying as heterosexual.

Scholars have noted that identity is not a stable, inherent attribute and that identities change historically and cross-culturally.[3] Some have even noted that an individual's identity can change over the lifecourse.[4] I suggest that we can go to an even smaller unit than the lifecourse and look at how identities can shift even over a single week or day.[5] That is, we engage in microtemporal everyday shifts in identity. The notion of identity commuting helps to point this out.

Commuting is, itself, a microtemporal instance of liminal transition.[6] Van Gennep (1960) argued that liminality marked a transitional period between shedding an old status and adopting a new one. He used this concept with respect to lifecourse transitions, but it also applies to everyday microtransitions in identity.[7] Identity commuters divide their social life into spatial and temporal zones that they keep separate. Rather than live in marked identity spaces, they live in "generic social space" and travel to "do" their marked identity.

---

3. On sexual identity, see, e.g., Chauncey (1994); D'Emilio (1983); Plummer (1981); Weeks (1985).
4. See Esterberg (1995:259) on sexual identity; see Gergen (1991) on identity more generally.
5. See Nippert-Eng (1996) on daily transitions from a home to work identity.
6. Ibid., 119.
7. See also ibid., 119–23.

When asked what they liked or did not like about the suburbs, many informants suggested that they both liked being within close driving distance of two major cities and disliked having to drive everywhere. As one explains:

> I like the proximity to major cities, and I like the proximity to scenic rural areas. I like the sense that you can get in a car and be in New York or Philadelphia . . . but that you can also be driving through beautiful country roads looking at the fall colors. I like the variety aspect of [living in the suburbs]. What I dislike is the feeling that to do anything you have to get in the car and maybe spend an hour getting somewhere and dealing with the Holland Tunnel or the PATH trains if you're going into the city.

Like most suburbanites this gay commuter enjoys the proximity of the suburbs to the city, but also like most "suburban commuters" he hates the "commute." He differs from the more traditional commuter in that his commute is more likely to be on Friday night than Monday morning.

Having a car was especially important to gay commuters with respect to driving to find other gay men. Tim says he was able to start seeing guys only after he got his car. He commuted to "be gay" during his high school years: "In high school I was straight in the day and I dated girls. Then at night I would drive forty miles to [another city] to be gay. I was basically straight by day and gay by night." Although the traditional way one might interpret this statement would be to assume that Tim was "really" gay, but just did not yet have the courage to express his "true self," this is not what Tim is saying. At this time in his life, Tim experienced his daytime heterosexual self as just as real as his nighttime gay self. His commute was not between a façade and a "real self" but between two different but equally "real" selves. Tim was even heterosexually engaged at the time and fully expected to marry his high school sweetheart. He claims that he negotiated both sexual worlds with a good deal of "success" and was envied by counterparts in each arena because of his ability to attract good-looking partners.

In these commutes, individuals are essentially slipping back and forth between a "straight identity" and a "gay identity" on a weekly, daily, or even hourly basis. And in Tim's case, during his high school years, he literally saw himself as a "part-time gay" and believed his "core self" was straight. Tim was able to maintain a straight "core self" in part because he relegated all his gay experiences to marked times and spaces. His everyday reality was still permeated with "doing straight" and his gay experiences were pushed to the peripheries of time (late at night) and space (forty miles away). The spatial and temporal distance he put between this self and his everyday self allowed him to bracket his gay identity as a peripheral part of his overall identity. It was only after he met a man in college with whom he started having a relationship that extended into the daytime that he began to redefine his "core" everyday self, first as bisexual, then two years later as gay.

Identity Distance: Traveling to Different Selves

The temporal and physical length of one's commute to a gay identity can tell us something about how much cognitive distance they put between different selves.[8] Some informants had maintained a "straight everyday self" for several years while making a long commute to perform their "gay leisure self." They bracketed their gay self into faraway spaces and late times at night. For many individuals who were grappling between adopting a full-time gay identity and maintaining their straight self, a long commute between straight and gay worlds allowed them to experiment with a part-time gay identity while hanging onto a straight everyday self. The further one drives to be gay and the later one comes out at night appear to be related to the identity

---

8. See Zerubavel (1991: 7, 25–28) on how we experience "mental distances" through the use of physical distance. See also Nippert-Eng (1996:117–32) on how commuting helps us make the transition between "different selves."

distance one places between his gay self and his not-gay self. That is, the spatial and temporal distance one travels to be gay measures, in part, one's distance from an integrated or full-time gay identity.

Many gay men I interviewed mentioned, for instance, that early in their coming out process they traveled to gay bars in other suburbs or cities rather than their own suburb. As they became more accustomed to their "gay self," they began to go to bars closer to their own town, thus shortening their commute to a gay identity. These commuters reinforced the mental distance between their everyday and gay selves both physically and temporally. In addition to traveling across space to be gay, they only expressed their gay selves at night. As a general rule, the later one comes out at night the greater the degree to which his nocturnal self[9] differs from his diurnal self. Likewise, a person who came out only on weekends generally experienced a greater distance between his daily self and his gay self (or "weekend self") than someone who commuted to the gay world on weekdays as well as weekends. The presence of a nocturnal self or a weekend self or a vacation/holiday self allows many men who engage in homosexual sex to maintain a heterosexual everyday self while commuting to a gay self only during marked times. Moreover, a long commute or coming out very late at night indicates greater identity distance than a short commute or coming out in the early evening.

If one looks at the temporal progression of gay activity during the course of a day one finds that it increases after dark and continues to increase as the night ages. Moreover, as the night becomes gayer, it attracts more and more identity commuters. In Northgate, the most rigidly commuting of all homosexual activity—"tearoom-style" anonymous sex at a late night "cruising street"—does not usually begin until after 3 A.M. (Humphreys, 1970). Although this cruising street attracts some men who come out earlier in the night to gay bars, it also attracts a number of het-

---

9. See Grazian (2000) for a discussion of how blues club travelers construct a nocturnal self that is bracketed from their everyday self.

erosexually married men and other daytime heterosexuals who will not set foot in any gay space before 3 A.M. Their bracketing of homosexual activity into the latest margins of the night allows these men to maintain a significant distance between when they are doing homosexuality and when they are being their diurnal heterosexual self. Avoiding any hint of "gayness" before 3 A.M. allows them to keep a comfortable divide between their unmarked diurnal self and their marked nocturnal self. The sexual commute of married daytime heterosexuals to a very short-duration homosexual self is a fleeting and exclusively sex-focused identity commute. Other commuters travel across space earlier in the night to take on longer, less sex-focused, more culture-oriented gay identities in a bar or gay ghetto.

Although we normally think of coming out as a linear process that occurs at the level of one's lifecourse, it can also be a cyclical weekly or daily process. Many informants tried on their gay identity several times before officially accepting it and adopting it as their core identity. In the early stages of trying on a gay identity, when informants said they had to drive somewhere to be gay, some of them meant it almost literally, not just metaphorically. More specifically, it was something they felt they could turn on and off like a switch or up and down like the volume knob on a radio. For instance, Tim explains that "I used to believe I was straight, but I'd sneak out to a cruising street really late at night. And it was just like the song, 'the freaks come out at night.' The gays come out at night too, and I used to come out at night." Although Tim now regards himself as gay all the time, in his transitional period between shedding his straight identity and adopting a gay one he basically came out as gay on a nightly basis and went back to being straight the next day. Thus, while we usually think of coming out as a macrotemporal process, Tim's experience suggests that we may also look at "coming out" as something gay men do many times at the daily level before deciding to do it as a more permanent lifecourse decision. Ray also saw gay identity as something that suburban gays activated like a switch, turning it on at night and off in the daytime:

> The norm among gays here is to rigidly draw a line
> between their social life and the professional world so
> that they are gay at the bar and then they are not gay at
> work. Like some guy will be Joe the gay guy on Saturday
> night but then on Monday he's just Joe who works at
> AT&T and that's it. He's not Joe the gay guy anymore.

Although Ray did not mean that the person was literally no longer gay when at work, he nonetheless points to the importance of seeing identity as something one does (verb) rather than just something one is (noun). We need, therefore, to think of identity as something that does not reside in the individual alone, but that resides in the interaction between the individual and his or her social environment. If we envision someone's identity as their "true colors," we might think of identity commuters as chameleons. Their colors change across time and space, and they are constructed in their interactions with their environment.

Identity Chameleons: Rising to the Occasion of the Setting

Whereas the lifestyler's gayness is omnirelevant, the commuter's identity is *omnicontextual.* The commuter is versatile and mobile. He prides himself on being able to fit in anywhere and on being able to get along with anyone. Among workers he is the best worker he can be, among Midwesterners he is the best Midwesterner he can be, among students the best student, among gays the best gay, among neighbors the best neighbor, among partiers the best partier, among sports fans the best sports fan. His "impression management" (Goffman, 1959) is flawless. He adapts to his social setting and takes pride in his ability to blend into a variety of social environments. The commuter's motto is "When in Rome do as the Romans do"—or more accurately, "do as the *best* Romans do."[10]

---

10. The Woody Allen movie *Zelig,* wherein the main character literally morphs into his various environments, provides a good caricature of the ideal-typical commuter.

While the identity lifestyler never sacrifices his principles to blend into an environment that is incompatible with his gayness, the commuter never sacrifices harmony to impose one of his selves on a habitat that he believes it is ill suited for. The commuter's identity is malleable across social space and lacks the fixity, the nounness, of the lifestyler's identity. For the commuter the salience of each ingredient of self varies with the context. His gayness is activated only when he is in gay space. Rather than a permanent master status, the commuter activates his gayness as a *temporary master status* in identity settings that evoke it, such as gay bars and pride parades. Outside gay settings, the commuter turns off his gayness and turns up other facets of his self. Like Clark Kent changing into his Superman costume, the commuter will change into his auxiliary characteristics and become "supergay" when he is called upon to do so, but he will change back out of the auxiliary characteristics when he leaves gay space. For the commuter, auxiliary characteristics are a uniform that one wears only in appropriate settings and that one is quick to shed when one leaves the identity setting. Just as occupational commuters change out of their work uniform when they leave the workplace,[11] gay commuters change out of their "gay uniform" when they leave the gay identityplace.

The key characteristic of commuters is *identity mobility*—the ability to move from place to place and fit in anywhere. Several of my informants said they would not want to move to New York City because it was a source of pride to them that they could fit in anywhere—that they didn't have to live in a gay ghetto. As one explained:

> You know I can go into the clubs in the city and be a queen for a night if I want to, but I can also just be a regular guy right here. And maybe some people who are queens, they have to live in New York because they don't

---

11. See Nippert-Eng (1996:132–42) on the importance of changing uniforms to change into "different selves" (e.g., home and work selves).

> have a choice; they just can't live anywhere but a gay neighborhood. But I don't have to live there because unless I want you to know you're not going to know that I'm gay.

Characteristic of commuters, he takes pride in being able to play up both his gay queen persona in New York club spaces and his regular guy identity in the suburbs.

Daytime Identity Work: Playing up the Generic and Downplaying the Marked

For the lifestyler being gay is full-time identity work. For the commuter gay identity is just one of many part-time identity jobs. Gayness is identity work he commutes to on a night or weekend shift, while he performs other identity work during the daytime or the work week. For the commuter, identity is a verb. He blends in like a chameleon, taking care to match his presentation of self with his surroundings. For him, identity work is "shift work." This strategy involves foregrounding or playing up environmentally encouraged facets of his self, while muting or playing down those that are discouraged in the setting. In unmarked spaces, blending in requires both playing down one's marked facets and playing up one's unmarked ones. Gay commuters, for instance, submerge their gayness and foreground the generic when in nongay spaces.

There are both structural and social psychological reasons for identity commuting. For some gay commuters, masking gayness and playing up the generic is done out of necessity because they live or work in an oppressive environment where they are afraid to be openly gay. Such individuals would likely choose to be full-time gays if their social space allowed them to. In interviews such people tended to refer to their gay persona as their true colors, implying that their daytime colors were only a protective façade.

It should be noted that in a culture where the default assumption is one of heterosexuality, even marginal performances of heterosexuality would pass in most straight environments. Yet many commuters play up their heterosexuality, demonstrating themselves as not just marginal or ordinary heterosexuals but among the *best* heterosexuals. One former fraternity member, for instance, pointed out that he not only passed among his brothers, but had a reputation as one of the studlier and more heterosexually accomplished members of his house. Although one may assume that he was playing the stud to overcompensate for fear of being perceived as gay, this is not necessarily the sole explanation. Since being a stud is the prime measure of status in fraternity culture (see Martin and Hummer, 1989), being the best fraternity member entails playing up one's masculinity and heterosexual stud persona, regardless of the members' "core" sexual identity. That is, playing up these auxiliary characteristics of a frat guy identity is something a commuter might do even if he weren't gay. Just as his gay identity is a momentary master status in gay environments, his fraternity identity is a temporary master status in fraternity environments. Even his heterosexual fraternity brothers play up the auxiliary characteristics of their fratness and thus manifest an exaggerated heterosexuality in the fraternity that they too submerge, at least partially, in other contexts.

The public everyday performances of commuters represent chameleon presentational strategies. These contrast with the peacock (or conspicuous display) strategies that Queer Nation employs in its use of generic public space. Presentational strategies serve as identity markers for others to judge one's social type and thus assess one's relative social value.[12] Commuters' blending-in presentations consist of playing up their positions of highest social value given the context and submerging positions of low or irrelevant social value. In ordinary suburban space, for instance, the "gay commuters" I interviewed played up such attributes as masculinity, employment status, and middle-class propriety and submerged their position of social disadvantage as homosexuals. They temporarily took on the cultural mask of hegemonic mas-

---

12. For more on the concept of social value, see Durkheim and Mauss (1963); Schwartz (1981); Williams (1990).

culinity (Connell, 1987) to blend into the conventionally masculine heterosexual environment of the corporate work world.

Conspicuously Generic: The Art of Being 120 Percent Average

The chameleon is not necessarily less active in playing up identity characteristics than the peacock. He simply plays up the expected characteristics of his unmarked environment with the same fervor with which peacocks play up the unexpected ones. Whereas the peacock is conspicuously marked, the chameleon in unmarked space is *conspicuously generic.* In generic unmarked space he plays up attributes that he has most in common with the unmarked majority rather than his marked minority.

Some gay chameleons, for example, play up their masculinity or their class status to deliberately overshadow any pretenses of a tainted identity. In his study of gay professionals, Woods made the following observation about one of his informants who lived a double life even to the point of being heterosexually married:

> As he shuttles between home and office [a sixty-five-mile commute from suburban New Jersey to Wilmington, Delaware], between his social and professional worlds, Eric undergoes a dramatic transformation. With gay friends he feels comfortable and authentic. He speaks candidly about the man he is dating, about gay political issues, and about the frustrations at home. Then, from nine to five, he becomes the office "superstud." Like the other men in his office, he swaggers and flirts, teasing the receptionist about her shapely figure, asking when it's "his turn" for a date. (Woods, 1993:109)

Using West and Fenstermaker's (1995) notion that individuals "do identity,"[13] we can see that even gay men may "do heterosex-

---

13. I broaden their original formulation of "doing difference" to "doing identity." Their concern was with how racial, class, and gender identities

uality" when confronted with the demands of living in heterosexualized spaces. Thus, Eric is able to play the superstud heterosexual as effectively as his heterosexual male coworkers. Eric, however, is more conscious than they are of the fact that playing the superstud heterosexual is a performance. He knows he is doing this identity, as a "verb."

The verb quality with which commuters actively do their identities to match their environmental settings demonstrates that identities are socially constructed and reconstructed at the micro level of everyday interactions. Some informants even expressed pride in how well they were able to pull off their performances of heterosexuality. For instance, Tim points out that he was highly successful in his life as a heterosexual and had sex with many women before he "became gay." True to the commuter type, Tim suggests that not only can he live in the gay world, but when he was still heterosexual he could compete and excel in their world as well.

In order to blend in when not in gay space, commuters conceal their gay identity while playing up heterosexual auxiliary characteristics. They live double lives, manifesting a heterosexual persona during afternoons and weekdays and a gay persona at night and on weekends. Their life is carefully divided into separate straight and gay spheres. Ray describes the pattern:

> I think that [there are] pressures of living in a very suburban area where it's family oriented—a lot of areas around here are blue-collar. I think that puts pressure on people in the gay community to decide "I do need to draw the line between my social life and my professional world and everything else, where I live, where I go to eat, etc." And I feel like a lot of people can only be gay at the bar, like that's the only place where I can be identified that I am

are reproduced in everyday interactions. Thus, they were studying how we do difference. I prefer the phrase "doing identity," since "doing difference" implies that identity presentation necessarily involves foregrounding only difference and not sameness.

gay, or at someone's house party or whatever. And that the rest of it, "Nope, now I am not [gay]," because those are the terms.

This pattern is particularly evident in the workplace, where many men carefully manage their identity to avoid discovery. Although it may not be obvious to heterosexuals, many informants point out that the most pervasive topic of conversation at the office is heterosexuality. Spouses, dates, weddings, and the like make up the lion's share of office gossip in many places, and this becomes a source of discomfort. Randy explains that one of the biggest problems he has as a divorced gay male in his thirties is that his office mates are always trying to set him up with a new woman. He deals with these attempts with a generic rather than a gay-specific answer: "Oh, I don't do blind dates anymore. I don't like to be set up, it never works out well for me." So far this reason has satisfied his workmates.

Others engage in more elaborate measures. A few men brought a female friend to work-related parties to pose as a girl-friend. In some cases, gay men brought a lesbian friend to their work functions and reciprocated as a stand-in boyfriend when she required a similar favor at her workplace. Ray says that one of his friends simply substitutes a woman's name for his lover's whenever he talks about his private life at work:

> I have a friend of mine who created a girlfriend. He had a live-in lover who he was dating for three years. His lover had five kids from a previous marriage that ended in di-vorce and he still refers to him as—I can't remember the name, let's just say Diana. [He] refers to the boyfriend as Diana and talks about their problems, talks about they had a fight, realistically talks about the five kids, the whole bit. But it's Diana, not his boyfriend's real name.

For Ray's friend, talking about his lover as though he is female gives his life the mundane appearance that allows him to pass as straight. Given that heterosexuality is the default setting and that fathers are generally assumed to be heterosexual, few of his coworkers probably even think to question his sexual identity.

Although commuters can "queen it up" with lifestylers in marked identity spaces, their most conspicuous feature in un-marked suburban space can be their ordinariness. One strategy some commuters use in unmarked space is to be blatantly aver-age. These commuters are not only ordinary in generic suburban space, they are *conspicuously average*. They manifest a suburban lifestyle that includes appearing masculine but not overly so, ex-pressing politically moderate views, attending church but not be-ing religiously zealous, and being civically involved. In contrast to when they are overwhelming others with their high-density spiciness in marked identity spaces, these commuters foreground their blandness in the generic spaces of suburbia. Some inten-tionally define their everyday lives as bland, ordinary, or average. Louis explains, for instance, that no one suspects him of being gay because his everyday life outside the gay bar scene is "too or-dinary":

> I'm basically only out to the gay community. I'm not out at work or to my neighbors and friends here, or to most of my family yet. And fortunately no one really suspects [I'm gay] because I don't really act very gay. It's funny but I'm just—I'm just not interesting enough to be gay [laughs]. I mean who is going to wonder about a regular average guy like me?

Although he does admit to letting his hair down in gay bars, the rest of Louis's life is nothing out of the ordinary. Outside of spaces where he openly expresses his sexual orientation his life appears quite "generic."

Perhaps no facet is more carefully managed for genericness among some gay commuters than masculinity. Being just a regu-lar guy or masculine but not overly butch was among the desir-able gender presentations of the suburban gay men I spoke with.

Their goal was to be as ordinarily masculine as possible. As one explains:

> I like to be butch but butch in a good way, not your super-beefy "I'm so macho" kind of butch guy, because that's a gay stereotype too. Sure, they're good to look at in a club, but who wants to stand out as being so butch? I mean, I'm just your ordinary masculine kind of regular guy. And when people see me, you know, I'm just a guy. I'm not a body builder and I'm not a queen, I'm just a guy.

Notable about this statement is that the individual is playing up the generic ("just a guy") as a socially desirable and valued attribute. He is consciously marking the ordinary and unmarked as desirable and preferable to the exceptional. When around "ordinary people" in unmarked space he will play up his ordinariness and commonality with them. The commuter finds what he has in common with the rest of the group and foregrounds it. Being around bland people he highlights blandness as his own most distinct flavor too.

There is an interesting split among commuter strategies in unmarked space between those strategies that play up the extreme types of the unmarked category and those that play up the modal types of the category. Among gay commuters, for instance, some play up the extreme superheterosexual persona such as the frat stud or the office superstud to score points in unmarked space, while others play up the modal heterosexual to blend into the crowd. Rather than play up the superheterosexual persona, they play up their superaverage persona (e.g., mild-mannered Clark Kent).

Coming Out at Night: Weekend Warriors to a Gay Identity

Several gay commuters spoke of letting their hair down or showing their true colors at night and on the weekends. Dave, for instance, maintained very separate gay and straight worlds. He explained that he was highly successful in blending in with the straight world, but at night he liked to come out with his true colors.

> What do fags wear outside the bar? Anything from a business suit to overalls on a tractor. Anything. Gay people are chameleons; we adapt into the scenery by day and like peacocks we come out with our true colors at night.

Dave feels his true identity is gay, and yet he is allowed to express his gay identity only in a few places and times. Consequently, when he does turn on his gay identity, he turns it on high volume. For commuters such as Dave gay identity is manifested as a high-volume, low-duration identity. He spreads his identity across very few spheres of his life, but he presents it in a heavily concentrated form. Turning up one's gayness at night and in the bars is a common practice among commuters. In fact, Dave was not the only one to use the peacock metaphor to describe gay men at night. Ray also described the bar scene and its high-intensity displays as "a bunch of peacocks in a bar showing their feathers. Like 'Hey, look at me!'" Larry elaborated on the peacocks-by-night phenomenon:

> I think that a lot of gay men have an identity that no one else may notice but they have, they create an identity where they're repressing the whole aspect of their sexuality [most of the time], so when they do go out they act like big screaming queens because they just let it all out. Because they are allowed to, you know, and they think "Oh, finally I can act like this because no one is going to judge me, and it's so much fun." And they end up putting on spandex clothing and putting on three bottles of gel in their hair, and they just do things that they don't normally associate themselves with, whatever. But then, in the day, they are accountants who are wearing suits and they are totally calm. It's kind of like letting out the darker

> side. . . . But to you, because that's what's important to you as a person, when you are repressing something, you are creating an identity based on that. And plus you do, you know, there are certain stereotypical mannerisms and speech patterns you're very careful of, to *only use in the right places* [emphasis added].

As Larry suggests, the zoning of gay identity into a very small sphere of one's life leads many men to present that identity in a highly concentrated form when they are able to let it out. They carefully manage gay auxiliary characteristics such as mannerisms and speech patterns so that they are activated only in the right places. As commuters limit their gay persona to society's few marked spaces reserved for homosexuality, many express it with added volume and density when they do turn it on.

Identity commuters use temporal zones such as night and day and weekend and weekday to bracket their separate selves. They also maintain separate daytime and nighttime social networks. Greg's segregation of his gay social networks into the night is apparent, for instance, when he states "like I told you, most of my gay friends I haven't seen in the daylight [laughs]." Greg maintains two selves and two social networks: a nocturnal network for his gay self, a diurnal one for his everyday self. Both the night and the weekend are marked social times, and it is in these times that social actors themselves are more likely to do markedness. At night one is somewhat more freed to flip the switch and turn on one's "true colors" or "darker side." The night has long been associated in lore with transformation of everyday workaday people into exotic others when the clock strikes midnight and the moon is full. The night is a temporal zone for doing markedness. It is a territorial frontier into which stigmatized groups can retreat. Melbin (1987) suggests, for instance, that just as settlers and deviants once escaped to the sparsely populated sections of the spatial frontier to escape persecution and stigma, today's marginalized groups can retreat into the temporal margins of the night. Unlike the early settlers, however, today's identity travelers need not en-

gage in a permanent move. They can travel back and forth between mainstream society in the day and the margins at night. In
essence they can be nighttime travelers and weekend warriors to
a marginalized identity.

"New York Is a Nice Place to Visit, but I Wouldn't Want to Live There": Commuting to Do Identity Work

Commuting from the suburbs to the city to do occupation work is
just one form of commute; individuals may also commute from
the suburbs to the city to do identity work. Commuters enjoy traveling to the gay ghettos, but they also like the separation between
their gay identity world and their ordinary suburban world that
the commute gives them. Although urban enclaves provide a territorial haven for gay men and those in other marked categories,
commuters do not necessarily express interest in moving to New
York. Many prefer temporary travel over a permanent move to a
gay-specific enclave.

Although some commuters may wish to be urban lifestylers,
others do not necessarily want to live in gay-friendly spaces such
as New York or San Francisco. Some commuters, in fact, take
pride in the fact that they do not live in the gay ghettos. Jacob
(who grew up in the South, attended college in the Midwest, and
moved to San Francisco after college) moved from San Francisco
to Northgate because he wanted to prove he could live in heterosexual space:

> [In San Francisco] there was just no respect for being a
> simple working person or a simple professional-type per-
> son. And I just felt like it was time for a change and time
> to see if I could live somewhere else where it wasn't gay
> all the time. And so I think I pretty consciously chose to
> come to New Jersey because I thought, What could be
> more manly than New Jersey. . . . In other words, Can I be
> myself? Can I pass? Can I be manly? In other words, I'm
> playing around with things as well, where especially in my

> early years of coming to New Jersey [I was] wanting to
> pass, [I was] getting off on passing.

He says his time in San Francisco was necessary for him to experience the full intensity of gay culture, which he enjoyed greatly at
first. But after a few years he determined that he no longer wanted
to live in a "fortress" apart from the rest of the world. Indeed, the
conformities of San Francisco's gay world eventually bothered
him as much as the conformities of the straight world he had escaped. Northgate provided the ideal compromise, since he could
still travel in and out of the gay world but no longer had to be "on
gay" all the time.

Many commuters, of course, have never lived in a big city. Nor
do they necessarily have any desire to. Like Jacob, other gay commuters also referenced their ability to live in suburban space as a
source of pride and a sign of maturity. Most of the suburban commuters I interacted with agreed that New York is fun, but several
also expressed a view of urban ghetto gays as the "free-roaming
adolescents of gay identity" and thus not to be taken too seriously. Some informants stated that they didn't have to live in
New York or be on gay all the time as a tacit indicator of their
mainstream respectability and, therefore, relatively higher "social
value" than that of more lifestyle-oriented gay men. A common
sentiment used to distance oneself, in part, from lifestyler culture
was to suggest that "New York is a nice place to visit, but I
wouldn't want to live there." Many informants had both positive
and negative things to say about New York. The positive comments tended to be voiced when speaking about visiting while
negative ones surfaced when informants were asked if they
would want to live in New York. One individual who traveled to
New York explained, "I wouldn't want to live in New York because there is too much diversity." Given New York's glamorous
image as a mecca for gays and other marked identities, one might
be surprised to hear this view from someone in a category we
would expect to value diversity. It is important to recognize, however, that one's markedness is just one facet of one's identity and

essence as a human. Like their heterosexual counterparts located in similar social locations, other attributes such as where they grew up, their class background, race, and occupation also weigh into where gay men prefer to live. Among the various reasons for not wanting to live in New York informants gave were that there was too much crime, "it's too crowded," "there's too much traffic," "it's expensive," "it's unsafe," "it's dirty," "it's a big city," "it's noisy," and "it's too impersonal." Some found the city intimidating and preferred to be a "big fish in a smaller pond," both socially and occupationally. As one computer graphics artist explained, "In New York there are a thousand people who can do what I do. It's hard to be the best at anything in New York. Whether it's the best queen in the bar or the best graphics artist or whatever, it's way too competitive." It is noteworthy that his statement expresses the commuter's desire to excel in both arenas—the bar and graphic arts.

Although a small number of the men I talked to had lived in cities, the majority grew up in suburbs, and a few even came from rural areas. Their past history as lifelong suburban or rural denizens generally washed over their "gayness" in determining whether they chose to move to a large city. When I asked Richard to elaborate on his statement that he would much rather live in the suburbs than in New York, he responded:

> Why would a gay person want to live in the suburbs?? Because we can! We don't all wear black leather—all of the time. I think we prefer the suburbs for the same reason anyone else would. The reason we're here is because we were raised in the suburbs and that's where we want to die. And I think we always have been suburban dwellers and from small towns. My partner and I travel on gay vacations hosted by gay cruise lines or Club Meds with seven hundred to two thousand people and those people are from Knoxville, Tennessee, and they're from somewhere in Alabama. They're from Podunk, Alabama. And we met people from small towns in Wisconsin and from Alaska.

> They certainly don't [all] live in big cities. They were from those kinds of places and we didn't really meet anyone from New York or San Francisco.

Using humor, Richard associates living in identity-specific space with the popular cultural image of an urban leatherman "lifestyler" to suggest that he, as a nonlifestyler, does not need to live in a gay enclave. In saying "we don't all wear black leather—all of the time," he hints that he may play it up in leather sometimes if he pleases, but he does not have to be "on" all the time. He has the *mobility* to move in and out of the gay persona and turn it up and down as he wishes. His identity-based vacations also reflect his ability to travel to escape heterosexual space when necessary. Note too that at least in his view most of his fellow identity travelers also come from nonurban environments.

Even those who regretted the oppression of their gay-unfriendly towns did not necessarily desire to *live* in the city even though they enjoyed *traveling* to the city. Dave, for instance, who laments having lived more than an hour from New York City while in high school, says he had to be straight in high school because he was not able to travel to places where he could be gay:

> Here if you're under eighteen, being gay is very difficult. There's no place to go. Generally, a lot of people underage stick to themselves. I did. It depends on the size, the number of people in the community, and how open they are. If you're young and live in Staten Island, you can go to the Village. If you live [here], you don't say a word to anyone. You go out with [straights] and you do whatever they do. If you are in the suburbs you try to be straight.

Although Dave likes Manhattan, it is interesting to note that he mentions Staten Island rather than Manhattan as an example of an ideal place for gay youth to grow up. He considers Staten Island's youth fortunate because they can easily commute to Manhattan to "be gay." Implied in his comparison between Staten

Island and his hometown is that living in gay space is not critical, but being able to travel to it is. A gay lifestyler would not consider Staten Island ideal and would contrast growing up in Dave's town with living in Manhattan rather than with living in suburban Staten Island.

Conclusion

Traditionally, we think of gay identity in terms of the closeted-out continuum and of marked identities more generally in terms of invisibility and visibility.[14] Although the closeted-out continuum is useful, there are advantages to looking at the identity process differently. The closeted-out continuum implies that there is a single axis (visibility) along which identities evolve and that high visibility is necessarily always the endpoint. As the example of Jacob (the ex–San Francisco lifestyler turned Jersey commuter) shows, this is not necessarily the case. Identity strategies do not always follow a trajectory from closeted to out. Moreover, although commuters are closer to the closeted end of the continuum than lifestylers, not all commuters are necessarily closeted nor are their lives necessarily miserable from oppression (though some are). Rather, commuting is a strategic choice by which they manage their marked identity while living in an unmarked environment. Commuting allows the individual to try out his identity, to act it out when freed from the constraints of the larger society, and to maintain as separate realms the gay and straight worlds. It also allows the individual to become acculturated into and enter his new world and new identity gradually. He may move back and forth between gay space and unmarked space until he feels fully comfortable in gay space.

Additionally, the concept of identity commuting allows us to extend our knowledge from observations of gay subjects to make

---

14. See, for example, Goffman (1963b:48–50) on the importance of visibility to "deviant identity."

analytic conclusions about social life that extend beyond the realm of gay sexuality and identity. Queer theorists have been arguing for some time that studies of gays, lesbians, and queers should inform the structuring of the social world more generally,[15] but this argument has so far been ignored by mainstream sociology. Perhaps moving away from the metaphors of the closet and invisibility to new epistemological angles will refresh the need to consider gay and other marked subjects as relevant to the analysis of social life in general and not just to the analysis of sexuality or "deviance."

Although there are certain to be differences between how gay identity and other identities are experienced, these differences alone should not lead to theoretical ghettoization. An analysis of how gay identity is managed in unfriendly space informs the study of all identity work. While not all marked groups suffer the same magnitude of discrimination and oppression, nor do they share the same degree of ascribed or achieved status, the concept of commuting to do identity is relevant to any social category. The degree to which commuters play up generic regular guy and other unmarked identities outside gay spaces also informs us of how identity work occurs even with respect to mainstream identity performances.

Commuters treat their identity as a verb. They "do unmarkedness" in generic public space and thus spread their markedness across very few spheres of their social life. They organize their marked identity to have a low duration and a high concentration. It is off most of the time, but when it is on, it is in a highly concentrated form and may be turned up all the way to high volume. Commuters invade spatial ghettos and the temporal extremes of the night to turn their marked identity on. They retreat back into the modal spaces of society and turn it back off by morning. They define their ability to fit into generic space as something that distinguishes them from lifestylers, whom they perceive as lacking

---

15. See especially Seidman (1996:13).

the mobility to move out of the gay persona. Their ability to live outside marked identity spaces is something they assert as a source of pride. Unlike lifestylers or unmarked members of society, commuters can move to either end of the identity spectrum. They can successfully pull off performances in both marked and unmarked space. As such, they have something over both life-stylers and the unmarked members of society. They can fit in at either end of the identity spectrum. Commuters, by passing in both contexts, show that both the marginal and the mainstream are engaged in performances of identity.

»4«

"Gay Defines Only a Small Part of Me"

Identity Centaurs

When I put a label on myself, "gay" is way down on the list as to how I define myself. When I think to myself "Who is Charles?," saying "Well, he's gay" is as accurate as saying "He's six-foot-two" or "He has brown hair and brown eyes." That's a minor part of who I am. I'm more proud of the things I've developed and accomplished myself than the things I was born with. You know, being gay or being six-foot-two and having brown eyes and brown hair are things I don't have control over anyway. I identify myself much more with the parts of me that I developed myself.

Charles, a gay integrator

Charles views himself as a mixture of multiple attributes and thus does not feel his identity can be pinned down to any core attribute or master status—gayness is not the leading component to his self. Unlike the lifestyler whose other attributes flow hierarchically down from and reinforce their master status, the integrator combines attributes that are not necessarily associated with one another.[1] In the integrator there is no central at-

---

1. I classify seventeen of my thirty primary informants as closest to the integrator ideal type.

tribute around which all other attributes, tastes, and views are organized. Whereas the lifestyler sees gayness and suburbanness as unrelated or even incompatible attributes and the commuter travels between his suburban self and his gay self as though they are mutually exclusive, the integrator is a hybrid of gay and suburban attributes that are manifested at the same time. The suburban gay integrator is an identity centaur whose suburban and gay sides mix to create a worldview that is neither exclusively suburban nor exclusively gay.

If we envision identity attributes as ingredients of the self, we might think of gay as a spicy ingredient, while unmarked facets such as suburban might be considered the more bland ingredients. The integrator dilutes the flavor of his markedness by adding bland unmarked traits to the recipe. From this perspective, the statement "I'm all gay!" has more potency than the statement "I'm an accountant, I'm middle-class, I'm a good person, I'm a neighbor, I'm suburban, and I'm gay." In the latter statement, mixing in a variety of unmarked ingredients dilutes some of the spiciness of the original recipe. By mixing in other adjectives, integrators dilute the salience and importance of gayness as a defining ingredient. Unlike the commuter, the integrator spreads gay identity evenly across all spheres rather than concentrating it heavily in one or two spheres of his life. As a consequence, its overall salience in any one sphere is relatively low.

While the integrator's marked identity is turned on all the time, it is on low volume. It is background instrumentation, not lead guitar. His marked attribute never becomes his single defining feature. Gay identity always represents a percentage rather than the entirety of the integrator's self. Existentially, for the integrator, gayness is always a *complementary status,* never a master status. But unlike the commuter, whose gay identity is a fraction of his whole self because he brackets it to a separate sphere of his life, the integrator's gay identity is a fraction of his whole self because he spreads it thinly across every sphere. Whereas the ideal-typical commuter concentrates, for example, 100 percent gay into 15 percent of his life, the ideal-typical integrator spreads 15 percent gay across 100 percent of his life. In the end, the commuter and integrator may do the same overall net amount of "gayness." The commuter, though he does gay identity only a small percentage of time, does it in a highly concentrated form. And the integrator, though he does gay identity in a diluted concentration, does it all the time.

As an integrator, Charles considers his sexuality relevant to who he is, but not omnirelevant. He defines it as something that occupies a small patch rather than the entire territory of his self:[2]

> [Who I like to have sex with] is such a small part of the whole picture. To say that my sexual orientation defines who I am is just silly. I would say that in most ways I'm not any different than my straight neighbors. And even where I am [different] it's not necessarily because I'm gay.

As he does not consider his sexuality omnirelevant, Charles sees differences between himself and his heterosexual neighbors as not necessarily being explained by their different sexual identities. Charles also suggests that he has far more in common with his straight neighbors than with publicly visible drag queens, activists, and leathermen. He considers his life relatively conventional and far removed from the exotic images of New York's and San Francisco's gay cultures. Integrators such as Charles label themselves as "ordinary," "plain," "bland," or "boring" as a way of distinguishing themselves from the flashy, spicy public image of gay life. When I was interviewing Jerry and Roger as a couple, for instance, I laid out a set of flash cards listing various social types within the gay community that other informants had identified, such as queens, butches, leathermen, and activists. They quickly pointed out that, for them, the most important category— "boring"—was missing:

---

2. Seidman, Meeks, and Traschen (1999:29) also found gay interviewees who defined their homosexuality as "a thread" rather than the core aspect of their identity.

Jerry: You're missing "boring." That's the biggest category right
there.

Roger: Right. Everything is just plain old people. I mean [look]
what's missing?! What category do we fit into actually??

Jerry: Yeah, because I don't fall—I'm definitely not a queen.
Butch maybe?—but not really because I'm kind of middle of
the road. I mean you could put "androgynous" down here as
a category. Not that I'm really androgynous either, but it
means neither overtly queeny or overtly butch.

Roger: Right. Just your normal kind of masculine person.

Wayne (the interviewer): So if you were to label yourself, if you
had to put a label on yourself, what would you use?

Jerry: Suburban.

Roger: Just a regular Joe fag.

Jerry: That's right. I think regular Joe is good.

As this discussion shows, both men have a hard time finding a
term from existing discourse that captures their social type. There
are no readily available cultural labels for their segment of the gay
population. The visible extremes of the gay community such as
activists, drag queens, and leathermen are more heavily articulated in the popular culture. The "boring" members of the community remain unnamed and thus largely invisible within extant
cultural discourse.

In a society where the category gay is associated with the exotic and extraordinary, showing that one is, in fact, just ordinary
can, itself, be a source of pride or even resistance. For integrators,
pointing out their own ordinariness is a way of saying "Yes, we're
gay, but we're also all these other things, so the salience of our
'gayness' isn't going to overwhelm you." It's just one spicy ingredient mixed in with an otherwise relatively bland recipe. When
asked how they would label themselves with respect to their
social type, such informants chose a variety of terms such as
"workaday gay," "regular Joe," "just an ordinary fag," "workaday
schmo," and "just a regular guy who is gay." Also common was
"[occupation] who just happens to be gay."

The appeal to being ordinary or just a regular guy was commonly expressed in the desire to be around good people regardless of sexual identity. Virtually all integrators said the number-one criterion for being their friend is "that you are a good person, period." Their friendship groups consisted of mixed social networks. Indicative of their integrator mind-set is that several had to think for some time before arriving at what proportion of their friends are gay. As Richard put it when answering what percentage of his friends were gay and what percentage were straight: "Off hand I'm not sure, [because] I don't think of it in those terms." Whereas the gay lifestyler chooses his social networks based on sexual identity and the gay commuter separates his social networks by sexual identity, the gay integrator organizes his social networks along other dimensions. Thus, for instance, while Richard could have come up with an answer to my question, to do so he would have had to reorient his classification logic to recognize sexual identity as the first attribute by which to categorize his friends.

"We're Just Ordinary Workaday Folks": Diluting Gayness by Mixing in Unmarked Attributes

Gay integrators articulate pride in being predominantly ordinary. They reject definitions of both the religious right and the queer left of gay men as extraordinary. The integrator does not regard himself as special, either in a positive or in a negative way. Unlike commuters, who maintain a strong separation between an ordinary everyday self and an extraordinary gay self, integrators have just one relatively ordinary everyday self. They mix the bland and the spicy together in one identity presentation and thus attempt and somewhat succeed in neutralizing the negative stigma associated with the marked attribute. Jeffrey Alexander (2001:245) refers to the ethnic strategy of "hyphenation" as one where ethnic groups try to neutralize negative qualities by symbolically associating with the core. Similar to such ethnic integrators, the gay integrator attaches a number of hyphens or adjectives to his gay label in an attempt to neutralize stigma. The integrator presents himself as a multifaceted combination of adjectives. Thus gay itself is just one ingredient that conveys minimal information about the overall flavor of his whole self.

Alexander's (2001:245) observation that "ethnic hyphenation does not suggest the equal valuation of core and outsider qualities" and that stigmatization remains is worth keeping in mind, however. While the integrator reduces the stigma of his own overall identity, he does so primarily by claiming that *his* gayness is diluted rather than by directly confronting attacks on gayness. To the extent that integrating is a political strategy, it is an individual one of stigma management. Nonetheless, his strategy does have collective ramifications, for in showing that gayness is compatible with socially valued attributes he challenges the perception among homophobic individuals that a uniform set of auxiliary characteristics will apply to all gay individuals.

For the integrator, presenting oneself as just a regular Joe is not merely a calculated political strategy to assimilate into mainstream society. Instead, it is indicative that the integrator's multiple social locations and not just his most politically salient location shape his values, interests, attitudes, and worldview. As white, masculine, middle-class males raised in the suburbs, many gay integrators, for instance, have values similar to those of other white, middle-class, suburban-raised males. Moreover, their values are not necessarily contrived, but rather such values reflect the standpoint of individuals who have been shaped not only by their experiences as members of an oppressed group but by their experience as members of several dominant groups as well. Their marked sexual orientation is not itself enough to wash over their more "generic" and tacitly privileging attributes to produce an entirely new "gay" worldview.

Although the integrator's worldview may be partially shaped by his gayness, it flavors only a small part of the whole, just as his middle-classness, maleness, suburbanness, and other attributes

each comprise just a small section of the whole picture. He belongs to several different "thought communities."[3] Since gayness
takes up only a fraction of his self, his attitudes reflect a mix of
one liberalizing spice (gayness) and several conservativizing
buffers (middle-classness, suburbanness, etc.). The integrator
mixes all these modifiers into his overall composition of self.

A key difference between integrators and commuters, is that
commuters separate their marked self from their unmarked one
whereas integrators mix it all together. One might think of the
lifestyler's identity plate as being a one-course meal consisting of
a single spicy dish, the commuter's as being a TV dinner with separate courses placed into separate compartments, and the integrator's as being a salad or a soup where everything is mixed
together. This is also reflected in social networks. Whereas lifestylers have identity-exclusive networks and commuters have
separate diurnal and nocturnal social networks, integrators have
mixed social networks. The commuter does gay guy on the weekends and AT&T guy at work as if they are two mutually exclusive
selves; this makes perfect sense to him. For the integrator, by contrast, the notion of gay AT&T guy is not an oxymoron, since both
are adjectives that can appear with one another in defining who
he is. Larry, for instance, believes that one's gay sexual identity is
not in conflict with one's mainstream corporate work identity:

> I don't understand when [another] gay person says, "Oh,
> you're acting so straight." . . . It's like when a black per-
> son says to another black person, "You're acting so white."
> If you go to work in a suit and tie why is that acting white?
> Or why is that acting straight? It's not. You're just acting
> the role that your job expects from you. When an accoun-
> tant is at work and he's wearing a suit and being conserva-

3. See Zerubavel (1997:9–22) for a discussion of how we think as members of
multiple social groups, such as churches, professions, and generations, that
shape our worldview as a thought community. See Fleck (1979:45) for the ori-
gin of the term "thought community."

tive and formal he's not acting straight, he's just doing his
job. If you're in a business, that's the way you act at work,
and it's not a straight/gay thing because straight people
don't act like that when they get off work either. Everyone
is acting a certain way at work, so no, they are not acting
straight, they're still being gay. They're just being gay *and*
they're being an accountant.

For Larry being corporate is an adjective that goes equally well
with either a gay or a straight identity. In fact, his notion that
straights are also acting at work implies the performative character of unmarked identities that often goes unquestioned. It is usually only when someone from a marked category plays up an
unmarked identity like "corporate" that the display itself is ques-
tioned as an "inauthentic" performance.

Integrators mix in their unmarked positions of tacit privilege
such as being middle-class, conventionally masculine, male, suburban, and white to make strong claims to be members of the
larger society rather than outcasts from it. There are many instances where their membership in such unmarked categories as
middle-class appears to weigh[4] more heavily in their values and
worldviews than membership in the gay category. Since most informants also possess relatively privileging attributes, they often
implicitly affirm their positions of class, gender, and racial privilege as signs of their symbolic social value. They emphasize their
traits of unmarkedness as tacit reminders that they, for the most
part, are just ordinary ("generic") people.

Critical to the worldview of the integrator is the notion that he
is an ordinary part of humanity rather than part of an "exotic subset." He dislikes the "queer" label that celebrates only the "exotic"
side of a gay person's self. John describes the gay community in
general, as well as himself in particular, as being mostly mundane
despite its extraordinary elements:

---

4. See Mullaney (1999) on how different identity attributes "weigh" differently in one's overall experience of self.

> Even with the drag queens, there's a lot of us [gays] alto-
> gether that just make us quite regular and quite mundane
> really. We're all a part of Western civilization. We all have
> a certain way of doing things. We wake up in the morning
> and have what you have [for breakfast]. When it comes to
> the majority of homosexuals out there, bisexuals, what-
> ever, they are just workaday gays. They have jobs. They
> have mortgages. There really is very little difference. I
> mean, I consider myself so assimilationist. There really
> isn't any difference between me and my heterosexual
> friends other than the fact that I want to date men. But
> getting married, getting the condo, townhouse, whatever,
> growing old together, building a career, these are all the
> same kinds of aspirations and goals that I have.

John emphasizes the common ground both he and the gay community as a whole share with humanity as a generic category. He
admits that there are spicy elements to the gay community, but
that when one mixes in all the mundane gay men with the few
drag queens the end result is pretty bland and only slightly different from "generic humanity" as a whole. Interestingly, he does
with gay identity at a collective level what the integrator also does
with his own identity at the individual level; he does not hide the
spicier elements of the community, but he attempts to neutralize
the spice by emphasizing how many more moderate elements
there are. Just as he is comfortable with his individual marked attribute as a gay person, he is not ashamed of the more exotic elements of the gay community as a part of the whole. In both cases,
however, he neutralizes the potential stigma of these marked elements by playing up blander elements of himself (individually)
and the gay community (collectively). He sees himself as an individual, as being shaped only slightly differently from the "generic
human" by his "gayness." The vast majority of his goals and aspirations make him almost indistinguishable from his heterosexual suburban counterparts. Similarly, in his view, although the
extremes give it a bit of flavor, the gay community as a whole has

similar goals and aspirations to the human community writ large. He expresses a similar view of himself:

> I am not just like a straight person in every way. There are things about being gay that make me different, so I'm not going to say, "Hey, I'm just like you." But on the other hand I am just like you in *most* ways, and where there are differences they aren't large.

For the integrator, gayness slightly modifies one's overall self to produce a self that is neither completely unmarked nor very marked.

Integrators emphasize the weight of their genericness more than that of their gay-specific uniqueness and position themselves closer to "mainstream culture" than to "gay subculture–oriented gays" (as they call lifestylers) in defining their core selves. Suggesting that they maintain gayness in only a diluted concentration, integrators stress their difference from more heavily concentrated manifestations of gay identity. Whereas lifestylers consider their gay identity omnirelevant and at the very core of who they are, integrators see their gayness as a modifying adjective rather than an all-encompassing noun.[5] Jacob, for instance, emphasizes the characteristic of being career-minded as something that aligns him with the "generic mainstream culture" and alienates him from what he sees as "typical" of gay persons and "gay culture":

> I don't consider myself a typical gay person because— what I don't like about gay people is they're not career-minded, they're like not smart, they just don't seem like— I mean this is going to sound really bad, but they just

---

5. Note that I am using the words "noun" and "adjective" as analytic templates. Informants themselves do not typically use these terms to refer to one another or their "identity management styles."

don't seem like normal people. But I do consider myself a
normal person. There are certain things I want, certain
middle-class values I was raised with, and those have not
been shaken out of me.

Another way integrators emphasize their generic humanity is by
asserting that sexual identity is value-neutral and thus irrelevant
to whether or not one is a "good person." This challenges both
the religious right's assertion that being gay makes one immoral
and the gay subculture's celebration of gay or queer identities as
automatically a positive moral affirmation. Mark, for instance,
says:

> I don't identify with gay subculture–oriented gays. They
> act in a very stereotypically gay manner, and I don't relate
> to that. I don't like that straights treat gay as a value-
> negative thing but then subculture-oriented gays treat
> straight as a value-negative thing and gay as automatically
> a value-positive thing. I want my sexual orientation to be
> treated as value neutral. It's not a good thing or a bad
> thing. My problem with gay lifestyle–oriented gays[6] is that
> their central core of essence is that straight is bad, so
> down with the mainstream. But I don't want to be down
> on the mainstream because I am the mainstream. If you're
> down on mainstream people, you're not just attacking
> straights, you're attacking me too.

Integrators object to the notion of gay identity as a noun because
they think the noun status of gay identity unnecessarily heightens
the salience of gayness and diminishes other aspects of the self.

---

6. It is worth noting here that I never used the words "lifestyler," "commuter,"
or "integrator" in any of my interviews. Thus, when Mark refers to "gay
lifestyle–oriented gays," it was a part of his own categorizing scheme before
he met me and not something he came up with to conform to my research
categories.

They also have a problem with the heightened salience that verbing gay identity creates. Although Mark's complaint about gay lifestyle–oriented gays appears to apply only to lifestylers, his criticism of gay subculture–oriented gays can also be seen as applying to commuters. The fact that he uses the terms "lifestyle-oriented" and "gay subculture–oriented" interchangeably suggests that he sees the ghetto natives and the ghetto-oriented tourists as part of the same high-density gay phenomenon.

One can see the adjective quality with which integrators treat identity in their political attitudes. Contrary to the notion that gays are necessarily a voting bloc aligned around issues of gay rights, AIDS, and similar "gay issues," most integrators did not see their sexuality as a primary factor behind their politics. Even those who identified as Democrats said they did so for reasons other than their sexuality. Others defined themselves as moderate independents and several defined themselves as Republicans. Regardless of party affiliation, few informants took a deep interest in politics.[7]

Richard's statement "the gay issue is only one issue" reflects a parallel to his organization of his self. Since gay is just one of many adjectives that describe him, its salience in his political attitudes is limited. Like many others in his income bracket, Richard favors getting people off welfare, balancing the budget, and lowering taxes. He defines himself as somewhere between a moderate Republican and a conservative Democrat. Although his gay identity influences his support for funding AIDS research and for some gay rights initiatives, it is not a significant factor in his overall voting patterns. His competing positions of stigma and privilege are apparent in their balancing of politics. In determining his own politics, Richard's privileging class status often washes over his sexual identity. Although support for gay rights is not irrelevant to his vote, it falls behind taxes, welfare, crime, and

---

7. Some gay men I spoke with had never heard of the AIDS activist group ACT UP (AIDS Coalition to Unleash Power), and several knew little about their own political leaders' stands on gay-related issues.

other typically suburban issues in his determination of whom to vote for. He is patriotically pro-American and heavily favors lower taxes. When asked what he would want me to write about, he played up his class status and downplayed the otherness of his sexual status:

> Tell [your readers] that my partner and I pay seventy-five thousand dollars a year in federal and state taxes, and I want something back for my money. I promise we won't upset the family structure [laughs]. We're not un-American. We are upstanding taxpaying Americans who believe we have the best system [of government] in the world.

He objects to the public discourse that attempts to discredit him because of his sexual identity. He attempts to wash over the markedness of his sexuality by emphasizing that his other attributes include such socially valued positions as being wealthy, a taxpayer, and a patriotic American. If one imagined a voting district that had a 20 percent gay population but also consisted of 20 percent wealthy voters, 20 percent patriotic constituents, 20 percent business leaders, and 20 percent life-long suburbanites, one would have a pretty good sense of the internal voting district that populates Richard's mind. He votes as a member of all of these demographic groups. Thus while his politics have a slightly gay flavor, his internal gay vote is often cancelled out by his internal coalition of wealthy, patriotic, suburban, and business votes.

Mixed Social Networks and the Nuanced Self

While the lifestyler's identity strategy is to present one singular unidimensional self and the commuter's strategy is to present different selves for different contexts, the integrator's strategy is to present a nuanced multidimensional self. Simmel (1955:150–54) argues that multiple group memberships and a web of overlapping group affiliations characterize the modern individual. Because of this, the demands on his self come from many competing identity affiliations. The commuter balances these demands by traveling to different selves, while the integrator balances them by mixing ingredients to form one complete self. With the many affiliations we each belong to, no two individuals are likely to share every affiliation; thus, although the spice of gayness may influence the worldviews and experiences of all gay men, the salience of that spice will depend on other ingredients. Whereas the lifestyler retains all of the spice by avoiding other ingredients and the commuter retains the spice by putting it on a separate identity plate, the integrator dilutes the spice by mixing in a variety of other ingredients.

On such continua as those of "daily lifestyle," "gender presentation," and "cultural values," gay suburban integrators emphasize the unmarked characteristics that place them close to the suburban center rather than to the presumed "gay-specific" poles. One is generally more likely to find suburban gay integrators mingling in the social networks of the corporate work world, backyard neighborhood barbecues, and local churches than at gay political demonstrations or pride parades. Their social networks are made up largely of heterosexual neighbors, coworkers, and others who lack the spicy edge found in the identity-exclusive networks of the gay ghettos.

Some gay integrators noted their commonality to integrators of other identity traits. Mark explains, for instance, that he sees his situation as similar to that of a suburban black friend who treats his black identity as an adjective:

> I have a black friend and he can't relate to the urban black
> mind-set just like I don't relate to the whole New York gay
> subculture mind-set. I draw an analogy [between urban
> gays] and inner-city black kids because the way they talk,
> the way they act—and then there are the suburban black
> people who can't relate to that. Like, I have a very good
> friend who is a black guy who cannot relate to that inner-
> city mentality and he's like, "I want to be around people I

> like." And I feel the same way. I want to be around them if
> they're man, woman, gay, straight, whatever. I associate
> with [gay people] because I like who they are, not because
> they're gay. And [likewise] I like straight people not be-
> cause they are straight.

Mark's objection to both the mind-set of the gay ghetto and that of
the inner-city ghetto is that, in his view, they are too exclusive. He
views mixed social networks of good people from multiple identity categories as a healthy balanced diet of social affiliations. In
his view ghetto gays and inner-city blacks lack this balance and
are thus too one-dimensional. He downplays the division between "gay" and "straight," focusing on other axes of identity. For
instance, although Mark and his friend have different sexual and
racial identities, these differences are insignificant compared to
their similarities as suburbanites, integrators, and men in their
twenties. Mark views ghetto gays as putting so much emphasis on
gayness that they fail to consider other similarities and differences. For him, sexuality does not provide a sufficient or necessary criterion to guarantee common ground.

Integrators frequently bring up the issue of common ground
with straights to explain their many nongay affiliations. Charles
explained, for instance, that he attends heterosexual clubs four
times as often as gay clubs. He elaborated on his reasons:

> Well, for one thing the music is much better in a straight
> bar! And my point is—look, you're heterosexual, but yet
> you and I like the same [heterosexual] bars for the same
> reasons, and I'm sure we have a lot of other things in com-
> mon too. That's my point. What I do in bed isn't necessar-
> ily going to decide what I like to do when I'm not in bed.

For Charles "gayness" is enough of a player that he'll attend a gay
bar one-fifth of the time when he goes to bars, but it is not enough
of a player to dominate his club life. His taste in music usually
overrides his sexuality in determining where he'll go. His dislike
of the disco, pop, and house music played at the local gay bar is

something he shares with many nongays. Similarly, Charles asserts his common ground with fellow *suburbanites* by noting that his home is "very suburban."

> [My partner and I live in] *the* suburban home. We don't have a gas grill anymore, but we used to [laughs]. We have three cats, a sports utility vehicle in the driveway—what else?—a bread machine, a little garden. Everything about us is just typical suburban. There's nothing obviously gay about it, it's just your average suburban town house.

Rather than speaking of uniquely gay tastes and aesthetics, Charles quite consciously notes how suburban his tastes are. One look at his typically suburban home and one can see that when it comes to housing tastes, Charles and his partner share significant commonalities with the larger community of suburbanites. Being suburban is a significant facet of their selves—as much so as gayness.

In fact, the face of gay suburbia looks pretty much like the face of heterosexual suburbia. Inhabitants are Republicans and Democrats, athletic and nonathletic, teachers, police officers, doctors, accountants, mechanics, fraternity brothers, and just about anything else. Although there is no one specific type of gay suburbanite, they are on average fairly conventional and somewhat conservative, just like their neighbors. For an integrator, gayness explains only part of his whole self, just as suburban, male, middle-class, alternative music fan, and northeastern would each explain only part of himself. Although "gay" may be a political master status, within the larger culture and within the gay subculture it does not override other variables in the way integrators form their social networks and live their lives; it merely flavors it.

Always Out but Never Obvious: High-Duration, Low-Density Gayness

The integrator does not hide his gay identity, nor does he foreground it. It is neither irrelevant nor highly relevant to his overall worldview. He presents what many would regard as a toned-down gayness. He is gay but lacks obvious auxiliary characteristics. Auxiliary characteristics increase the density, volume, visibility, and coloring of one's identity. Because the integrator lacks the requisite auxiliary characteristics, his gayness is diluted, quietly manifested, barely visible, and of a dull hue; it is subdued by the constellation of his other attributes. Gay suburban integrators used volume and visibility metaphors to describe themselves. Ted, for instance, says, "I don't hide it, and I don't do the bells and whistles either," indicating that he is neither invisible nor on high volume in his presentation of gay identity. Consistent with integrator language he sees himself as someone who neither abstains from nor goes to excess in presenting a gay self. In his view, he does gayness in moderation.

Representative of the integrator's suburban life of quiet but not invisible moderation is Jerry, who leads a very different lifestyle from his older brother Joe (who lives in San Francisco). Now in his thirties and very much an integrator, Jerry lives in a large suburban house with Roger, his partner of five years. White and upper middle-class, Jerry has lived in the suburbs of the area his entire life, never living more than thirty minutes from where he grew up. His brother is the family rebel—a single, free-spirited artist who moved across the country to live in the libertine spaces of San Francisco. Living in a studio apartment with a view of the Golden Gate Bridge and just blocks from the gay Castro district, Joe enjoys the big city. Jerry describes Joe somewhat in jest as "a free spirit who is content to live in a studio apartment with a few paintbrushes and whose biggest thrill in life is to find the biggest greatest [marijuana] joint he can find." Although Jerry admires his brother's free spirit, he admits that he himself is "too grounded" to cut loose like him. Moreover, he enjoys being "down to earth." He describes the differences between himself and his more flamboyant sibling:

> I want things and I want money and I want people in my life and I want the best of what I can afford and . . . he's

[just] got his artwork, his art table, and all of the pastels and markers and pencils and a view of the Golden Gate Bridge. That's all he needs pretty much at the moment, and I envy that. That's sort of cool. He can take off in directions I can't because he's not grounded really. He's a bit of a free spirit, which is nice. There's certainly a group of people who exist like that. I think it's great. [But] I couldn't do it. I couldn't. I need a little more structure. But it's nice to know people like that and sort of live vicariously through them.

Unlike his brother, Jerry prefers not to live in a big city. He says he doesn't have the tolerance for city life and dislikes the crime, excessive competition, and overall rat race of urban living too much to move away from the suburbs. Moreover, in the suburbs he and his partner can afford their own house, have a nice yard, and live in a safe neighborhood—things that they enjoy and consider important.

Jerry contrasts his moderation in the suburbs to Joe's flamboyancy in the city to illustrate how grounded his own lifestyle is. Whereas his brother leads a life that is more typically associated with being gay, Jerry leads a life that is more typically associated with heterosexuals. Neither Jerry nor Joe represents his sexuality in the culturally expected way, however. Jerry is gay and Joe is straight. In the cases of Jerry and Joe, the standard cultural cues and auxiliary characteristics people use to attribute sexual identity might very well lead to the wrong conclusion for both.

The integrator sometimes finds that not all recognize his subtlety and nuance. In many cases, individuals I interviewed found their gay identity was invisible to others even when they didn't intend it to be. Their lack of gay auxiliary characteristics made it difficult for many to perceive them as gay. As Ray explains, his "gay identity" is invisible at work through no design of his own:

I don't try to hide that I'm gay at work but it doesn't matter because unless you flaunt it everyone assumes you're

> straight. Since I don't wear homosexuality like a badge
> and I don't have a rainbow-colored mouse pad at my com-
> puter, no one thinks I'm gay.

Many integrators explained that they didn't want to be in the
closet, but they also didn't want to go out of their way to "make
an issue" of being gay. As Drew explains:

> I don't want to hide that I'm gay, but if people can't figure
> it out what am I supposed to do? It's awkward to say "Hey,
> by the way I am gay," because then I'm making an issue of
> it and my whole point of wanting people to know is be-
> cause it's not that much of an issue to me. But if I come
> out of the blue and say "I'm gay," then I'm saying "Hey,
> it's an issue." And that's not the point I want to make. I
> don't want my sexuality to be a big deal and I don't want
> to hide it. But if I mention it I'm making a big deal out of
> it, and if I don't mention it most people won't figure it out.

In his desire to keep his sexual identity an adjective rather than a
noun, the integrator is faced with a dilemma. In a culture where
people assume heterosexuality as the default identity unless an
ocean of auxiliary traits suggests otherwise,[8] they find it difficult
to make their own gay identity visible without appearing to make
a big issue of it. Moreover, because the low visibility displays of
integrators often go unnoticed, their moderate image as representatives of the category gay also generally remains unnoticed.
Lacking the visibility and volume of gay lifestylers, integrators fail
to figure prominently in perceptions of what auxiliary characteristics are associated with gay men. This becomes particularly evi-

---

8. See Brekhus (1996:516–17) on the "entire ocean rule" and how we
typically assume an unmarked identity unless a multitude of cues suggest
otherwise.

dent in the case of Mark, who spent over an hour coming out to a heterosexual friend. Mark recalls:

> I told him, and he laughed and said, "Oh, good one," and I said, "No, I really am gay," and he still thought I was kidding. And this went on and on. He just couldn't believe I was gay and we had to go over and over it again. "But you don't act funny and you don't talk like a gay person and you're not this and you don't do that," and I'd be like, "Well, yeah, I don't act like a woman and I don't talk funny and I don't do this and I don't want to be a hairdresser but I am gay," and he'd be like, "Yeah, but if you're gay?" and I'd be like, "Look, I am gay, OK."

In his earlier days Mark feared discovery, but he found that his relatively standard masculine appearance and his mainstream social values were so incongruent with public perceptions of who is gay that even claiming his gayness was unconvincing to his friend. His friend had bought into the high-density image of gay men as being clearly distinct from the ordinary average unremarkable person.

Conclusion

Contemporary debates over gay identity have generally lumped integrators in with the assimilationist side of the assimilationist/separatist debate. This categorization, however, limits our full understanding of the ways in which gay integrators attempt to manage their identity. First, the term "assimilation" assumes that the individual is accommodating to the values of another group. This is misleading since gay suburbanites who lack what are perceived as gay values may not be accommodating to straight values so much as they are following the suburban part of their integrated self. As an identity centaur with both a suburban and a gay component, the gay suburban integrator attempts to satisfy both attributes simultaneously. Second, while integrators are often invisible to others, they are not consciously and deliberately so. Rather, in a culture where identity groups are seen as discrete and mutually exclusive entities, only excess is easily recognized as an example of "doing identity"; moderation goes unnoticed.

The integrator possesses a nuanced self that is shaped by his "multiphrenic" (Gergen, 1991) social location among many simultaneously competing social affiliations, identity groups, and thought communities. The gay integrator's membership among gays is just one of many affiliations, which he combines into one complete multifaceted self. Unlike the lifestyler whose "political master status" becomes his overriding identity affiliation or the commuter who separates his identity affiliations, the integrator mixes his politically salient and nonsalient ones. The integrator's gayness lacks the high-density concentrations of both lifestylers and commuters. Unlike the lifestyler who concentrates his gayness all the time, or the commuter who alternates between bursts of concentrated gayness and long stretches of abstaining from gayness, the integrator spreads his gayness in a diluted form across every sphere of his life.

The concept of the identity integrator is an important one beyond the realm of gay identity. The integrator is an important ideal type to understand, for his or her treatment of identity attributes as adjectives is almost certainly the most common identity grammar for most attributes. Although the more excessive displays of the lifestyler or the most-of-the-time abstinence of the commuter draw theoretical attention, much of managing identity involves neither abstinence nor excess. The integrator's constellation of overlapping and even competing social attributes is an important reminder that all of us are mixtures of many different attributes, worldviews, social networks, and standpoints. The integrator shows us that identity is complex and subtle and that categories are rarely as discrete or homogeneous as we pretend. Even while integrators themselves generally eschew identity politics and activism, the image they present is the one that would most upend social stereotypes.

»5«

Contested Grammars

Gay Identity Disputes

In the previous chapters we examined the different presentational strategies of gay lifestylers (peacocks), commuters (chameleons), and integrators (centaurs). The lifestyler does identity as a noun and values *identity dominance;* the more fully exclusively committed to a gay identity, and the more "100 percent concentrated pure gayness" one exhibits, the better. The commuter does identity as a verb and values *identity mobility.* He is proud of his ability to move in and out of different identities and to fit into multiple social contexts. The integrator does identity as an adjective and values *identity moderation.* He likes to moderate his gay attribute with his unmarked attributes when emphasizing his own composite self. Each of these grammars (noun, verb, and adjective) is based on a different set of values (dominance, mobility, and moderation), and these values inevitably clash. There are contentious debates and disputes over the "proper" way to perform a gay identity. These debates often underlie the conflicts over whether people should treat a marked identity as a noun, a verb, or an adjective.

From a researcher's (or etic) viewpoint, one can see lifestylers, commuters, and integrators as falling along three corners of an equilateral triangle built around three axes (duration, density, and dominance) that can be represented as continuums from high to low (see figure 2). On the continuum of duration commuters occupy the low-duration end (e.g., 15 percent duration) while lifestylers and integrators share the high-duration end (e.g., 100 percent duration). On the continuum of density integrators occupy the low-density end (e.g., 15 percent density) while lifestylers and commuters share the high-density end (e.g., 100 percent density). And on the continuum of dominance, commuters and integrators share the low-dominance end (e.g., 15 percent dominance) while lifestylers occupy the high-dominance end

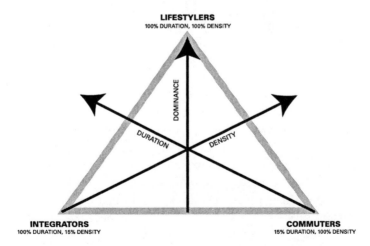

Figure 2: Identity triangle.

(e.g., 100 percent dominance). As analytic ideal types, lifestylers, integrators, and commuters are each the same distance from one another. From each insider's (or emic)[1] point on the triangle, however, the world of identity looks more like an isosceles triangle. That is, rather than viewing each type as equidistant from the others, as in the figure, representatives of each social type are likely to express a worldview in which they occupy the vertex angle of a thin isosceles triangle and the other two types are far away from them and close to one another at the opposite end of the triangle. The lifestyler will lengthen the dominance arrow and thus see himself at the top of a tall isosceles triangle with the commuter and integrator close together at the bottom of the triangle. He sees himself as very different from both the commuter and the integrator but sees only a small difference between the commuter and the integrator; in his view both are inauthentic because they lack the *dominance* that lifestylers believe the identity merits. The commuter will stretch the duration arrow and thus push the lifestyler and the integrator far away from him and closer to one another at the opposite end of the duration arrow. The commuter sees himself as very different from both the integrator and the lifestyler, but sees the lifestyler and the integrator as similar to one another because they both lack the mobility to travel between separate worlds and identities on the axis of *duration*. The integrator will extend the density arrow and thus push the commuter and the integrator to the far end of an isosceles triangle away from him. The integrator perceives himself as very different from both the lifestyler and the commuter, both whom he perceives to be excessive in letting a single identity attribute consume to much of his presentation of self on the axis of *density*. Each of these types transforms our ideal type equilateral triangle into an isosceles triangle by emphasizing and lengthening one axis.

---

1. For more on "etic" and "emic" see Pike (1967). Pike describes the broad conceptual analysis of a social structure from the outside observer's vantage point as the etic point of view and the insider's embedded and relational perspective within the social structure as the emic view.

Yet even though each point of the metaphorical triangle views the other two corners as close together, the occupants of any two corners will have some complaints about the third corner in common. From the lifestyler's standpoint his own undivided singular commitment to gay identity as a noun makes him the most authentically gay; commuters and integrators view the lifestyler's dominance unfavorably as one-dimensional. From the commuter's standpoint, his own treatment of identity as a verb is the most mobile and flexible gayness; but lifestylers and integrators view his mobility as hypocritical or two-faced because, in their view, he hides his "true self" behind whatever façade his environment demands. Moreover, they see the commuter as uncommitted to a "core self" because he moves promiscuously between different selves. The integrator prides himself on moderation; lifestylers and commuters view his low-density gayness as conceding too much and selling out to the straight world. Incidentally, the combined and paradoxical tendencies to conflate opposing corners of the triangle with one another and to have separate complaints about each of the other poles can lead to a good deal of talking past each other and feelings of being falsely accused. Recognizing these differing standpoints along the identity triangle, we can see that disputes within the gay community (and within any other identity group for that matter [see chapters 8–10]) are really *grammar disputes* over whether one should treat one's identity as a noun, as a verb, or as an adjective. These grammar disputes form around the issues of duration, density, and dominance.

Identity Natives and Identity Tourists: Duration Disputes over Gay Identity

Lifestylers believe that one's commitment to an identity should be undivided. They possess a greedy identity—an identity that requires exclusive and undivided identity work. Central to the lifestyler view is an identity politics model that considers gay invisibility a defining factor in the oppression of gays. From this perspective, high-duration gay visibility is critical to overall cultural visibility and acceptance. To the lifestyler, the commuter who resists high-duration gayness is part of the problem, for his invisibility perpetuates the oppression of gays. These disputes over gay identity duration are tied to larger identity politics debates within different sections of the gay movement. This analysis focuses, however, on the individual worldviews that arise out of these larger debates. One might consider this an analysis of the micropolitics of gay identity in everyday life that derives from larger political and social debates.

The lifestyler perceives those who do an identity only part-time as uncommitted opportunists who merely "play" the identity when it is safe to do so. The lifestyler views himself as an identity native and the commuter as a mere identity tourist. This divide can also be seen between lifestylers and commuters in the lesbian community. One of Stein's (1997:162) informants, for instance, accused some women of lesbian "tourism" or ideological "play," asserting that they were fakes who were merely posing as lesbians on low duration. From the lifestyler's corner, the commuter is a poseur—a weekend warrior to a gay identity who only "plays the identity" because he lacks the full commitment to "live it."[2] The lifestyler dismisses commuters as "pretenders" or "wanna-bes," or worse yet as "hypocrites" because they show their "true colors" only when it is safe to do so.

Some gays in New York City, for instance, refer to suburban identity commuters as *tunnel and bridge gays*.[3] From the New York lifestyler's perspective the tunnel and bridge gay is tainted by his association with straight suburbia and his lack of sophisti-

---

2. This occurs generically across identities. In different identity contexts, one hears of "weekend soldiers," "part-time punks," "Sunday Christians," and "wanna-be gang members."

3. I have heard this term used by gay men in New York City. Some of my suburban informants who commute to New York City complain that some New York gays are "cliquish" and will avoid anyone who they know is "tunnel and bridge." Levine's (1998:51) gay New York clones also used the term in the eighties to refer to suburban gays.

cation regarding the culture among natives. From the perspective of some urban gays tunnel and bridge gays, like "tourists" to any culture, do a poor job of following the local customs and thus fitting into the native culture. Indeed, those very customs may be there for the express purpose of separating the inner circle from the wanna-bes.

Part of the urban lifestyler's objection to tunnel and bridge gays is that they turn off their gay identity as soon as they pass back through the tunnel into the heterosexual world. The commuter's gay life consists of fleeting weekend bursts of gay identity in the city followed by long stretches of mundane suburban living. The duration of his gayness is too short for the lifestyler to take him seriously. From the lifestyler's perspective he won't be a "true gay" until he "goes native" and abandons the straight world. As long as he is only commuting to or vacationing in the city he is not a true insider but merely a curious spectator to the gay subculture. The lifestyler expects total immersion in gay culture not just on the weekends but all of the time. Moreover, the lifestyler views anyone who is only a part-time gay as uncommitted to his "core self." The lifestyler views individuals who repress this all-important part of their identity at some times and in some places as "self-hating." Signorile (1993), for instance, refers to the closeted gay, in which category his definition includes the commuter, as a "self-loathing homosexual" who allows his entire self to be dominated by oppression most of the time. The gay lifestyler, who views gayness as a noun, sees any act that does not openly proclaim one's gayness as a betrayal of one's true inner "core self." He believes the chameleon has sold his soul and betrayed his true colors every time he turns in his bright urban gay colors for the bland straight colors of mundane suburbia. The lifestyler views the identities of commuters as impure and inevitably tainted by their high-duration contact with the profane nongay world. For instance, Levine's (1998) informants perceived suburban commuters, who failed to adopt the full dress code of clone culture, as visual pollutants to their "authentically gay" environment. Some queer theorists have adopted the lifestyler's position on duration as their own analytic position, suggesting that the closeted homosexual, again defined to include commuters, suffers from a polluted self-image.[4]

The commuter views his duration differently. Rather than seeing low duration as a lack of authenticity or commitment, he sees it as an abundance of mobility. From the commuter's view, "full-time gays" (lifestylers and integrators alike) lack flexibility. For instance, identity commuters express the view that there is a difference between a "part-time queen" and a "full-time queen." As Bill states:

> Now there's a difference between [being] a queen and [acting] queeny.[5] A person can be queeny but not necessarily a queen. I mean a queen is a queen *all the time,* and that's what they are. They're defined by it. Those people who are Joe Blow but they can be queeny at times, that's a little different. They can act effeminate at times but a queen has made it their life.

For Bill, someone who can be queeny at times is superior to someone who can only be a queen, because the queeny person also has the flexibility to be Joe Blow if he wants to. Although Bill's disdain for "queens" may not be clear from the above quote alone, his attitude toward queens was highly unfavorable.[6] By contrast he had a higher regard for the queeny person because, in his view,

---

4. See, for example, Signorile (1993); Vaid (1996).

5. In a somewhat parallel example among lesbians, one of Esterberg's (1996:266) informants similarly distinguished between "playing" butch and "really" being butch.

6. This was reflected in both his sarcastic voice inflection when saying "all the time" and a "queen has made it their life" and in his general attitudes toward queens in other parts of the interview. Incidentally, he had a similar attitude toward women, but did not put men who occasionally act "queeny" in the same category as "queens" and women because they could be "manly men" if they wanted to. He values masculinity and regards femininity as weak and inferior.

the queeny person is engaging in play and thus his "core" is still masculine. The commuter views being defined by a full-time queen status as an unfortunate state of affairs that only afflicts those whose femininity is so overpowering she can never be anything else; her flavor is always the same. In the commuter's eyes the queen is frozen because she can never change into Joe Blow or anyone else; she is one-dimensional, a noun. By contrast the queeny person has the flexibility to slip out of his queeny persona and into other personas, including generic ones. In fact, for some commuters the generic ordinary Joe rather than the gay queen is their default identity. One suburban gay who defined himself as a regular guy, for instance, argued strongly for the low duration of his gayness in saying that "*very few minutes of the day* are defined by who I like to have sex with." Far more minutes a day, he went on to suggest, are defined by his position as an "ordinary guy in an ordinary suburban neighborhood."

The commuter views the full-time gay's sin as his inability to turn off his gayness in nongay spaces. For the commuter the lifestyler's inability to be anything but gay can be embarrassing. As Scott explains:

> Some people are more tolerant [of queens], and I'm probably a little less tolerant. And it might depend on location. In some gay groups I'm not as put off by effeminate gay men as when I'm in a public restaurant and someone comes up to me who was overly effeminate. [In that case] I might feel a little embarrassed.

Scott's primary concern is with queen displays that extend into unmarked times and spaces. He tolerates effeminacy in gay spaces "where they belong" but is embarrassed when such displays cross over into the nongay realm. For him and other commuters, the always effeminate gay man threatens his boundaries between gay and nongay time and space. Gay commuters worry that effeminate men may hinder their own mobility to move between a gay self in marked times and spaces and a nongay one outside those spaces.

Brian worries about the potential staining effect of spending too much of his time around gay lifestylers. A new traveler to the gay scene, Brian feels he can tell some people are gay by that little flamboyancy in their voice that he believes they have acquired from hanging around too much in all-gay environments. He likens picking up a "gay accent" from hanging around in New York's gay spaces to picking up a regional accent:

> I don't want to say that people choose to talk feminine, but when it comes right down to it, it's learned to talk that way. Kind of like if you were a Texan in New Jersey you would lose your accent and if a New Jerseyan went to Texas they would gain an accent. So I think it's kind of like gaining an accent. So that's why I'm not particularly fond of hanging around very feminine people [too long]. I mean they're fun and everything but—yeah, I talk a little bit more feminine joking around with some of my [gay] friends at times, but then I'm like, "stop that."

Brian is content to be a traveler to peacock gay spaces and to even play it up a little himself when he is there, but he fears that too much time in gay space will cause him to pick up the "native accent" of gay lifestylers. Since he still has to turn it off in his life outside gay space, he worries about the potential spillover effect of spending too much time in the presence of queens and effeminate gay men. Like other commuters, he wants to be able to move between the two identities and their separate spaces.

The commuter views full-time gayness as a problem because it invades inappropriate times and places. For the commuter, weekends, nighttime, and vacations are the proper times to let gayness take over and become a master status. The commuter believes other times should be reserved for his unmarked identities. Commuters I spoke with, for instance, often disparaged gay politics as something for people "whose only goal in life is to live a gay lifestyle." They argued that they themselves held "real jobs" and thus were above what they saw as the immaturity of full-time gay activists. Andrew says, for instance, that while he agrees with the goals of gay activists, he thinks it is "silly how much *time* they let it consume." He goes on to say that people who take their jobs seriously don't have time to be "politically gay all of the time":

> People who are working just don't have time to be on these panels or [in] these groups fighting for causes. . . . Gay politics never really concerned me. It never really interested me, and I never felt the desire to do anything about it. It's nice for these people who are graduate students and they don't really know what to do with their lives. I know a lot of people like this. This is their goal in life: to be gay, to be politically gay. But, ah, my life goes on.

For Andrew and other commuters, the problem with gay activists is that they devote too much duration to their gay identity and thus do not leave enough duration to other identities such as their occupational identities. For many gay bar patrons like Andrew "being gay" is a nighttime activity. An activist gay politics would likely extend beyond the duration and the confines of the bar scene and thus impinge on activities reserved for his diurnal self. Underlying Andrew's distinction between "people who are graduate students" (student lifestylers with the auxiliary characteristic of political activism) and "people who are working" is a temporal distinction between the full-time gay and the part-time gay. This same concern among commuters that a full-time gay identity pushes out other important identities came through when Bill explained his view that a queen is superficial because, unlike a queeny person, she can never talk about other facets of self: "queens are superficial because the only thing they ever talk about is gay life; they never talk about anything of substance like work or sports." Bill equates work and sports with substance because they are ingredients beyond one's nighttime self and beyond the auxiliary characteristics of gayness.

Like the lifestyler, the integrator has a problem with the part-time aspect of the gay commuter's identity. However, while the lifestyler complains that the gay commuter is only being true to himself in gay space, the integrator complains that the commuter is never being true to himself because he is always bracketing a part of himself. For the integrator neither suppressing one's gay identity nor foregrounding it and suppressing one's diurnal self are true displays of oneself. Warren expresses the integrator view:

> I don't like that some gay people I know, they are in the closet and they hide it . . . and they'll even say homophobic stuff just to fit in . . . and then—but then you go to the bar and they are the biggest queen in the bar. I mean if you're going to be gay why not just be gay? I mean just be yourself *and* be gay. Don't hide it, but don't make a big deal of it either. If you don't act [the way you act in a gay bar] normally, what makes you think you should act that way just because you are in a gay bar?

For Warren and other integrators, the commuter is problematic because he overcompensates for low duration with high density. He questions why the commuter cannot commit to one "core self" instead of shifting between two identity poles. He wonders why the commuter cannot just be one everyday gay self all of the time instead of a part-time everyday self and a part-time gay self. In the integrator's view, the commuter is untrue because his whole self is never present. He is always bracketing something off and hiding it from view. In contrast, all of the integrator's identity attributes are always accessible. Whereas the commuter divides his different identity commitments into separate temporal and spatial domains, the integrator mixes all of his commitments together into every minute of his life. One might think of the commuter's identity plate as resembling a TV dinner (all separate dishes compartmentalized into separate spheres so that only one dish can be accessed at a time), while the integrator's plate resembles a salad or a soup, where everything is mixed together. (The lifestyler's plate would have one giant habanero pepper—all spice with no moderating flavors.)

An integrator's view on the durational problem of commuters is exemplified by Bawer's complaint against gays whom he perceives as choosing to "shout on high volume" one day a year rather than put in the time to convince people "quietly" 365 days a year—that is for a display of too short duration and too high density:

> At Gay Pride Day Marches, some gay men and lesbians, like the Stonewall Rioters, have exposed America to images of raw sexuality—images that variously amuse, titillate, shock, and offend while revealing nothing important about who most of those people really are. Why, then, do some people do such things? Perhaps because they've been conditioned to think that on that gay high holy day, the definitively gay thing to do is to be as defiant as those heroes twenty-five years ago. Perhaps they do it because they can more easily grasp the concept of enjoying one day per year of delicious anarchy than of devoting 365 days per year to a somewhat more disciplined and strategically sensible demonstration designed to advance the causes of respect, dignity, and equality. (Bawer, 1996:10).

Interestingly, both lifestylers and integrators attack commuters for their short binges of gay display. They differ, however, in that the lifestyler views the bursts of gayness as the commuter's true colors and the rest of his duration as problematic, while the integrator views the commuter's short binges as the problem and his "364-day self" outside the parade as closer to his true colors.

On the issue of duration, commuters favor a mobile self while lifestylers and integrators favor a unitary self. For the commuter the self is flexible and fluid enough to blend in anywhere. The lifestyler conceives of the unitary self as organized hierarchically around a master status with all other facets of self as auxiliary characteristics. The integrator's unitary self, by contrast, is composed of constant adjectives arrayed in a flat, modular nonhierarchical way around the nebulous label of "human being." The lifestyler and the integrator cannot understand the commuter's constantly changing self since it shows little commitment to a "core self" of any kind. The commuter, by contrast, cannot understand the frozenness and inflexibility of his lifestyler and integrator counterparts, who refuse to adapt and respond appropriately to changes in their social environment.

Identity Purists and Identity Moderates: Density Disputes over Gay Identity

Disputes over identity are not just about the time one spends doing an identity; they are also about the purity with which one manifests an identity. In the view of gay purists (lifestylers all of the time and commuters when their gayness is activated), for instance, one must, to be authentically gay, organize all other identity attributes in an auxiliary manner that is consistent with being 100 percent gay. The purist sees all other aspects of the gay self as deriving hierarchically from one's sexual identity and thus expects gayness to be a defining feature in realms of behavior other than the sexual. The gay purist may insist on "gay" lifestyle tastes, "gay" political leanings, and "gay" occupational and avocational interests. The purist may claim, for instance, that an urban, liberal Democratic artist is more authentically gay than a rural, conservative Republican auto mechanic. The low-density gay (integrator), by contrast, does not see his gayness as necessarily flavoring his tastes in nonsexual areas.

The density debate today often takes the form of a debate between difference and sameness. The *identity purist* is committed to the distinctiveness of one's identity and thus emphasizes difference from other identities. The *identity moderate* emphasizes that his gayness is just one small piece of himself and that absent the slight flavoring of the attribute, he is no different from anyone else. Both the lifestyler and the commuter prefer identity purity and want high-intensity, unadulterated gayness when one is being gay or performing a gay identity. They view the integrator as letting other parts of himself wash out too much of his uniquely gay self. The integrator, by contrast, views identity in moderation rather than identity purity as the important issue. In his view the lifestyler and commuter are both excessive and let gayness consume too much of their overall selves.

These density disputes are tied into larger political conflicts between different organizations and factions of the gay movement that have developed competing political analyses of the nature of and solution to gay oppression in the United States[7]; thus, while I focus primarily on individual views at a particular historical moment, these views are shaped by that larger cultural and political context in direct and indirect ways.[8] More specifically, the idea that expressing 100 percent concentrated gayness is the best way to be gay arose out of an identity politics centered around coming out within gay liberation that saw cultural invisibility as a defining dimension to the oppression of gays and thus saw visibility as liberatory and politically necessary.[9] Although only a small handful of suburban gay men are involved in political activism, their attitudes are shaped, in part, by exposure to the public cultural debates among activists and the portrayal of these debates in media, arts, academia, and other arenas.

Some proponents of the purity side of the density debate favor the use of the label "queer" to describe and define themselves against mainstream cultural views and to increase their cultural visibility. In their view difference from the mainstream culture is critical to being purely gay; if a gay person is not different to the point of being queer, then he is so "diluted" that he is advancing

---

7. For an empirical analysis of the strategic political uses of emphasizing difference and sameness in the lesbian and gay movement and on how those strategies varied across different institutional and historical contexts, see Bernstein (1997).

8. For an ethnography that captures historical and cohort effects on identity debates within the lesbian community see Stein's (1997) analysis of the life stories of lesbian baby boomers.

9. I thank Elizabeth Armstrong for this observation and for suggesting that I briefly situate these disputes in their larger sociopolitical and historical context.

gay cultural invisibility and might just as well be straight. This is the view of BRATS (Big-Honkin' Radical Anti-Assimilationist Terrorist Super-Queers):

> We have declared war on heterosexism and homophobia. This of course means hets, but also the mainstream, nicey-nicey, assimilationist, "We're just like you nice straight folks except for who we sleep with" gay and lesbian bowel movement. This movement needs to be flushed, and we are the tidy bowl queers! We will target many with our random, unpredictable, terrorist attacks who are deserving punishment. Hateful breeders who bash us and assimilationist scum that *water down* our angry voices and channel our efforts into a system that oppresses us are both cause to pull out the ammo and come out shootin'. [emphasis added]. (quoted in Davis, 1995:295)

From the queer lifestyler's perspective, the integrator *dilutes* his gayness and *pollutes* his essence by converting it from a noun to a weak adjective. Notice that in the above view the mixed metaphor of "watered down" and "scum" equates dilution with pollution.[10] For the most adamant lifestyler, the integrator is a turncoat whose gayness is so diluted and whose self is so contaminated with the dirt of mainstream society that it no longer matters; he might as well be straight since his minimal concentration of gayness lacks any real potency to challenge the profane dominant culture.

While some lifestylers and commuters favor the label queer, integrators oppose it on the grounds that it stains their entire self with the color of one tiny adjective among many in their nonhierarchical arrangement of attributes. Many objected, often strongly, to individuals who they saw as letting their gayness consume too much of their identity. Ted explains, for instance, his objection to "queers":

---

10. For more on "pollution" terminology as it relates to identity, see Douglas (1966).

> Being gay is an important part of who I am. But if there's
> one thing I do have a visceral reaction to it's this whole
> queer thing. . . . This whole queer business turns me
> off . . . because it *dilutes* our humanity. It says we're not
> a whole person, we're just queer and that's it. It really
> overemphasizes one part of our personality to the nth
> degree. I mean being gay does shape who I am, but it
> doesn't define me. (emphasis added)

It is interesting to note that whereas the lifestyler and the commuter perceive the integrator as diluting his gayness, the integrator criticizes the lifestyler and the commuter for diluting their humanity by oversaturating it with queerness at the expense of other ingredients. For the integrator the queer label is threatening because he feels it washes out all his other attributes. Ted's complaint that it takes one part of the whole self and multiplies it to the nth degree is a complaint about transforming an adjective into a noun.

The perspective of integrators is that gayness is a good thing, but only in moderation. In the recipe of one's self, integrators want a moderate blend, somewhere between completely bland and overpowered by spice. The integrator views the commuter, for instance, as ruining his recipe by letting the spice overwhelm every other ingredient and totally dominate his entire flavor of self. Larry's complaint that some gay men let their gayness engulf far too much of their entire self echoes the perspective of many integrators about commuters:

> You go into certain clubs and you get very annoyed be-
> cause you see people running around, looking ridiculous,
> you know with fourteen pink triangles all over themselves
> and their little rainbow flags waving in the air and you're
> just like, "calm down!" I think they're really letting it con-
> sume far too much of themselves.

While the commuter perceives gay space as the appropriate place to crank up the volume on his gayness, the integrator believes that it should remain at a calmer volume level at all times.

Integrators are at odds with those who play up their identity as a verb. They find some commuters' playing up of gay identity overblown and unnecessary. In their mind, one does not have to do something special to show that they are gay. Consequently, some integrators see the verbing of gayness as an unnecessary capitulation to stereotypes. Bart, for instance, believes that the "effeminate parts" of gay men are not as "real" as their "masculine parts"; they are only acts to conform to the societal image of who is gay. Seeing his gay identity as something that is always a small part of him, Bart does not understand those who play it up with effeminate speech and mannerisms:

> Some of my friends are queens and they're real people just like anyone else, though I don't know how real the effeminate parts are. I'm not sure why they act that way but I think it's because they either want to be in people's face or they're so insecure that they have to create an identity of someone else. That's how they get attention. That's how they get noticed. That's how they can be in the spotlight. So for whatever reasons they feel they have to act that way.

Integrators report being embarrassed by the more flamboyant, high-volume displays of gayness that occur at pride parades and other gay-oriented gatherings. They view such displays as "flaunting it," "wearing it like a badge," and "waving it around like a rainbow flag." Some claimed that large gay events reminded them of Halloween or a giant costume party, since even the people who are playing it up do not normally act in such a manner. Their complaints echo those of Bawer (1993:155–56), who laments that at New York's gay pride parade "it seemed as if people who wore suits and ties the 364 other days a year had, on this particular morning, ransacked their closets for their tackiest, skimpiest, most revealing items of clothing. . . . [The parade] presented homosexuals less as human beings than as *sexual* beings" [italics in the original]. Bawer's concern reflects a primary density concern among integrators. The gay integrator does not want the marked flavor of his sexuality to wash over his generic flavors. He wants to be recognized as a member of the nebulous category of generic humanity rather than as a member of a sexuality-specific subset of humanity.

Integrators frequently alluded to the density issue by complaining about concentrated displays of gender. In their view a quiet masculinity that isn't hypermasculine is the appropriate low-density display of gender. Unlike commuters, integrators make little distinction between part-time and full-time queens. The integrator lumps them together as excessive displays of concentrated effeminacy. While the queeny commuter takes issue with the full-time queen's lack of flexibility and mobility, the integrator takes issue with both for their high-volume displays. Several integrators described queens as "loud" or "screaming," making clear their association of effeminacy with excessive volume. As with political activism, integrators view the gendered presentations of "butch" and "queen" as too high volume. They sometimes lumped gender radicalism and political activism together as though they are necessarily connected. The word "flaming" was used to refer to both queens and political activists, implying that both were too loud; integrators prefer subtler, more subdued forms of gender and politics. In one of the stronger examples of this sentiment Tim[11] equates activism, effeminacy, and flamboyance as though they are necessarily intertwined: "I'd rather not associate with these flaming fags running down the street or these people who are trying to do their civic duty and work in ACT UP. . . . I don't like the way [those] gay people act." Suburban integrators often place high importance on mainstream

---

11. The reader may recognize Tim as the high school– and college-age commuter (chapter 3) who enjoyed being conspicuously heterosexual in straight space and conspicuously gay in gay space. Tim's current attitudes are much more those of an integrator—a case in point that shows that these strategies change over the lifecourse as social circumstances change. His social networks also reflect this change. I discuss lifecourse changes in identity grammar in the next chapter.

respectability, which they see as requiring low-volume displays of gayness. Both activism and effeminacy defy a sort of suburban noise ordinance.

For the gay lifestyler and the gay commuter, gayness trumps other identity attributes and thus, when played, is always the dominant card in the deck. But for the integrator, gayness is a weaker identity attribute that can be trumped by other social attributes (e.g., one's occupational identity or one's gender identity). In the integrator's view gayness is one card of moderate value in a deck of many cards.

Identity Univores and Identity Omnivores: Dominance Disputes

In addition to disputes over duration and density, grammar wars occur over the issue of dominance. The key dominance issue is between *identity singularity* and *identity balance.* For gay lifestylers, one's practices, worldviews, and tastes must remain singularly connected to gayness as the central defining factor. They are *identity univores,*[12] committed to a singular and specific identity diet and to one attribute as their core ingredient. The commuter and integrator, by contrast, are both *identity omnivores;* the commuter's diet shifts from identity entrée to identity entrée, and the integrator's mixes all his attributes together into one dish. They are committed to a broad and balanced identity diet. For the identity omnivore, gayness is just one of many ingredients in his recipe of self. It is, perhaps, technically more accurate to define the commuter and the integrator as identity multivores since they

---

12. I expand upon Peterson's (1992) notion of the *univore* as someone who is committed to one cultural taste that overrides all others. For instance, Peterson (1992) and Bryson (1996, 1997) have shown that some musical genres, such as country and heavy metal, have fans who are more likely to be univorous than fans of other genres, who are more likely to be omnivorous in their musical tastes. Peterson's univore-omnivore distinction, developed in the context of musical and social preferences, is a useful one that is worth considering in the context of identities as well.

do not take part in all identities. I use the omnivore label because of its cultural association with diet. Moreover, to the extent that integrators try to include all of their ingredients at once in their self-definition and that commuters attempt to be "all things to all people" by changing from setting to setting, the omnivore metaphor fits.

The lifestyler maintains a univorous identity diet and values identity singularity and focus over identity plurality. In his view one must be committed to a dominant gay identity attribute. For him, gay is the core noun that defines one's "true self," and all other ingredients are subordinate auxiliary characteristics that follow inevitably and naturally from his noun. He likes the arts because he is gay and gays like the arts; he likes disco because he is gay and gays like disco; he is a Democrat because he is gay and gays are Democrats. All of his other facets of self trickle down from his gayness. His interests, tastes, and political views all derive directly from gay culture and are never independent of his gay self. His possession of derivative gay auxiliary characteristics is his proof that he is being authentically gay and thus true to himself as first and foremost a gay person.

The identity univore finds it easy to label the central attribute of his self while the identity omnivore considers his self defined by so many competing attributes that it is hard to choose the most important one. From the gay univore's point of view, the identity omnivore lacks focus and commitment to his gay identity because he has too many competing commitments. The gay univore's focused identity diet can be seen in the social spaces he inhabits and interacts in. Unlike the mixed spaces and networks that the omnivore lives and interacts in, the univore is able to maintain a more gay focused life.

Commuters and integrators, however, see the lifestyler's singularity as one-dimensional and lacking balance. They view multidimensionality as more desirable than commitment to one attribute and all its accompanying auxiliary characteristics. A singular commitment to a fully gay lifestyle, in their view, requires them to jettison too many parts of themselves that do not necessarily align with gayness as a master status. Rather than load up on gayness and its auxiliary attributes they desire a more balanced diet of identity attributes. Commuters balance the spice of gayness by having some bland attributes to travel to when they are done sampling the spicy ones, and integrators balance their spice by diluting it with blander ingredients.

Because they emphasize balance in their constellation of identity traits, identity omnivores sometimes found it hard to define themselves by any label. Jacob, for instance, simply says "I'm just a guy, I'm just whatever, I'm just there. OK? I'm not an anything. I'm someone, but there's a lot of substance to me and so, yeah, I'm hard pressed to label myself, period." Moreover, for Jacob it is clear that his identity is intertwined with the identity of the social space in which he is located. He defines his moving to suburban New Jersey from San Francisco as a test to see if he could live in generic everyday space. Implicit in this test was also a test to see whether he could live a "balanced lifestyle" in place of the all-gay existence he lived in San Francisco. Whereas most informants said that if they were writing this book they would focus on how ordinary they were, Jacob actually emphasized how ordinary suburban New Jersey itself is:

> I think you should focus on: "Where are we here?" I mean I love New Jersey. I really love New Jersey. I've barely explored it. It's a great state. It's so small and there is so much diversity. And yet it is so nowhere. It is so nothing. It is so—I mean I don't know what it is. It's everything and it's nothing.

For Jacob, focusing on where we are also tells us something about who we are. He marks Northgate as special precisely because it is not overly exceptional.[13] Moreover, his description of New Jersey

---

13. In an article about gays leaving San Francisco for other parts of California, gay journalist Rex Wockner ("The Wockner Wire," *Planet Out*, April 21, 2001)

as "so nowhere, so nothing" directly corresponds with his own statement about himself: "I'm not an anything." The statement that one is not "an anything" is a claim that one is not a noun. Interestingly, the notion that one is everything and one is nothing can fit both the integrator and the commuter definition of self. The integrator, having no singular defining trait but rather a constellation of nonhierarchical adjectives that make up his self, is composed of all of these adjectives and thus "everything." At the same time having no defining trait but his ordinariness and no easy labels to draw upon, the integrator is also "nothing in particular." The commuter is "everything" because he can be all things to all people, yet he is "nothing" because there is no "core self," only multiple shifting selves. In describing New Jersey as both everything and nothing, Jacob emphasizes that there is no core trait of New Jersey that stands out. That he passed the test and blends into his suburban New Jersey environment also implies that no core trait of his personal identity stands out. The commuter side of Jacob is evident in his liking New Jersey because it is both small and diverse. This diversity within a small area allows one to encounter and take on a variety of different identities by traveling across a small amount of space. One can establish a "generic" lifestyle in everyday suburban space and not be marked as anything specific while accessing diverse nearby spaces that allow for a broad range of identity-specific displays. Commuters are conscious of the identity settings they are in. As they manage impressions to match the setting, they cognitively mark all social spaces. Jacob's notion that suburban New Jersey is so nowhere explicitly marks generic space precisely because it is ordinary.

A common theme among my interviews was that the suburbs are an ideal site to live a balanced multidimensional life. Many informants defined the suburbs as a place where they could live a

---

expresses similar sentiments about the identity of non-gay-specific space. Having moved to San Diego seven years ago, he describes it as a "funny place to be" because after "seven years I still can't tell you exactly what San Diego is about, what its identity is."

balanced life between what they saw as the restrictive singularity of rural areas on one extreme and what they saw as the all-gay unidimensionality of the Village on the other. Several informants who enjoyed traveling into and out of the Village said they enjoyed its proximity but wouldn't want to live somewhere where it was all gay, all the time. Although their impression of the Village as "all gay, all the time" is an exaggeration, it does point out the degree to which they wanted a balanced life. Some referred to the suburbs as a "balance between two extremes," "a nice middle-ground,"[14] or "a place near the middle of everything, but not at the center of anything." As one integrator said:

> I like it here [in the suburbs] because it's not a big city
> and it's also not a town in the sticks. Those are the social
> opposites and I'd rather be in the middle of those extremes.
> I want a life partner because I don't want to be alone, so
> I wouldn't want to live in the sticks. But I don't really like
> being in a city much either. I would prefer to be in a some-
> what suburban area close to a city rather than actually liv-
> ing in a city.

Just as gayness and a general cosmopolitanism both play a role in his own personal identity, Northgate is a space where each has a role but neither has the lead core role. In general, both commuter and integrator informants viewed living in the suburbs as showing that they had balance in their lives. Both liked the proximity of New York, either for its effect in mildly flavoring the suburbs (integrators) or for its direct offering of a spicy subculture that one could travel to on the weekends (commuters).[15]

---

14. Similarly, Wockner defines San Diego (while not a suburb) as "a workable middle-ground" between San Francisco's gay enclaves and less urban areas like rural northern California and Palm Springs.

15. Note that these are not necessarily gay-specific reasons for liking to live in the suburbs. Most nongay New York suburbanites would likely have similar attitudes about the benefits of living near, but not in, New York.

Whereas lifestylers express pride in their identity singularity and focus, commuters and integrators value their identity balance. John shows a shift in his life from a more lifestyler to a more integrator viewpoint, for instance, in expressing satisfaction in the fact that his friendship circle has evened out after previously being nearly exclusively gay:

> I am having a party coming up soon and I was writing all the names of the people who I was inviting, and it came out to be fifty-fifty [gay and straight]. And that made me feel really good. It made me feel that I had balance in my life again. I've gone from the side of my life that has to be surrounded by gays to get the sense of community to a life that is more diverse now. I mean, I know a whole gamut of people, and I would say it's probably around fifty-fifty.

John's use of "diverse" indicates that he is starting to prefer an omnivorous identity diet over a univorous one. He now sacrifices some focus and commitment for balance. Jerry reflects a similar appreciation for balance in stating, "My straight circle is widening a bit, which is a good thing because I was pretty much exclusively gay oriented in terms of friends a while ago." The ideal-typical lifestyler, by contrast, sees this balance as a lack of full commitment to the identity and as watering down the intensity of one's gayness by associating with the enemy.

There are two roads to balance. The commuter strikes a balance by being a part-time gay and a part-time straight. When he is being his gay self, only gay men surround him. But he balances his life by limiting his gay self to specific contexts. He has two sets of friends—his gay friends and his nongay friends. He balances his identity diet by having two or more sets of friends and social networks to rely on. His interactions in each social network are very focused on a particular identity when in those networks, but he focuses on other facets of his self when in other networks. The integrator, by contrast, has only one diverse social network; he does not bracket sets of friends into different spheres of his life or different identity networks. He integrates his gay and straight friendships and does not define them as separate sets of friends. Mark shows the integrator's view toward identity-specific networks in his dislike of gay-specific bars. He dislikes gay bars because, in his view, the environment is too unbalanced because it defines him solely by his sexuality:

> I don't care for gay bars. I don't like the whole gay bar
> mentality. I would much rather prefer to be around my
> friends than in a gay bar where I'm going to be defined by
> the fact that I am gay. It might be harder to meet someone
> because I don't go to a bar, but those aren't necessarily the
> type of people I want to meet anyway.

Mark's statement that "those aren't . . . the type of people I want to meet anyway" is indicative of the integrator's view of univores and identity singularity. Even though Mark shares gayness with gay bar patrons, he prefers to be in mixed multidimensional social networks where people are defined by a range of attributes.

In fact as I went through my interview with Mark it became clear that he valued his association with identity integrators of all stripes and all axes of identity (e.g., race, religion, ethnicity). He had black friends who were integrators, Jewish friends who were integrators, and a diverse range of friends with broad demographic backgrounds but relatively weak commitments to those backgrounds. Showing the integrator mind-set across attributes, Mark expressed parallels between his view of gay lifestylers and his black friends' views of African-American lifestylers. As an integrator, Mark views both gay and African-American lifestylers as one-dimensional for basing their whole culture and value systems on an oppositional identity. He complains, for instance, that lifestyler cultures are organized one-dimensionally around their oppressed position as a minority:

> If your whole culture is based around resistance to your
> oppressor, and this is true for racial minorities too, if your

thing is "the white man is bringing me down" or "the
straight man is bringing me down," what happens when
the straight man is not bringing you down anymore, the
white man is not bringing you down anymore? Your whole
system of values, your whole culture is built upon that
oppression. If the oppression is not there and you're still
doing it, you have a problem. You're hurting yourself in a
way. Well, the straight people don't understand [they're]
like, "Why are you doing this? No, no [we] don't have a
problem with you. Whatever, get over it." Gay subculture–
oriented gays act in this very stereotypical manner. It's like
an inner-city black manner except for gays, and I don't
relate to that. That doesn't speak to my system of beliefs.

Mark is not entirely opposed to resistance to the straight culture,
but he is against organizing a subculture specifically around such
resistance. He believes that there is a place for gay and minority
politics but that it should not consume every facet of one's life.
Mark wants his sexual orientation to be taken for granted (unmarked), and he feels gay lifestylers draw too much attention to
gayness as different and oppositional from the mainstream.

It is worth noting that Mark was in his early twenties and in
college in the mid-1990s. He is growing up in a historical period
when gay invisibility is not the pervading social reality that it was
for older cohorts of gay men. Unlike some of those older men, he
feels less connection to the strategic identity politics of gay visibility and views the more important struggle as one of gaining acceptance and integration. He is aligned with forms of gay strategy
that emphasize sameness over difference. In his integrator worldview, he sees the high-density gay-specific politics of gay visibility
as passé and thinks gay identity should be neither value-negative
nor value-positive but an unmarked value-neutral attribute:

I'm tired of people being surprised that a normal person is
gay. The cliché "we're just like everyone else" is really
true. Most of us are not interesting. We really are just bor-

ing, everyday people. Being gay should be a value-neutral thing, it shouldn't be a negative thing. Yes, there are promiscuous gay people but there are also promiscuous straight people. Being gay or straight should be irrelevant. People should be judged on whether they are good people or not.

Mark objects to an overall evaluation placed on his whole personhood by his sexual identity. In his view, his sexual identity is too minor an ingredient to tip the scales[16] by itself in either a value-positive or a value negative direction. His multidimensional social networks with integrators across the various demographic axes reflect the degree to which his gay self is integrated with and balanced by other attributes. He has a complex identity where multiple ingredients, including gayness, share the same phenomenological space.

Conclusion

As the grammar disputes in this chapter illustrate, there is far less coherence among social groups and less uniformity in their worldviews than many people assume. In fact, gay lifestylers, commuters, and integrators disagree on the basic values around which to express a gay identity. The lifestyler believes that a true gay must live the identity as a noun. Anyone who lacks either the duration or the density and thus the dominance required of a noun is a mere pretender who is lacking in identity authenticity. The commuter believes that identity is something you create by doing. He values flexibility and mobility among identity attributes and regards those who noun or adjective their identity as frozen and unable to change to keep up with the times (or the spaces). The integrator believes that identity should be expressed

---

16. See Mullaney (1999) on how we "weight" different acts in attributing identity.

in the moderation and permanence of an adjective, rather than in the permanent excess of the noun or the temporary excess and fluidity of the verb.

Each sees his own identity strategy as more advanced than the others because each defines the ultimate goal differently. The lifestyler defines the goal as full realization and commitment to the identity as one's core self. The commuter defines the goal as the ability to fit in anywhere and to adapt to each of one's different social worlds. And the integrator defines the goal as the ability to combine worlds and to integrate one's markedness into their overall mix of self.

Whether one chooses to live his identity as a noun, do his identity as a verb, or incorporate his identity as an adjective is dependent on a number of factors. In chapter 6 I look at some of the lifecourse and structural elements that influence one's gay identity grammar. In chapters 7 through 11, I demonstrate that what gay lifestylers, commuters, and integrators show us about identity is in fact relevant to a general theory of identity. The worldviews and identity management strategies of gay lifestylers, commuters, and integrators inform us about the ways all social actors organize and create a social self, present and transform their identities, and construct symbolic moral boundaries.

»6«

Shifting Grammars

Lifecourse Changes in and Structural Constraints on Identity Management

I moved from San Francisco to here because I got tired of having to be on gay all the time.[1] It was gay all the time and for a little while that was great. But you know, I'm not a queer activist, and I'm not HIV+, and I'm not very bohemian, so after a while I'd rather just be around ordinary people like me whether they're gay or not. Here you get the best of both worlds, because it's still close to New York, which is gay friendly, but it's also just an ordinary place to live. And I have to say that while being gay is a central aspect of my personality, I can't live an all-gay existence. And certainly in San Francisco it was possible to do that. But it is not possible for me to do that now. I need to live out in the world as a gay person.

Jacob

Jacob's move from San Francisco's gay community, where his networks were mostly gay, to the suburbs, where they are mostly straight, illustrates that the ecological organization and grammatical strategies of one's identity can shift over the life-

---

1. Jay Quinn makes a very similar point in an interview with Jesse Monteagudo for the on-line publication *Gay Today,* where he says he left South Beach for the suburbs because he was "gay-ed out" and "in the suburbs there isn't the same pressure to be specifically GAY all the time" (emphasis in the original). From http://gaytoday.badpuppy.com/garchive/people/070600pe.htm.

course. Jacob described his time in San Francisco as "living a gay lifestyle" and estimated that his social networks there were 80 percent gay and 20 percent straight. His portrayal of San Francisco as a place where you have to be "on gay all the time" suggests 100 percent duration. Moreover, in his view, it was a place that expected someone "on gay" to demonstrate requisite auxiliary characteristics, and thus high density, such as activism and bohemianism. In San Francisco, Jacob's overall package of predominantly gay social networks (a dominance indicator) and his high duration of being on gay suggest a point closest to the lifestyler corner of the triangle (the density of his gayness was between that of the integrator and that of the lifestyler, with the environment encouraging a higher density; after a time, he no longer desired to continue living at that density). After several years in San Francisco, he moved to the suburbs and abandoned his predominantly lifestyler grammar for a low-dominance combination somewhere between the commuter's and the integrator's point on the triangle.[2]

Because Jacob's shifting identity grammars are illustrative of the role structural and demographic factors may play in identity grammar, it is worth providing some biographical detail to put his move into context. Jacob grew up in the South and went away to a public university in a small Midwestern city, where he first came out of the closet to those around him during his junior year. He spent the summer of his junior year in San Francisco and subsequently moved to its gay community immediately after college. After a few months' stint at a small business in a service industry moderately related to his college degree, he began to work freelance in the same area; he did so for over seven years before leaving San Francisco to move to Northgate to continue his education.

---

2. He described himself as out to some people and not out to others and his social networks as 30 percent gay and 70 percent straight with only a little overlap. Initially after the move he was mostly a commuter, but has become more of an integrator over time.

Although this chapter's epigraph implies that he left solely for identity reasons, he also left in part because his particular job market began to bottom out; this, combined with San Francisco's high cost of living, provided a strong economic push to make a lifestyle change that he had been considering anyway.

Another key demographic factor in the changes that took Jacob from the closet to the ghetto to the suburbs is his age. First, while growing up he lived within the larger conservative heterosexual culture of the South. In his early twenties he moved to San Francisco to live a gay life segregated from the mainstream culture. In his late twenties he eventually grew to dislike the conformities of San Francisco's gay world nearly as much as the old conformities of the mainstream heterosexual society of the South; he moved to a New Jersey suburb, where he first attempted to reconcile the dominant and oppositional cultures by adopting a more commuting approach. Over time in the new area, he has gradually adopted more of a hybrid between a commuting and an integrating approach.

Although Jacob considers having lived in San Francisco a necessary stage in his life, he defines his move away from its gay subculture as a sign of maturity because he feels he now has the flexibility to interact in and fit in in both the gay and the straight worlds. He contrasts his mobility with that of a gay friend he met in college who moved to New York after college and who still lives there, where Jacob perceives him as still being stuck in that "big city gay lifestyle":

> We're still friends now although not as good friends in recent years, and he's sort of just being an East Village queen and working out and just that whole thing, and I don't think New York for this long has been good for him because he's just—you get hard and bitter after awhile; you know, those bitter New York queen faces. And it was the same way in San Francisco. It's just, it's a hard lifestyle to live, that big city gay lifestyle.

In Jacob's view, his friend's error is staying a lifestyler in New York for too long (a duration issue) and not moving on to what Jacob perceives as a healthier identity grammar for later in the lifecourse. Interestingly, one can interpret the commuter's definition of the mobility to move through both gay and straight cultures as a sign of maturity and a healthy self, as a folk challenge to models of identity that see the only logical development of gay identity as going from closeted to fully out.[3] Jacob experiences what others, including his friend, might call a partial retreat back to a more commuting (and partially closeted) approach as moving forward in his life, not backward.

I introduce this example as just one of many changes one's identity grammar can undergo over time. These trajectories are related to other variables such as occupation, income, age, historical cohort, gender,[4] relationship status, composition of one's social networks, race, ethnicity, and geographic region. The individual examples I provide merely provide a window into some of the possible ways these factors might interact in one's decision to lifestyle, commute, or integrate and in one's decision to maintain or shift identity strategies over time. The variables can interact in different ways and, although some directions are more common, there is no set path or single direction of progress to one kind of identity strategy.

Returning to the grammar disputes discussed in the previous chapter, one's view of "progress" or "maturity" varies depending on what identity grammar one practices. Gay lifestylers see their point as the logical endpoint on a continuum from low dominance to full-time, full-density commitment. In the lifestyler's view, progress in accepting a gay identity can be measured by his move from low commitment (either in duration or density) to full

---

3. See, for example, the psychological development models of Lee (1977) and Troiden (1979).

4. Here I use "gender" to include different forms of masculinities (see Connell, 1995) and femininities rather than as a dichotomous variable such as male and female.

commitment to the identity. For him, anything less than full commitment is less than full self-acceptance and complete maturity. He views the commuter as an unfinished lifestyler. The commuter is trying out the gay scene as a tourist, but he won't have fully matured until he accepts his gayness on a full-time basis. From the commuter's standpoint, however, he is at the end of a continuum from low mobility to high mobility because he has the flexibility that lifestylers and integrators lack. His progress in accepting a gay identity can be measured by his move from immobility (having to live an all-gay or all-closeted existence) to flexibility and mobility (being able to access both worlds). The lifestyler defines progress by commitment, the commuter defines progress by mobility, and so each talks past the other in conversations about personal progress, success, and maturity.

Although Jacob saw lifestyling as the transitional phase between the closet and his mobile life between two worlds, others see commuting as a transitional phase. For some suburbanites, commuting to the city to be gay in short-duration bursts eventually contributes to a desire to go native and become a lifestyler rather than a tourist in the gay ghetto. Still other commuters find the high density of the gay scene difficult to maintain and spread out their gayness across more spheres of their life while diluting its salience in any one sphere. They expand the range of places where they are known to be gay but diminish the density of their gayness. This strategy is often associated with things such as becoming partnered, becoming self-employed, or moving to a secure employment situation that makes it easier to be openly gay.

When I first met Jerry in the early 1990s he was very much a commuter to the gay world. Over the course of the decade Jerry moved from a low occupational position and a social life dominated by the local gay bar scene to a very high ranking position in a small company and a social life dominated by a mixed social network of gay and straight friends. Also contributing to this shift to integration was his having met a man who occupies a similar management niche in another small company. They purchased a large house together in a quiet nonstudent neighborhood not far from a college campus. Although they get along with their neighbors, like many suburbanites they do not interact with most neighbors on a deep level. Instead, most of their contacts are friends from their workplaces (mostly heterosexual) and friends they have kept in touch with from the gay bar scene. Their friendship circles overlap, and their own private parties as well as most of their social gatherings consist of both straight and gay people, an overlap that would have been unthinkable for Jerry four years earlier. The greater freedom his occupational position gave him allowed him to have a live-in partner without fear of occupational reprisal, and the reputation he established over time among heterosexual peers at his company gained him respect and acceptance that washed out what negative opinions some coworkers might have of "gays" as a category. All of these factors allowed for a significant shift in his identity grammar to that of an integrator.

This shift also led to changes in his worldview that reflect the integrator's greater acceptance of bridging the gay and straight worlds. In the past he wanted to keep those worlds bracketed, and he avoided queens at the local gay bar who, among other things, he feared might blow his cover if they approached him outside the bar. He ran in a masculine clique at the bar that defined itself against the "bar queens." Although when I attended the bar with Jerry, he and some of his friends would occasionally use feminine pronouns to refer to one another and "queen it up" as "play," they did this only periodically in any given night and did not do it in public space. In 1992, when Jerry was most closely aligned with the commuter corner of the triangle, he strongly disliked queens, whom he saw as threatening to his own mobility and as staining the reputation of the entire gay community. At this time his objection seemed to relate to the queen's "inappropriate performance" in front of straight audiences (a duration issue). By 1996 he had adopted a somewhat more tolerant, though not entirely accepting attitude toward queens. His more recent objection to queens, however, in implying that the queen has a temporary and chosen affectation, seems to collapse "queens" and "those who act queeny" (as distinguished by commuters) into basically the same thing:

> My opinion has sort of changed over the years. I used to be really turned off by [queens]. I [still] am not turned on by them now. [But] I mean [I was] turned off in the sense that I was actually sort of repulsed, and I think that was more as a gay person lumped with them, a gay person wanting to distance myself from that. . . . They don't turn me on sexually. I don't have many of them as friends. I don't click with effeminate men very well just because I can see through that affectation. It's like, "get over it." So I don't ever even bother with them. However, I don't deny them their freedom to exhibit that because that's at this particular point in their life, that's their only way of being able to assert themselves into the world as gay men. I wish they weren't—I wish people didn't have to take on affectations, but some people do.

While Jerry no longer worries as much about distancing himself from queens, since a more flexible attitude toward difference is a part of his identity strategy in his diverse and multifaceted social circles, he also makes clear that he believes "queens" are just unfinished integrators who haven't yet matured to the point where they can assert themselves as gay men without taking on high-density affectations. His view is that "queeny" behavior is a mere affectation and that if the queen were true to himself he would not be so hung up on playing up just one facet of himself. Whereas the lifestyler views being a queen as being true to himself, and the commuter admires the gay man who can "do queeny" as a context-appropriate gesture (but is bothered by "queens" because of the inappropriate duration of their high-volume identity display), the integrator views playing up this auxiliary characteristic as an affectation that betrays a more complex, multifaceted self.

Jerry's change in attitude toward the extremes of the gay community (both in the specific critique of them and in the tendency to tolerate them as category members) was not uncommon among people who had gone from a more commuting gay identity to a more integrating one. John, for instance, says that he used to distance himself from "obviously gay" men when he was younger, but now wants to include the extremes as well as the averages in the gay community:

> Most of us are just ordinary workaday schmoes like me. And you'll never see us in the media because we don't stick out. No one is going to want to take pictures or show twenty minutes of film footage of regular schmoes like me walking down the street because it's like, who cares? Who the hell wants to see boring, ordinary people?! So they focus on the fringe, and I used to dislike queens and leathermen and the extremes because of that. But not anymore. I'm not interested in kicking one group out of the gay community to make me look better and make me more acceptable. I'm not going to play the good gay/bad gay game where I'm going to say to the straight community, "look if you accept me, you know, I'm normal. I hate these damn big flaming queers too. Accept me and I'll reject them." I really despise playing that game.

As an integrator John no longer feels the commuter's need to identify entirely with the straight community in straight space and with the gay community in gay space. He believes he can be himself and be gay while still accepting other gays whose self is spicier than his own. John's live-and-let-live attitude came about after he read about the history of Stonewall and recognized that low-density workaday gays like him benefited from the political struggle of high-density cross-dressers and other extremes within the gay community. Prior to his becoming more of an integrator, he wanted to bracket the queens and leathermen from the majority culture's view of who gays are. Now as an integrator he feels no desire to separate the more visible elements of the gay community from the overall mix.

Equally revealing on the role of structure in identity grammar are cases where an individual expresses a desire to switch identity grammars but continues to pursue the same grammatical strategy because of occupational or other constraints. Marshall (a thirty-one-year-old white male) believes that his "true self" belongs in San Francisco rather than the suburbs. Working from home for a San Francisco–based national gay on-line service, Marshall admits he would rather move to the Castro than continue to cyber-commute and periodically travel there:

> If it were up to me I would be living in the Castro right now. My partner and I travel to San Francisco a lot, and the only thing that is stopping me from moving there permanently is that he would have to start all over at the bottom of his job if he moved. So he can't move and that's the only thing stopping us, because I feel that's where I really belong. That's who I really am. That's where I can "be myself." It is pretty funny because I am working for this big San Francisco gay community organization but I'm working [from home] in a small suburban town that is far removed from San Francisco.

Constrained from freely choosing an identity management strategy, Marshall expresses a "true self" that would be happier in the gay lifestyler space of the Castro. But because his partner would have to start over at the bottom of his occupational niche, they are confronted with the constrained choice between the place with the better occupational fit and the place with the better identity fit. Ultimately, Marshall's valuation of being a supportive partner overrides his interest in living out his "true gay self" in San Francisco. Consistent with the constrained choice to stay in the suburbs, Marshall's identity strategy plays out in a somewhat unusual way. He is out to his many gay friends in San Francisco and other parts of the country that he has met through his job, and he has a male partner and a gay-specific occupation, but he is not out to the majority of heterosexuals that surround him in his immediate community. For commuters like Marshall and his partner, the opportunity costs of lifestyling are greater than the costs of organizing a gay identity around short-term commutes and longer travel.

We have looked at examples of variations in progression from one identity grammar to another or expressions of desire to vary a grammatical strategy as they relate to other factors. In addition to looking at lifecourse shifts, we can look at some of the ways different variables may impact identity grammar. These trends should be regarded as speculative hypotheses to be tested rather than definitive conclusions. I also show the ways some factors can be complicated by the introduction of other factors.

Both high occupational prestige and income afford an individual more freedom to choose an identity grammar. Lifestylers cluster in occupations with unusually large numbers of gay men, in small organizations run by gays, and/or in firms centered around providing services to the gay community. Many of those men I spoke with who had low to medium incomes and occupational ranks commuted to and from a gay world, keeping their private lives and their public lives distinct. Some of those who commuted included, for instance, a thirty-one-year-old tech support worker in a company with three thousand employees, a twenty-four-year-old temp worker at a large pharmaceutical firm, and a twenty-seven-year-old computer graphics designer. Working at a large company with many employees seemed to be associated with a high number of commuters, whereas smaller companies appeared to increase the likelihood of integrating. The smaller company was more likely to produce tighter and more enduring social networks with less job turnover and with a situation wherein one's coworkers became relatively close, multiplex ties and part of one's outside social networks rather than the more impersonal weak ties of a large company's middle to lower echelons. Some individuals took the job because friends already worked there. Others developed coworker friends who came to judge them as a whole person based on a cumulative resume of self; this allowed them to then insert their gayness into the equation without spoiling their self-identity.[5]

Although for some people the economics of high city rents appears to constrain them to commute to a gay space to express their gay self, it is worth noting that at the very high ends of occupational prestige and income, there were also gay commuters who used their financial resources to make frequent identity commutes not only to places like New York and Fire Island, but even several times a year to places such as Key West, New Orleans, San Francisco, and Toronto. Some occupationally high-ranking single men kept their nongay and gay lives separate this way. Yet when asked if they would move to the places they commute to, they pointed to the positive advantages of mobility. The suburbs give Allen, a thirty-year-old white professional, a home base from which to travel to more specifically gay spaces and networks:

> I like living in the suburbs because it gives me an anchor.
> It keeps me grounded. Here I am close to everything and—
> but I can choose to go where I want when I want and I
> don't feel trapped in one spot, you know. I don't feel like
> I have to live a particular way, and I can be gay, and I can
> be in New York City just like that if I want to, or even
> Philadelphia . . . but I don't have to be. I can just stay at
> home, you know, and it's nice to have those options.

Just as the frequently traveling heterosexual businessman and politician have more freedom to commute to satellite sexual selves and other satellite selves because of their wealth, high-income gay men have opportunities to commute to a satellite gay self. Thus, one might plot the tendency to identity-commute

---

5. Goffman (1963b) would describe their form of managing an identity after coming out as "covering" rather than "passing" because they managed stigma by admitting a "discrediting identity" but by avoiding the more discrediting elements of the identity.

against income and occupational status as a U-shaped curve, high at both extremes and low in the middle. Although most people recognize the role of oppression in producing commuters, it may be interesting to consider the degree to which privilege may also paradoxically produce double lives. Integrating, by contrast, seems to be a strategy that clusters at the middle. Middle-class couples seemed to be the most integrated—a characteristic that is generally true among couples of their social standing.

Being partnered as opposed to being single also increases the likelihood of integrating. After all, commuting is sometimes an expression of trying on an identity, just as dating is a strategy for trying on a relationship; in fact, many people use dating itself to experiment with new potential identities in a relatively bracketed relationship. As such, commuting tends to be an especially common grammar among unattached younger men. The commuting strategy allows men to try on a gay identity at night before either adopting or not adopting it as one's full-time self. Indeed, some commuters bracketed their gay experiences and still maintained a core identity as heterosexual while they sampled the gay identity and decided whether or not to become full-time members of the new identity. Tim, for instance (see chapter 3), commuted between a satellite gay self and a home straight self for a while before finding a male partner caused him first to integrate his gay and straight selves into a bisexual self and later redefine himself as gay and integrate his partner and his gay life into everyday life. Lifestyling, because of the identity dominance and singularity required, and the doubling of potential structural deterrents to lifestyling in a partnered relationship, is also a strategy that is most easily followed by the unattached. Although some partnered couples can and do commute or lifestyle, partnership presents unique problems for such individuals. The lifestyler, for instance, will have to make compromises with other facets of self if his partner is not also a lifestyler.

In an interesting twist, however, one interracial white and Asian couple claimed that they were able to live together and still pass in their predominantly straight surroundings by letting conventional social attitudes about race and difference work in their favor. As Samuel (a white professional) explains:

> Being an interracial couple, we have more invisibility in the neighborhood because people, I think, like if we all travel collectively, five white guys and an Asian, the first one will hand all the boarding passes to the stewardess but as soon as Lee walks on, her arm goes up because there's this preconceived notion that he's with someone else. So I think when people see us living in the house, there's the assumption we're [just] roommates because we're different. So I think we blend in because people form these cognitive structures where they don't make the connection.

Samuel views his partner's status as a racial minority as helping them blend in as roommates. Were he coupled with a white man, he believes the neighbors would more easily make the connection. But the idea that they are living next to a couple that is both gay and interracial is a difficult connection for them to make. On the other hand, being partnered with this particular man who commutes away from the gay identity at his high-level position at a large firm has nudged Samuel closer to the commuter corner of the gay identity triangle, showing that partnered status is not always predictive of integrator strategy.

In chapter 5 we looked at grammar disputes among segments and individuals within the gay community. These interpersonal identity grammar disputes over whether to treat identity as a noun, a verb, or an adjective are often tied to larger structural, demographic, and lifecourse issues such as one's social class, occupation, race, relationship status (single or coupled), age, historical cohort, and other structural and demographic factors. Structural variables also influence the intrapersonal shifts that people make in their identity grammar over time, for just as identity grammar is contested terrain at the collective and interpersonal level it can become a contested and shifting terrain on the

intrapersonal level during the lifecourse. One's grammatical treatment of gay identity (and, I will posit, of other identities) is sel-
dom static over the course of a lifetime. It is not unusual, for
instance, for a college student on a liberal campus to live as a gay
integrator or even lifestyler while in college only to become a gay
commuter after college. Similarly, men who move to the city to be
gay lifestylers in their early adult years often move to the suburbs
to become integrators or commuters later. Likewise, many gay
commuters eventually decide to go from commuting to the city to
living in the city and becoming lifestylers.

This chapter has examined the structural changes affecting individual gay men's experiences and identity strategies and associated standpoints in intragay identity conflicts. Chapters 8 and 11
will elaborate on general patterns, hinted at in these men's experiences, by which structural factors, singly or in combination, can
influence variation and change in identity grammar strategies
across all social identities.

»7«

Vegan Peacocks, Christian Chameleons, and Soccer Mom Centaurs

Identity Grammar beyond Gay Identity

The conceptual insights gained from studying how gay men organize different facets of their identity should not be limited to the field of gay studies; they are also significant to the general study of identity. Too often gay studies and queer theory have been ghettoized and their relevance to mainstream social theory ignored. Since gay identity is currently salient as a marked attribute, gay men are likely to be self-consciously aware of the way they manage their identity across time and space; this makes them an ideal case study for identity management. My informants reveal the general process of identity management. It is not a uniquely gay enterprise; the ways gay men organize their identity ought to also reveal something about how Christians, Democrats, feminists, doctors, bird watchers, mothers, African Americans, Italians, southerners, Gen X'ers, baseball fans, vegetarians, drug dealers, kindergarten teachers, and jazz musicians organize their identities.

The framework that we have examined in some depth in the case of gay suburbanites has universal breadth; it extends across all dimensions of social identity including profession, religion, political affiliation, race, religion, status, ethnicity, institutional rank, gender, recreational subculture, age, class, occupation and sexuality (not only gay sexuality). If these categories of lifestyler (peacock), commuter (chameleon), and integrator (centaur) apply to other identity categories, we should be able to see the same identity disputes over duration, density, and dominance that we see among gay men. In the following chapters I draw on anecdotal material from a range of data sources such as newspaper articles, letters to the editor, books, academic studies, and personal observation, to show that we can in fact find the same kinds of identity disputes and conflicts over whether identity is a noun, verb, or adjective in other categories. These examples are gathered in a less systematic, but topically broader and even more analytically driven,[1] manner than the grounded theory/analytic fieldwork case study laid out in chapters 2 through 6 that prompted these theoretical insights.

Peacocks, Chameleons, and Centaurs across the Identity Spectrum

Walking through the streets of Manhattan, one can experience lifestyler (peacock) identity spaces almost everywhere. One will find gay lifestylers on Christopher Street, bohemian lifestylers near NYU, student lifestylers in the NYU dorms, Goth lifestylers

---

1. Again, see Black (1995:843) for more on the epistemological rationale behind this method of data gathering.

around Saint Marks Street, S&M lifestylers at the Hellfire Club near Fourteenth Street, Christian lifestylers at one of the many storefront churches, ethnic lifestylers in Chinatown and in Little Italy, wealthy lifestylers on the Upper East Side, and so on. These identity peacocks are visible and often fascinating to nonlifestylers. Moreover, they do the important political task of carving out social space and an identity-specific subculture for members of their category to enjoy the identity in its most concentrated form. Lifestylers provide the spaces to which commuters travel and the political clout that allows integrators to perform their identities at high durations. Peacocks are aware of their contributions, and they act as spokespersons for the identity as well as the enforcers of the proper standards for identity purity and authenticity. They wear their identity membership loudly and proudly.

Walk through these same social spaces and one is also likely to encounter tunnel-and-bridge identity chameleons who are commuting to the city to play up an identity that they submerge elsewhere. They will be decked out in their most authentic identity costumes, expressing their identity in a very visible and densely concentrated form. In their high-density colors they may be indistinguishable from their lifestyler counterparts. Their alternative chameleon color as a mild-mannered kindergarten teacher, or a suburban accountant, or a parent of two, or whatever other persona that they adopt outside the marked identity space will be submerged and invisible in the urban habitat in which one encounters them. Should one later cross over the tunnel or bridge into the suburban spaces of New Jersey or New York's outer boroughs, one may encounter the same commuter again. Only this time one will see the good neighbor, the lawn-mowing supersuburbanite, the English-speaking physical therapist whose mother lives in one of the city's ethnic enclaves, and the community pillar on the flip side of the identity divide. These chameleons change colors as they cross the tunnel and bridge from one identity habitat to the other.

One who continues through the suburbs will find Italian-

American integrators who neither hide their Italian heritage nor appear overly committed to it, relatively ordinary suburbanites with a few Goth CDs on their shelves, semibohemian folks who hang out with bohemians and nonbohemians alike, and suburban couples who incorporate mild dashes of S&M into an otherwise vanilla sexual diet. These identity centaurs combine two or more adjectives to construct their unique version of a whole self.

Traveling across space we can find individuals who approximate the ideal types of lifestylers, commuters, and integrators in any conceivable social category. It is worth looking at each of these categories more closely before turning to the grammar wars over identity among these different identity types.

One Hundred Percent Pure Concentrated X: Lifestylers

Every identity category has its lifestylers. They set the standards for the identity subculture; they are the movers and shakers of the category. When people think of an identity, they generally think first of its lifestylers. Lifestylers are the vanguard and the cultural arbiters of any identity category. They carve out identity-specific spaces and create a community that commuters can travel to and that integrators can take subcultural cues from. They shape the cultural perceptions of an identity and are its primary entrepreneurs in creating self-identification and sustaining the identity category as a positive affirmation. Where there are identity-specific enclaves one can be sure there will be lifestylers. The following characteristics signify a lifestyler identity: (1) a full-time commitment to the identity that encompasses all times and spaces; (2) an essentialist view of one's identity and the belief that it is one's "calling" or "true self"; (3) the accentuation of auxiliary characteristics to the main identity and a conspicuous distancing of oneself from characteristics seen as conflicting with the identity's auxiliary characteristics and; (4) a home in an identity-exclusive space, enclave, or ghetto, and identity-exclusive social networks used to maintain the unitary self. These characteristics result in a hierarchically arranged unidimensional social self.

Identity lifestylers separate themselves from the profane world through the use of physical space. Because oppression and intolerance or the desire to be around others with common interests and values drives them to find identity-exclusive social networks, lifestylers often live in or move to identity-specific spaces such as enclaves, ghettos, communes, dorms, and other similarly exclusive spaces. The lifestyler is someone who responds to oppression by adopting solidarity among other lifestylers of his or her identity and by limiting ties with the oppressive or threatening outside culture. Having been marked for discrimination and unequal treatment by the larger society or having found that society's typical demands on its members conflict with his or her requirements for an acceptable life, the lifestyler accepts his or her designation as specialized and different but assigns a positive rather than negative social value to this difference. Lifestylers derive their spiritual, mental, or physical sustenance from being enmeshed in the social networks of "their own kind."

In the category of ethnicity, lifestylers can be found in such ethnic enclaves as Little Italy, Spanish Harlem, Chinatown, and other similarly ethnically marked neighborhoods. Language, cultural barriers, and oppression are conducive conditions for the formation of ethnic identity lifestylers.

Along the dimension of class, wealthy peacocks can be found in gated communities[2] and in wealthy-exclusive ghettos like Brentwood, California, and Grosse Pointe, Michigan. In the wealthy lifestyler ghettos certain auxiliary characteristics like owning expensive cars and an interest in golf may be assumed if not expected. McDowell (1995:92) highlights the unidimensional social network domination characteristic of wealthy lifestylers in describing the environments of London merchant bankers as a place where the worlds of work, finance, leisure, and lifestyle lead to a complete interpenetration of areas of life previously separated by

---

2. For a good discussion of gated communities, see Lang and Danielsen (1997).

boundaries. The existence of wealthy lifestylers shows that being a lifestyler is not necessarily always a response to oppression;[3] privileged groups too will maintain a noun identity as a master status and vigilantly police their boundaries. Such policing includes not only limiting access to the space through private security and keeping subway and bus lines out, but also includes being very careful with one's own social contacts and networks so as to only include fellow lifestylers.

Along the dimension of religion, cults will ensure exclusivity of social networks and a lifestyler identity by breaking off all non-cult social networks. Similarly, Christian monasteries will maintain an identity-exclusive space for only those whose commitment to the identity is undivided. Religious enclaves and communities represent a less extreme version of religious lifestyler spaces. Amish and Mennonite communities, Christian comunidades de base, and Hasidic neighborhoods represent religious lifestyler enclaves.

Along the dimension of occupation, there are university faculty ghettos, student ghettos and student dorms, military bases, blue-collar ghettos, diplomat enclaves, and migrant labor communities that host a number of people whose occupation is often a salient identity even outside the duration of work time and whose social networks do not expand far beyond their occupational circles.

Along the dimensions of subcultural tastes and hobbies one can find vegan vegetarian peacocks, who differ from vegetarian commuters and integrators, and cowboy lifestylers who differ from cowboy commuters and integrators. Geographically, there are artist and poet/writer lifestyler enclaves in some large cities, birder lifestyler enclaves in some rural habitats where local residents are strongly committed to bird watching and where lodges and bed-and-breakfasts specifically for birders attract commuters

---

3. It may be that wealthy lifestylers view burglary as the "oppression from below" that they are avoiding with their gated communities.

from thousands of miles away,[4] skier enclaves in Colorado that house skier lifestylers and host skier commuters, surfer lifestyler neighborhoods along some beaches in western California, grunge music lifestyler enclaves in Seattle, slacker lifestyler spaces such as the Sixth Street area of Austin, and fraternity lifestyler "Greek towns" on large university campuses. A lifestyler often advertises her lifestyle with vanity plates, such as "surfer," "luv2ski," or "ingodzi," that let everyone know what attribute most defines her.

Some situations virtually require a lifestyling identity while other situations allow enough latitude to make taking on the attribute at the level of a lifestyle a relatively free choice. A tenured professor or a mother with teenagers may have considerable choice whether to lifestyle, commute, or integrate their respective professor and mother identities, whereas first-year professors and first-year mothers may not. Mothers of infants, for instance, are practically forced to become mother lifestylers, as motherhood at that stage is a greedy identity that allows little room to commute to other selves or to integrate many other attributes. Whereas mothers of older children can lifestyle, commute, or integrate, the high-intensity, high-duration demands of a newborn infant and the high demands U.S. society places on mothers of infants to be full-time caregivers require the type of undivided high-density commitment that only a lifestyler can provide. Although we may value integration in other realms, most individuals in the United States want mothers of newborns to be fully committed to their mother identity, even at the expense of all other identities.

Politicians are another category whose members are con-

---

4. When I stayed in the small town of Portal, Arizona, for instance, I noticed that the town economy seemed to be based heavily on birding tourism. Lodging accommodations advertised the number of bird species available on the premises and provided personal bird feeders for their visitors; the town's only grocery store had as many aisles of bird food as human food. It is not unusual for lodging accommodations in June to be filled by January because of the area's popularity with birders. Several of the locals I met were ex-commuters to the area who decided to move there and make birding their lifestyle.

strained by their structural situation to have less leeway to commute or integrate. The president, for example, has little freedom to be anything but an occupational lifestyler. The controversy over George W. Bush taking a one-month vacation during his first year in office was partly based on the belief that presidents should not commute or have off time, nor should they integrate and work from home rather than from the Oval Office. Bush's long vacation was viewed as a lack of commitment to his identity as president. His shorter workday than those of other presidents further contributes to the perception among some that he is a commuter president. Similarly, much was made of the fact that Bill Clinton's sexual transgressions with Monica Lewinsky happened in the Oval Office. This made people especially uncomfortable not just because it was adultery but because he integrated his sexual self into a space where he was expected to be 100 percent committed to his presidential self. His taking of an official phone call while simultaneously performing his sexual self further demonstrated that he was mixing his sexual and occupational identities. While in other contexts many will admire the flexibility of the integrator or the mobility of the commuter, they prefer that a head of state have the lifestyler's rigidity, focus, and singularity of purpose.

In general, marked identities require more of a commitment than unmarked ones and thus produce more lifestylers. The presence of stigma at one extreme or considerable privilege at the other extreme often encourages one to limit one's social networks. The stigmatized may limit their social networks to their own kind to avoid the indignities that others visit upon them. The hyperprivileged, on the other hand, may limit their social networks to maintain their privilege. Making it to the top often requires being stingy with one's time and limiting one's social affairs to events among the kinds of people who will advance one's career and social position. The time commitment of a lifestyler outside of the identity is limited, and whether one's markedness is based on stigma or privilege is less important to an attribute's capacity to produce lifestylers than the presence of markedness itself.

Superman, Dracula, Cinderella, and Other Commuters

Every attribute or identity category also has its identity commuters. These are the travelers who commute to the proud world of lifestylers to spread their wings. Their high-intensity attribute remains dormant in most settings but when the time and place are right, the attribute is displayed in all its glory. The commuter has long held a significant place in popular culture. The dramatic transformations of Superman, Dracula, Cinderella, and other mythical figures are, in part, a cultural celebration of and a warning about the commuter whose surface appearances may be deceiving or whose "core self" may lay dormant beneath the surface. The commuter's ability to undergo dramatic changes in appearance and persona is the domain of both comedy films and horror movies.[5] We are both amused and disturbed by those who are not always what they appear to be.

The commuter escapes persecution and travels to the safe spaces that lifestylers have created, often under the cover of night. Traveling to the spatial margins of rural wildernesses and urban centers and to the temporal margins of the late night and weekends, the commuter uses these spatial and temporal enclaves to express his identity with the same intensity and pride that the lifestyler does all of the time. The night is a frontier that houses individuals who wish to escape the strictures and perceived or real oppressions of everyday living (Melbin, 1987:29–52). Both the night and the city represent havens for the commuter to make pilgrimages to. Like the identity of a religious pilgrim, that of an identity commuter takes on its highest salience in pilgrimage to the identity-specific enclave.

The commuting strategy is especially popular in literature and songs. Much popular music, for instance, has celebrated the commuter's pilgrimage to an identity. In their song "Subdivisions," for instance, the rock group Rush celebrate leisure commutes to

---

5. The close relationship between topics of humor and topics of horror is suggested by Simpson (1996:549–50, 557–59).

the city and decry the forced conformity of suburbs and their "in-
sulated borders" far removed from the freeing lights of the city.
The song is an anthem for suburban commuters of marked identity traits in suggesting that "nowhere is the dreamer or the misfit
so alone" as the suburbs and that the only temporary escape is to
drift like moths into the city and "light up like a firefly." Similarly,
many heavy metal songs celebrate the night as the time when
teenage outcasts can band together in their pariah status and express their identity proudly.[6] Such song titles as Judas Priest's
"Living after Midnight" and Dio's "Sunset Superman" and "Night
People" hint at the importance of life after dark for the heavy
metal pariah. Grazian (2000) has shown a similar commuting attitude among blues club travelers, arguing that both audience
members and amateur blues musicians at the clubs construct alternative temporary nocturnal identities that are radically distinct
from their diurnal selves.

Although the double life of people who shift between diurnal
and nocturnal selves is the most celebrated form of commuting in
both music and literature, most identity commuters live more
than just a dual life. Some live multiple lives, switching identities
repeatedly across time and space. Although day and night and
weekday and weekend are the most common cues that it is time
to commute to a different identity, there can be others. Moreover,
while oppression is a common reason for commuting, not all
commuters are merely reacting to oppression. Rather, for commuters life is organized around the mantras "when in Rome do as
the Romans do" and "out of sight, out of mind." The commuter is
ultimately an identity traveler who likes to take on the self du jour
of the setting.

A commuter identity is characterized by: (1) a part-time durational commitment to more than one identity; (2) a fluid view of

---

6. See Weinstein (2000:205–12) on the preparation in auxiliary characteristics
that many metal fans take before a concert; see ibid (199–235) on the commuter venue of the concert. The night is a key temporal variable in the heavy
metal commute, and many rock anthems celebrate the night for that reason.

identity as mutable across different spatial and temporal contexts, (3) the high-volume accentuation of auxiliary characteristics including specialized knowledge skills (insider knowledge) appropriate to whatever setting one is in; and (4) maintaining separate sets of social networks around separate identity attributes. The commuter is someone who responds to his surroundings by shaping himself to fit the context, and travels among contexts for this purpose. The commuter keeps his selves cognitively segregated by maintaining different social networks. The commuter is likely to organize his networks into separate categories such as "work friends," "weekend friends," "church friends," "bridge club friends," and "softball friends" without mixing the different networks. A parody of the identity commuter mind-set appeared in an episode of *The Simpsons;* when Bart and Lisa Simpson ask Reverend Lovejoy to help them find a particular rabbi, he responds "Yes, of course, let me check my non-Christian Rolodex." While meant as parody in this example, the keeping of separate appointment books and phone lists for different identity networks is a strategy that betrays a commuter's sensitivity to keeping social networks distinct.[7] Christena Nippert-Eng's study of people who either segment or integrate their work lives, for instance, shows that those who segment tend to keep separate phone lists, calendars, address books, and other items that are used to organize their social networks.[8]

Identity commuting occurs both with achieved attributes and ascribed attributes. Although research has focused primarily on

---

7. In another episode, devoted Christian follower Ned Flanders calls up the reverend for spiritual guidance late at night and gets an agitated and indifferent response from the off-duty Lovejoy. In the first example, while the reverend is on duty at the church, his consulting a non-Christian Rolodex is the kind of subtle marking of non-Christian outsiders that one might also expect from a lifestyler; in the second, his response to a high-duration Christian shows his mobility between a Christian and a secular everyday self.

8. See, for instance, Nippert-Eng (1996:149–51) for the ways that integrators and segmenters (her word for commuters) differ on a variety of organizational matters.

the mutability of achieved identities, ascribed identities can also be mobile across social contexts. Rockquemore (1999) shows, for instance, how some biracials take on a protean identity as sometimes black, sometimes white, and sometimes biracial depending on the social context. They are racial identity commuters who have the mobility to move "between and betwixt contexts and cultures freely and smoothly" (Brunsma and Rockquemore, 2000:16). But even when individuals do not fully change their racial category in a protean way, they can still commute from a virtually "unraced self" in some contexts to a racially salient one in others. Some African Americans at colleges and corporate workplaces, for instance, play down seemingly race-specific cultural tastes in an attempt to appear as generic as possible, but foreground their African-American cultural tastes when in exclusively African-American neighborhoods and events. Similarly, with respect to ethnic identity, some Irish-Americans blend in as nondescriptly white or "generic Americans" until Saint Patrick's Day, when they take down their American flag and put up an Irish flag[9] or travel to an Irish pub decked out in green to display their Irish colors loudly and proudly.[10] The ethnic chameleon may place an American flag in her public yard or place of business to play up the American aspect of her identity and to submerge the ethnic aspect that she foregrounds in more ethnicity-specific places and times.

Along the dimension of class, some members of the poor and the wealthy choose to foreground their class identity only where

---

9. A letter writer to a *Boston Globe* message board (http://www.boston.com/news/packages/underattack/message_boards/patriotism/messages9.shtml, retrieved December 28, 2002) explains that her parents put out the American Flag "EVERY DAY except St. Patrick's when they put up an Irish flag" (all caps in the original). It is noteworthy that they didn't fly both flags at any time and that the Irish flag received 1/364 of the duration of the American flag.

10. For examples of this and other methods that some Irish Americans use to play up an Irish identity on Saint Patrick's Day, see Waters (1990:123–24). For a critique of the low-durational Irish identity of ethnic chameleons, see Hayden (2001).

others around them share the same class position. Wealthy commuters, for instance, will play up other more generic characteristics and hide their wealthy background when in nonwealthy spaces, but will reemphasize their wealth when surrounded by other members of the privileged classes. One can see this in political campaigns, where wealthy candidates attempt to construct an "ordinary person" identity and to play down or even hide their position of class privilege among the general voting public. Similarly, when I was in graduate school some wealthy classmates attempted to hide their wealthy background for fear that their less well-to-do classmates would envy or resent their class privilege. When reacquainted with members of their wealthy-specific social networks, however, the commuters reverted back to showing the auxiliary characteristics of wealth that they suppressed around their nonwealthy colleagues.

Along the dimension of religion, there are weekend and holiday Christians—Christian chameleons—who attend church and play up their religiosity in marked religious times such as Sabbath days and marked religious spaces such as churches but play down their Christianity in unmarked secular time and space. Unlike the religious lifestyler whose religion is active all the time every day, the religious chameleon's religion is readily available only at religion-specific times and places.

Along the dimension of occupation, there are commuters who express their occupational selves only at work and never talk shop outside of work. The commuter mentality is expressed well in the *Jump Start* cartoon where Marcy explains that "working Marcy" and "weekend Marcy" have no dealings with one another. The occupational commuter segregates her work and home life and prefers to keep them separate.[11] Although low-autonomy, low-prestige occupations may be expected to produce more commuters who want to completely segment their work and home

---

11. For an excellent analysis of occupational commuting, see Nippert-Eng (1996:117–23).

lives (Nippert-Eng, 1996:182), the correlation between occupational autonomy and occupational identity strategies is not uniform. Many blue-collar workers, especially in male-dominated professions such as construction, extend their occupational social networks after work at the closest pub while some members of certain occupations divorce themselves as much as possible from their work life when off duty. One can think of the lawyer or doctor who hates being asked legal or medical questions at a party as falling on the occupational commuter side of the equation. Likewise, one can think of the difference between the professional chef who happily accepts invitations to cook something for a friend's party (a chef lifestyler) or the professional photographer who is asked to take a few pictures at the party (a photographer lifestyler) and the professional chef or photographer who will only do so if paid (chef and photographer commuters).

Along the dimension of subcultural tastes and hobbies there are any number of commuters for such diverse identities as tattoo collectors, white-water rafters, deer hunters, magicians, chess players, bird watchers, opera fans, and athletes. Watson (1987) shows that many women athletes, for instance, maintain very distinct on-court and off-court identities. They foreground an athlete identity on the court and then change back to foregrounding their woman identity off the court (Watson, 1987:443). Here the court and game time become the spatial and temporal cues to turn on the athlete identity; the locker room serves as the social phone booth from which to change between the super athlete and the mild-mannered female identity. Off the court, her athlete identity goes into remission and her female identity takes center stage. The negative sanctions placed on strong females cause many women athletes to downplay their athlete attributes in generic public space and to play them up only in specifically marked athletic spaces. Related to this idea of separate identities on the court and off the court, my wife's high school Spanish teacher said she loves the ability to immerse herself fully in Puerto Rican culture through the social network that language skills have allowed her to create because Puerto Rican culture allows her to "live out parts of myself" that her white southern culture does not. When immersed in Spanish culture she can, in effect, bring to the fore a different self that remains dormant when she is in her everyday world.

The commuter is someone who gives 100 percent intensity to whatever identity he is doing at the time but has too many separate identity interests to give 100 percent to a single identity all of the time. The bookshelf of a commuter will generally be neatly divided, like a TV dinner, by one's different ingredients of self. Each topic will be clearly separated from one another. Thus, for example, vacation guides, political books, chess books, sociology books, and reptile books are each purposefully stacked into separate bookshelves.[12]

Centaurs: Integrators as Composite Creatures

Unlike lifestylers, who are singularly committed to one dominant aspect of self, or commuters, who move between distinct selves, integrators are mixed and multidimensional creatures. They are centaurs: complex creatures whose uniqueness comes in the combination of their attributes rather than in the salience of any one characteristic. Unlike the commuter, who travels between an unmarked and a marked self like human/werewolf or Clark Kent/Superman, the integrator combines disparate parts into one unique multidimensional creature of self—a centaur rather than human/horse. Whereas lifestylers and commuters both give 100 percent to an identity at times, the integrator never commits herself fully to a single identity attribute. The integrator likes her overall combination and does not want to ever let any single ingredient dominate the self. The integrator's commitment never weighs heavily toward any single attribute; rather it is spread

---

12. This example is a description of my own home bookshelves. True to the commuter spirit I have strong sociological, political, reptile watching, and chess playing identities but keep my social networks in each of these areas separate.

thinly and consistently across a wide variety of attributes. Whereas the lifestyler defines the subculture and creates subcultural innovations for the larger culture and the commuter travels between the two worlds and spreads the innovation, the integrator mediates between the subculture and the general culture and brings innovations to acceptance in the larger culture by incorporating them in a low-key, nonthreatening way.

The following characteristics signify an integrator identity: (1) living in unmarked space with all of one's attributes including markedness consistently publicly available as adjectives; (2) viewing the self as coherent but multifaceted; (3) possessing very toned-down, low-density auxiliary characteristics; and (4) maintaining a single large mixed or multidimensional social network rather than multiple distinct networks. Unlike the commuter whose mantra is "when in Rome, do as the Romans" or the lifestyler whose mantra is "if a Roman move to Rome," the integrator's mantra is "when in Rome, just be yourself."[13] In contrast to lifestylers and commuters, the integrator does not feel one must be enveloped in the experience of an identity at 100 percent intensity to enjoy it. The integrator can enjoy the cultural experience of a public sporting event without wearing team colors, applying face paint, or cheering loudly. Similarly, the integrator can enjoy a gospel choir or charismatic church service without becoming especially animated herself in worshipping. She has broad interests but often lacks the depth of commitment that a commuter or lifestyler has to a particular interest.

The racial or ethnic integrator will generally live in a mixed

---

13. In a paper on Muslim women in the United States entitled "When in Rome, Do Your Own Thing," Obol (1994) describes the ways in which some Muslim women (whom I would consider located somewhere between Muslim integrators and lifestylers) maintain a Muslim flavoring in a predominantly Judeo-Christian society. I found this title helpful in advancing my own thoughts about the different ways in which one can act with regard to their identity in a context where some of their identity package is unfamiliar, marked, or foreign.

neighborhood. In the United States, an ethnic centaur will emphasize both the American and the hyphenated part of her identity. She may place both an ethnic and an American flag in her yard to signify a simultaneous commitment to both identities. Likewise, her social networks will consist both of those who are perceived as "ethnic" Americans and those who are perceived as "generic" Americans.

The class integrator will reflect her class tastes in minor ways but will also have many other interests that are not perceived as class specific. The class integrator's wardrobe will generally include a number of items that can be worn in a variety of different contexts and by a broad range of social classes. Her car is seen more as transportation than as status symbol.

With respect to religion, the integrator is religious but does not express her religion on high volume. Unlike the Christian commuter who dresses up in her Sunday best for church, for instance, the Christian integrator might wear the same clothes to church on Sunday as she wears during the week. Her social circles may be mixed among several denominations and might even include nonreligious people.

Occupational integrators will consider their job a significant part of their self but not necessarily their defining characteristic. A working parent, for instance, may reflect the combination of two selves in choosing not to foreground either his occupation or his parent status as more central to his core self than the other. Similarly, the soccer mom centaur may combine a number of different selves as a mother, a wife, a school board member, and a volunteer worker to manifest a multidimensional self with overlapping integrated social networks.

Along the dimension of subcultural tastes and hobbies, the integrator has a breadth of interests rather than one or two very deep interests. The integrator is a jack of all trades rather than the master of one domain. The integrator's bookshelf is a complex network without clear divisions; a frequent integrator complaint is "where should this book go? It could fit here, or here, or here!" On the integrator's shelf transitions flow into one another; novels blend into current events, current events blend into history, history blends into sociology, sociology blends into cognitive science, cognitive science blends into psychology, etc.[14] The integrator has a bookshelf with a wide variety of subjects and a CD collection with a wide variety of musical genres, but does not have extensive collections of books on a single topic or of CDs in a single genre.

Conclusion

In this chapter I have argued that the ideal types of the lifestyler, the commuter, and the integrator are instructive for the generic study of identity. On any axis around which identity is formed, individuals are likely to adopt strategies that approximate or incorporate elements of these three types. Although the real world is complex, and such types do not necessarily exist in pure, unambiguous forms, one can see elements and representatives of each type for any identity category. Even where some individuals fall squarely between two different types, recognizing these ideal types helps us to think about the underlying dynamics of identity organization and about the internal choices we make between treating an identity attribute as a noun, a verb, or an adjective. Both structural constraint and individual agency play into the type of identity strategy one adopts.

Lifestyling is a strategy often, but not always, created by oppression from the outside world. Pushed to the margins of society, the lifestyler creates a community and a sense of pride by forming identity-exclusive social networks and living in identity-exclusive space. For heavily marked identities, people expect the lifestyling response in the face of marginalization and oppression. Even those who actively marginalize the identity will often expect the

---

14. This example is a description of my wife's home bookshelves. True to the integrator spirit, her friendships and social networks overlap and her conversations flow from topic to topic freely without rigid boundaries such as "shop talk," "hobby talk," or "politics talk."

marginalized to "show their true colors" and "live among their own kind" rather than "hide who they are" and assimilate into the rest of society. Even powerful and nonmarginalized groups, however, have some lifestylers. Geographically, lifestyling is most often associated with the most urban and most rural extremes.

Commuting is a strategy often associated with oppression and with the need to pass. Although this is obviously a significant aspect of much commuting, some people commute to identity attributes even when the cost of integrating the attribute is extremely low. Some occupational and hobby commuters risk little more than surprise or mild ridicule by revealing their occupation to the people they share a hobby with or their hobby to people they work with, and yet they choose to maintain a separate presentation of self in each environment. Indeed we are all commuters to some degree. Goffman (1959) notes in *The Presentation of Self in Everyday Life* that individuals are social actors who attempt to manipulate their presentation of self to present the most favorable impression of themselves given the social environment they are in. We all mask some parts of our selves and foreground others when in important settings like job interviews, first dates, and class reunions;[15] indeed, those who are such integrators or lifestylers that they can't pull off a commute in such situations as job interviews and first dates often do not fare well in either marketplace. Geographically, commuting as one's dominant identity strategy is most often associated with mobile spaces that have easy access to transportation, such as suburbs and rural areas near freeways and urban areas near subway lines and airports.

Integrating is the strategy least associated with or connected to oppression. The integrator adopts neither a central defining attribute nor different personas for different contexts. She has one multidimensional self that is ever present for all to see. For unmarked social attributes, integrating is a more common identity

---

15. For an excellent analysis of impression management and commuting to a situated self at class reunions, see Vinitzky-Seroussi (1998:136–54).

strategy than commuting or lifestyling. This suggests that in a world without oppression or markedness that integrating would be the strategy of choice for most people. The integrator is perceived as well-rounded and possessing a variety of interests. Only some of us have the social option to be well rounded, however. The chronically ill person may not be allowed to take on any identities that rival his central defining feature as a sick person by the rest of society, for instance. The chronically ill person faces social as well as physical limitations to being well rounded and possessing a balanced identity diet. The master status of some attributes is so heavily weighted that the individual will not be able to have other attributes count toward their identity without tremendous effort.[16] Other attributes, by contrast, may require only a moderate effort to balance them out with other ingredients and some unmarked attributes may require almost no effort.

In the next three chapters I look at the disputes between lifestylers, commuters, and integrators with respect to identity attributes. First I look at duration disputes that pit the lifestyler and integrator value of identity stability against the commuter value of mobility. Then I analyze density disputes that pit the lifestyler and commuter value of purity against the integrator value of moderation. And finally I look at dominance disputes that pit the commuter and integrator value of balancing commitments against the lifestyler value of focused commitment.

---

16. For a detailed analysis of the process by which we weigh marked and unmarked attributes in determining identity, see Mullaney (1999).

»8«

Duration Disputes
Identity Stability vs. Identity Mobility

"I want to be English when I want to be," remarks an informant in Katharine Jones's study of English identity in the United States. Jones explains that

> his status as an English person in the U.S. seemed to give him a sense that he could *repudiate* or *exaggerate* his national identity at will. Speaking from a position of relative privilege, this young white man had a sense of control over the degree of Englishness he felt. National identity, for him, was dynamic and contestable. (Jones, 2001:1) (emphasis added)

The English immigrant to the United States has the identity mobility to turn up (exaggerate) or turn off (repudiate) his identity as he wishes. He can be a part-time Englishman. Although Jones provides an excellent example of an identity commuter, it is noteworthy that she associates repudiating and exaggerating identity with the agency and choice provided those with privileged identities. I find this account interesting because many people in the everyday world as well as the research community associate identity commuting with oppression and stigma. For them, the commuter is a fearful person who hides a stigmatized identity out of fear. Yet this is not at all what Jones is implying. By turning identity on its head and studying privileged English immigrants instead of negatively marked immigrants, Jones is able to show the "chosen" rather than the "forced" side of commuting.

One dimension along which members contest an identity is duration. The lifestyler values a high-duration identity. For the lifestyler, identity is a full-time commitment, and identity is essential and thus supposed to remain stable across time and place. The lifestyler views his "core self" as composed of a central defining ingredient and several complimentary ingredients arranged hierarchically downward from this ingredient. By contrast, the integrator views his "true self" as the entire composite of ingredients mixed in a low-intensity flat organization rather than hierarchically arranged. Still, though the lifestyler's self is high intensity and focused and the integrator's is lower intensity and multidimensional, lifestylers and integrators share one thing that separates them from commuters. Both believe that they have a "core self" that they should be committed to at all times. They value identity stability over identity mobility. With both the lifestyler and the integrator, for the most part, what you see is what you get.

The commuter, however, values lower-duration bursts of identity. Like a tourist who gets into the experience of each unique setting, the commuter takes on a range of identities across different social environments. He views his self as more interactive with the social environment—a fluid or claylike self that can be molded and reformulated easily to match different social settings. The commuter remains true to the social setting, once he's in it, while the integrator and lifestyler remain true to a stable core self that varies little from setting to setting. The commuter criticizes the other types for not making enough concessions to the setting, while integrators and lifestylers are critical of the commuter for not making enough concessions to the self.

These two views of the temporal relationship between self and social environment set up a conflict between self-oriented lifestylers and integrators on one side and setting-oriented commuters on the other. The arguments directed at the commuter are rooted in duration but often couched in language implying a necessary connection between time commitment and self-commitment: "authenticity vs. fakeness," "commitment vs. opportunism," "playing vs. living." The commuter, however, does not accept that the act of committing himself fully to an identity involves spending all his time in or on that identity; he frames his arguments in the durational disputes as issues of "flexibility vs. rigidity." Lifestylers and integrators believe suppressing facets of one's self in different contexts, as the commuter does, presents a false self, an identity façade. They do not respect the commuter's mobility and flexibility because they see the commuter as playing all sides and lacking commitment to a single, stable core self. The integrator believes the commuter is being inauthentic when he is playing up a particular identity to the nth degree and ignoring everything else, and the lifestyler believes the commuter is being inauthentic when he is *not* playing up an identity to the nth degree. Integrators and lifestylers may differ over which identity of the commuter they believe is a façade, but they agree that the commuter cannot be his true self if he is constantly changing appearances to meet the norms of the setting. They want the commuter to be monogamously committed to one stable core self rather than to move promiscuously between commitments to different selves. Ultimately the lifestyler and the integrator believe that the commuter is violating his core self when he plays to the setting, while the commuter sees the others as violating the setting when they foreground the self without ever making compromises to the setting.

Marked Settings as Battleground: Natives and Tourists, Full-Timers and Weekend Warriors

The lifestyler often moves to an identity-specific setting that allows him to be simultaneously true to both the self and the setting. Often to maintain a full-time self, the lifestyler moves to an identity island where he can be isolated from the influences and impurities of the outside society on a permanent basis. The commuter, by contrast, is only a tourist to the island; he goes there on a temporary (and often seasonal or cyclical) basis. As a resident of an identity-specific space, the lifestyler is free to live his identity as a full-time vocation rather than take part in it only as a temporary profound sense of identity—something that commuters find, for instance, in fleeting identity settings like conventions, parades, and rallies. The journey of the Puritans to Massachusetts Bay is a classic example of moving to establish identity as a vocation (see Erikson, 1966). It is noteworthy that idealist identity colonists like this still hold a cherished place in genre literatures such as science fiction and fantasy. Although in most contemporary instances, individuals cannot move to new continents or physical islands to lifestyle an identity, they do create symbolic and mental islands[1] that they then reinforce spatially through the use of gatekeepers and border patrol at identity checkpoints,[2] commercial and residential networking and segregation, or a host of other measures.

The full-time spaces that allow lifestylers to live their identity as a calling or vocation also create space for commuters to travel to their identity as a part-time occupation or recreation. These

---

1. See Zerubavel (1991:5–20) on "islands of meaning."

2. For instance, a gated community for wealthy lifestylers, a cult compound for religious lifestylers, and a militia compound for militant lifestylers.

spaces are often a key site of duration disputes over identity. The lifestyler may welcome the commuter as a member of the identity category, but he is skeptical of the commuter's commitment because the commuter only exercises his identity on a part-time basis. The commuter is only a "seasonal employee" to the vocation, which gives lifestylers cause to question his commitment in a number of ways either directly related to duration or extrapolated from it based on the lifestylers' assumptions and values. For instance, the lifestyler will sometimes confuse lack of duration with lack of intensity. The lifestyler criticizes the commuter for being only part-time, thus lacking a durational commitment to the identity, and for merely "playing the identity rather than living it," and for being a wannabe rather than an authentic member of the identity community. The lifestyler will use terms such as "poseur," "wannabe," "weekend warrior," "part-timer," and "amateur." Moreover, from the lifestyler's perspective, the commuter is polluted by the impurities of his other vocations; even though the commuter brackets these, the lifestyler fears that their impurities still remain active beneath the surface and are not entirely dormant.

Both lifestylers and commuters take pride in their pariah status while in marked identity spaces. They differ, however, in that the lifestyler chooses to live this status at all times, while the commuter is openly a pariah on only a part-time basis. For this reason, the lifestyling peacock accuses the commuting chameleon of opportunism since he is a "proud pariah"[3] only in spaces and times where his marked status is accorded a high social value. The lifestyler reasons that if the commuter were really true to himself, he would remain loud and colorful in all settings, whether his identity was valued or not.

A single identity attribute is the defining characteristic of

---

3. I borrow the term from Weinstein's (2000:93) study of the heavy metal subculture. She uses "proud pariah" to refer to the subcultural youth who willingly accept the stigma accorded their musical orientation as a badge of honor.

the lifestyler's essence. Identity is not something the lifestyler chooses, it is something he is, always has been, and always will be. Monster Kody Scott (aka Sanyika Shakur) expresses the view of a gang identity lifestyler: "[Being a gang member] was my career, my 'calling' as church folks say when someone does *one thing* real well" (Scott, 1993:40) [emphasis added]. Scott goes on to explain how he tried to validate his calling much like the early Calvinists validated theirs: "This was not some awkward stage of my life. This was a job to me, and I was employed full-time, putting in as much overtime as possible. Life from that vantage point seemed to be one big test of show and prove, pick and stick" (Scott, 1993:40). For the lifestyler finding the one thing that defines his "true self" and living his "identity calling" to its fullest is the goal. One must engage in identity work as a full-time commitment. For the lifestyler identity is vocation, not recreation.

The lifestyler views the undivided commitment to an identity and its auxiliary characteristics as the showing of true colors. Even with identities that appear so obviously chosen from the outsider's perspective, the lifestyler will insist that their identity was predestined. Blee (2002:52) points out, for instance, that Nazi lifestylers in the United States use essentialist logic, claiming that they were born that way and that their Nazi essence has always been with them no matter when they finally discovered it. Nazi leader Karl Allen, for instance, said that "Nazis are born not made" and that almost all his fellow Nazis believed it was a "cause they were born to serve."[4] Similarly, in Fox's (1997:343) study of "real punks" and "pretenders," the people she refers to as "real punks" (which I would call lifestylers) argued that they had *always* been punk on the inside: "Punk didn't influence me to be the way I am. I was always this way inside. When I came into punk it was what I needed all my life. I could finally be myself." Interestingly, Fox's own scholarly analysis accepts the punk lifestyler's values of commitment and authenticity as the terms of

---

4. Cited in Blee (2002:52).

the debate, and thus her own analytic categories of "real punks" and "pretenders" reflect the lifestyler vocabulary. For the lifestyler an undivided commitment to a singular identity is the definition of the "true self." Moreover, they believe that they themselves are the real and committed members of their category and that those who do not put in full-time commitment to the identity are mere pretenders or wannabes. Related to the commitment issue is the belief among lifestylers and integrators that the commuter cannot be taken seriously because of his lack of durational commitment. If the commuter were really serious and committed to the identity, they reason, he would not just display it a small percentage of the time. Fox's (1997:354–55) punk lifestylers, for instance, referred to commuting punks as pretenders: "All I know is that I live [punk] seven days a week, they just do it on the weekends" and "being punk to them is like playing cowboys and Indians." For these lifestylers, the temporal component of identity is the key between merely doing an identity as trivial play and authentically being an identity. No matter how well a commuter plays the identity, his duration is too low for the lifestyler to take him seriously as legitimate. In the lifestyler's eyes a commuter is a mere tourist while the lifestyler *lives* the identity.

The lifestyler believes that one must put in serious time and commitment before one can be considered a true member of the category. Across a number of identity categories the common criticism lifestylers level at commuters is that they lack commitment because they only do identity work part-time. The full-time military soldier views the part-time national Guardsman as a "weekend warrior"; the devoted full-time Christian views the Christian who plays up her Christianity only on Sundays as a "weekend Christian" and the Christian who attends church only on Christmas and Easter as a "holiday Christian." A bar regular views the Friday night binger as a "weekend drinker" and the once-a-year New Year's Eve binger as a "holiday drinker." I have heard both bartenders and regular bar patrons, for instance, refer to New Year's Eve as "amateur night." Similarly, the academic lifestyler looks down upon the commuting "conference academic" who does little research most of the year but shows up to the annual meetings every year and plays up an academic researcher identity for a few days; the sports lifestyler scorns the commuting "fair-weather fan" who suddenly decks himself out in team colors and talks smack when the home team is in the playoffs but whose commitment to his identity as a team follower was low-key or absent during the uneventful middle of the season; the Irish-American lifestyler views the "Saint Patrick's Day Irish" commuter as uncommitted because she only plays up her green colors once a year.

Frozenness and Adaptability: The Commuter's Perspective

Although lifestylers may consider commuters uncommitted, commuters see the duration issue differently. They see themselves as mobile, flexible, and able to adapt to different social environments. The lifestyler claims a monopoly on density because the lifestyler is monopolistic in duration, but the commuter does not see duration as a requirement for density. A primary dispute between commuters and lifestylers involves the tension between doing and being.[5] The individual who occasionally raves on weekends may see her "raving" as a verb, but will not see herself as a "raver" in its noun form. One who describes her occasional gambling in verb terms as "betting on the game" does not necessarily view herself as a "gambler" or a "bettor." Many commuters maintain their conventional identities while occasionally embarking on deviant identities as a verb at night, on the weekends, during holidays, or in identity-specific spaces. Murphy, Waldorf, and Reinarman (1993), for instance, describe some middle-class cocaine sellers as people who "had become adept at articulating the proper identity at the proper time." For example, "By day, one

---

5. See Mullaney (1999) on how others socially weight acts to determine when doing indicates a state of being and when doing is just doing.

woman dealer was a concerned mother at her daughter's kinder-garten field trip, and that same evening she was an astute judge of cocaine quality when picking up an ounce from her connection" (1993:468). Unlike lifestylers, commuters often maintain a con-ventional lifestyle outside of marked spaces. This very fact often renders them invisible as representatives of the marked category. Murphy, Waldorf, and Reinarman (1993:465) point out that pop-ular press descriptions focus only on the most visible street sellers thus representing only the extreme tip of the cocaine-dealing ice-berg. This complaint illustrates a familiar problem. Lifestylers are seen as representing entire identity categories since neither com-muters nor integrators have the same social visibility; as such, lifestylers become the media spokespersons of their identity groups even though most identity groups have more integrators and commuters than lifestylers.

The commuter views herself, with her ability to move among identities, as flexible rather than uncommitted or unstable. She rejects the notion of a single coherent self and sees no problem with a more malleable and protean self. Like the lifestyler, the commuter wants to take on an identity in its most intense form, but she prefers to sample multiple identity plates and play the field rather than choose a single favorite identity attribute and make a full-time commitment to it. She relishes multiple alternat-ing intense short-term commitments. For her, the ability to turn off one identity and turn on another is critical.

From the commuter's point of view both the lifestyler and the integrator appear self-absorbed because they pay more attention to their self than to the setting. Both are inflexible bores who do not alter their conversations and performances to suit the envi-ronment. For instance, while the integrator may consider herself well-rounded when she discusses her interest in raising cats at a softball team party, the commuter will interpret the integrator's directing of the discussion away from softball to talk about her cats as an indication that she is interested only in cats (a cat per-son lifestyler). Similarly, if an occupational integrator talks shop after hours, the commuter may easily mistake them for a workaholic (occupational lifestyler) who has no life outside their work. The following description of a biologist who had a reputation for talking shop inappropriately betrays a commuter's perspective:

> [H]e could be heard trying out his latest ideas on anyone who would listen; rumor had it that he was once overheard explaining some of the finer points of theoretical biology to the copier repair man. (Waldrop, 1992:101–2).

The commuter finds the high-duration self of both the lifestyler and the integrator a problem, because both will introduce attributes to a setting that aren't auxiliary to the setting, and thus, in the commuter's view, don't belong. Interestingly, while the commuter may work with relentless intensity and focus (as in the adage "work hard and play hard"), he does not see himself as a "workaholic" because he defines excess on durational rather than density grounds.

Commuting and Lifestyle Change:
Polygamy and Serial Monogamy of Identity

To understand the conflicts that lifestylers and integrators impute to the durational strategy of commuting, we can use the loaded terms "polygamy" and "promiscuity." We can think of the lifestyler as someone who is wedded to a single core identity attribute and whose commitment to that attribute is unfalteringly monogamous. The integrator lacks a strong commitment to any single identity attribute and, like the single person with lots of acquaintances but no significant other, does not ever need to give his time exclusively to any of them. The commuter, by contrast, is committed to more than one high-density identity attribute and must therefore divide his time between two or more identities. In short, individuals who have more than one strong identity commitment must find a way to negotiate their polygamous identity commitments or make a choice among the commitments. An example of someone who valued identity monogamy to the point where he could not cope with the dual strong identity commitments of a commuter is Dimitrius Underwood, a college football star, who in 1999 walked away from the Minnesota Vikings training camp the day after signing a $5.3 million contract, claiming that he was unable to balance two commitments: God and football. Although there are part-time ministers in the NFL who are able to excel at both football and the clergy, Underwood rejected this polygamous option. As he explains it, he had to choose between football and God and give 100 percent to whichever one he chose; in his view there was no room to do both.

> I was pretty fanatical, the type to sleep in the weight room. That shows I'm the type of person who goes for the gusto and gives 100% when I commit to do something. That's why this [conflict between choosing football or religion] happened. How can I give 100% to God and play football too?[6]

Notice that Underwood, in calling himself "the *type* of person who . . . gives 100% when [committing] to do something," admits that he is compelled to go all the way when making a commitment, not to integrate and give less than a 100 percent commitment. During his college years he was committed to football as a lifestyle even to the point of sleeping in the weight room. After college he felt constrained to choose between his two true loves, football and religion; he decided, after leaving the Vikings, to marry himself entirely to his religious identity and become a preacher. His family, however, pressured him to reconsider his choice and he honored their wishes by reentering football instead. Shortly thereafter he stabbed himself in a suicide attempt while chanting "I'm not worthy of God."[7] His friends and relatives blamed his temple, which they described as a cult.

---

6. See Bell (1999:14C).
7. Hoffman 1999.

Underwood's case is an extreme example of the conflict that can occur when two strong identities compete for the position of "core self." In contrast to Underwood's attempts to choose one lifestyle and commit to it, commuters balance their two commitments in time cycles. Interestingly, one of Underwood's would-be Vikings teammates—Chris Carter—is a commuter who is both an ordained minister and an all-pro wide receiver. Carter gives his all as a minister in the football off season and on the gridiron during football season. From Carter's perspective as a commuter it is possible to balance two very strong identity commitments by giving 100 percent to each in its respective season. Carter's case is important from the commuter's point of view because it shows that the divided identity commitments of the commuter need not always contribute to a strained and conflicted identity or to poor performances in divided fields. Indeed, while lifestylers and integrators often focus on the pathology of commuters and their double lives, commuting allows one to have a few strong identity commitments without being too unidimensional (as the commuter believes the lifestyler is) or too unfocused and spread too thin (as the commuter believes the integrator is). From this perspective, commuting offers a sensible middle ground.

The commuter maintains a strong committed relationship with two or more different selves. She can be fully committed to an occupational identity on weekdays, an erotically based identity at night, a hobby identity on weekends, a religious identity on Sabbath days, and an ethnic identity on key holidays. The commuter sacrifices the durational intensity of having one permanent lifestyle, but she also sacrifices the breadth of the integrator's many simultaneous overlapping commitments. After all, her church friends don't socialize with her ethnic friends, and she is unwilling to sacrifice her hobby time to take that computer course that meets every other Saturday. She temporally brackets her life into a few highly focused identities to avoid the integrator's lack of focus, but creates multiple courses in her menu of self to avoid the lifestyler's singularity.

In fact, commuters do not, as integrators and lifestylers assume, always feel torn by living a double (or higher multiple) life. Take for instance the nonchalant reaction of John Gross (2002:68) to growing up in England with a dual identity. In *A Double Thread: Growing Up English and Jewish in London* he describes his childhood as divided between two different lives but not conflicted:

> It wasn't only at school that Englishness was instilled. The whole town offered a daily lesson in the subject, simply by being what it was. And meanwhile my Jewish life at this period . . . was largely confined to home. The sense of contrast between the two worlds, English and Jewish, ran deep. I must sometimes have felt, even then, as though I had been assigned simultaneous roles in two different plays. Yet I can't recall being especially troubled by the dual destiny. What it principally suggested was not so much conflict as inconsistency.

Note the similarity between Gross's statement and those of my gay commuters in chapter 3. Contrary to the integrators' and lifestylers' view that an individual must have a stable, coherent identity, many commuters do not feel deeply conflicted about their mobile and changing identities. I would add to Gross's point that not only can one play a character in two different plays, but that the commuter may often play a lead role in both plays. Recall, for instance, how some gay commuters in chapter 3 could work their identity as the lead frat guy or the lead corporate stud during the day and then head out to work just as hard at being the biggest queen in the bar at night. Similarly, the "work hard, play hard" mentality of some successful career people[8] might also reflect how the commuter may excel in two different universes. We might look at the commuter as someone who does identity work

---

8. Auld (2002) finds, for instance, that heavy and moderate drinkers earn higher incomes than light drinkers and abstainers.

in shifts and who moonlights a second shift of identity at night or on weekends.[9] For the commuter, identity work is shift work.

In contrast to the commuter with her identity shifts, the lifestyler is completely monogamous in his identity commitments. He gives his undivided attention to a single core aspect of his being and finds little time for any attributes that conflict with his core. The idea that an identity can be like a monogamous marriage can be found in texts on identity and in the statements of identity lifestylers themselves. Ezekiel (1995:64) points out that among white supremacists, organizing their entire life around whiteness is metaphorically like being engaged to a lover: "organizing is the leader's jones. He has to have it. Like every jones, it is his world, his lover, his identity. Without it he is nothing; when engaged he is God." For the lifestyler the idea of balancing competing intense commitments is like being committed to more than one lover; it shouldn't be done.

Serial Monogamy, Identity Divorce:
Consistent Grammar with Changing Content

Like other relationships, the relationship to one's self and one's identity changes over time. Duration to an identity can thus be measured over the course of a life as well as over the shorter time units we have focused on so far. Although some lifestylers make a full-time commitment to a single core self and stay married to it forever, many others "mature out"[10] of a particular identity,

---

9. See Melbin (1987:101–16) on the connection between shift work and the night.

10. The term "maturing out" was first applied by Winnick (1962) to addicts who age out of addiction naturally without treatment because of changes over their lifecourse that make heroin use less attractive or less practical. The concept is also sometimes used to refer to juvenile delinquents who "mature out" of crime naturally without the intervention of the criminal justice system. In both cases, aging, lifecourse changes and a greater "stake in conformity" (Toby, 1957), because of new demands on the individual lead to the change. It is likely that changes in identity sometimes follow a similar process.

change commitments, or find a new identity to wed themselves to. Indeed some people seem to adopt a pattern of serially monogamous identity lifestyles, moving from one highly committed identity to another. Under such a pattern of serial monogamy each commitment is taken to its fullest when practiced, but is bracketed after the relationship with the identity ends. Thus, for instance, Monster Kody Scott went from a full-time gang member, to a full-time member of a self-help gang truce organization, to a full-time Muslim; he maintained an intense commitment to each when he was active in the identity, but dropped each commitment when he moved on to the next.[11] Although these different selves appear to contradict one another, Scott simply *divorced himself* from his old identities when he took on new ones. Moreover, whatever identity arena Scott played in, he had to be the "best" at it and not just an average player. One can look at Scott's career at each point and see him as a gang lifestyler, an ex–gang member lifestyler, and a Muslim lifestyler, but one can also see his career in toto as a series of long-term serially monogamous commutes from one lifestyle to the next. We are reminded that "lifestyler" is an ideal type, and that just as lifestylers can be viewed as intensified forms of integrators, they can also be viewed as long-term commuters to an identity.

In essence, we can see varying temporal cycles of identity commutes, ranging from those who commute to more than one identity daily to those who commute to different identities weekly, those who commute seasonally, and those who commute only a few times over the entire lifecourse. Whereas daily, weekly, and seasonal commuters change identity on cyclical bases, the lifecourse commuter makes a few radical changes during the course of a lifetime, usually on a linear basis. The magnitude of the time scale and the linear progression have the effect of creating a qualitative difference between lifestylers and commuters. Whereas some lifestylers can be seen as commuters at the very

---

11. See Scott (1993).

macro level, one might see the integrator as a commuter at the extreme micro level. She moves so rapidly between attributes and identity networks in a single conversation or setting, without the commuter's segregation, that her commutes are subtle and blurred much like the distinctions on her bookshelves and in her CD collections.

Returning to the issue of serially monogamous identities, consider columnist Carolyn Hax's response to a woman who is complaining that her best friend has made an abrupt identity shift from a radical "super feminist" to an antifeminist super stay-at-home mom:

> I can appreciate your frustration with her drastic philosophical flip, but it might be less drastic than you think. She couldn't just be a feminist; she had to be a super-lefty man-hater, right? Now she can't just be a stay-at-home mom, she has to be a super-homebody mom with the one perfect man. After this, expect her to be super-something else—I suspect she's extremely consistent in her need to be radically something.[12]

Note that the letter writer sees a radical identity shift in her friend because she focuses on the *content* of the identity, while Hax implicitly recognizes the grammatical *form* of identity in stating that the person is actually consistently a high-density lifestyler at whatever identity she commits to a long-term relationship with. Similar to Monster Kody Scott, this woman undergoes a radical change in identity every few years, but the grammatical form as a high-density identity-monogamous lifestyler remains consistent.

Similarly, the notion that identity can be mobile and flexible over the lifecourse in a series of serially monogamous relationships to an attribute is reflected well in the following letter from spiritual adventurer Elisabeth Lesser to Huston Smith:

---

12. *Washington Post,* May 18, 2001, C6.

As I have progressed along the path, I've not found it possible to pick just one organized religion. . . . I've noticed
this to be true for many other people, as well. I think that
if done with sensitivity we can follow a path that moves
through a variety of traditions. We don't have to make a
lifelong commitment to one faith in order to plumb its
depths and reap its rewards. I think of my own spiritual
life as one lived in "serial monogamy." I've made a serious
study of one faith (as well as other disciplines like science,
psychology, healing, work, etc.), and then moved on to
immerse myself in another tradition.[13]

Responding to this commuter's "cafeteria-style spirituality" is
Smith, who resides in a position on the lifestyler-integrator side of
the triangle:

I believe that it is most helpful for people to choose one
main meal, to commit [to] and focus on that tradition, and
then to add to it if the need arises. I am a firm believer in
vitamin supplements. Christianity is my main meal to
which I have added several supplements over the years.[14]

What is being debated here is not the content of one's religious
tradition but the *duration* with which one commits to a particular
tradition. For this near-lifestyler with some integrator supplements it matters not so much what religion the commuter commits to, only that she make a full-time commitment to some
religion or mixture of religious elements. For the commuter, however, duration is not an important measure of one's ability to
"plumb the depths" and thus "reap the rewards" of a religion.
Like the woman intensely attached to both her spouse and her
paramour in another city, the commuter believes that as long as

13. Lesser (2001:34).
14. Ibid, 36.

intensity is there and her attention is fully focused on whomever she is with, *her* romance with a spiritual identity can be fulfilling even if it doesn't last forever. Intensity, rather than length of commitment, is likewise seen as the most important component of identity monogamy for season-length commuters. On a sports message board, one avid fan explains why he doesn't take on his identity as a basketball fan or his central role as one of the leading posters on the basketball message board until baseball season is over: "I'm kind of monogamous when it comes to sports, [I concentrate on] only one at a time." As a commuter, he wants to show great depth and this, in his view, requires him to fully commit his attention to one sport—per season. His hedging "kind of" indicates a little ambivalence with calling what is essentially a longish-term commute "monogamous."

Conclusion

Many analysts lament the decline in the stable, coherent self and the increasing fragmentation of self-identity in modern society. At the same time some social actors—lifestylers—do carve out spaces where they can live a single identity in spite of a general societal trend toward multiplicity and fragmentation. Nonetheless, in modern society a permanent lifestyle commitment to a single identity is rare. Competing social networks make increasing demands on our duration and commitment. The permanence of an identity or social self can no longer be taken for granted. Identity promiscuity, identity divorces, and second-shift identity work are increasingly common ways to adapt to a modern heterogeneous society. Modern transportation and communication allow for more rapid commutes from one self or identity to another. In such a context, it is not surprising that disputes arise over the duration of identity.

Traditionalists, both lay and scholarly, yearn for some permanence of self and adhere to the idea of a core inner self that is stable and unchanging. They see identity as having an anchor and a core that is not easily altered by the social environment.

Postmodernists, on the other hand, emphasize the malleability of modern identity and suggest that the self is omnicontextual and ever changing. The debate between traditionalists and postmodernists over the temporal consistency of identity reflects the contested grammatical terrain of identity. Peacocks who treat their identity like a noun and centaurs who regard self-identity as a constellation of adjectives emphasize the permanence of their identity traits and construct or narrate a core self that is relatively fixed. Chameleons, who regard facets of their identity as verblike, point out the temporal and spatial mobility of their identity.

In addition to shifting identities on a daily or weekly basis, people can shift identities seasonally or over the life course. It is noteworthy that many people who commit themselves 100 percent to a single identity often find that upon abandoning that identity they commit themselves 100 percent to a completely new identity. The biker lifestyler who becomes a drinker lifestyler and then an AA lifestyler and then a born-again Christian lifestyler, for instance, maintains a lifestyler strategy but changes the content focus of his lifestyle several times. Thus he is, in some ways, a commuter on a much grander temporal scale. Likewise the full-fledged hedonist who suddenly becomes a born-again Christian fundamentalist in the middle of his lifecourse is leading the commuter's double life linearly at the macro level rather than cyclically at the micro level.

In addition to actual shifts in identity content, individuals may also shift their grammatical strategy within the same identity category over time. Some commuters, for instance, go native, eventually moving to the identity islands they visit, to become lifestylers. Other commuters give in to the struggles of maintaining separate social networks and eventually become integrators. Likewise the sociology-of-deviance concept of maturing out asserts that many young "deviants" slowly become more mainstream and tone down and limit the volume of their deviance (drug use, drinking, etc.) as they get married, get jobs, develop mainstream social networks, and run out of energy and support for their earlier activities; this suggests that for some identities, lifestyling is an option more accessible to the young and single. Although a move to integrating appears to be a common trajectory for people who change identity strategies, it is not the only one; grammar shifts occur in different directions and are related to social structure and life course in myriad ways.

»9«

Density Disputes

Identity Purity vs. Identity Moderation

In *How Race Is Lived in America* (2001), correspondents of the *New York Times* provide glimpses into the lives of individuals as they negotiate their racial identities in the United States. As I read these accounts I was struck by how much the identity strategies of people negotiating their racial identities resemble those of negotiating a gay identity. Although the content of the identity is different, the form in which identity is organized is quite similar. Take, for instance, the identity strategies of Brian Smith:

> Smith says he is giving his sons a racial grounding before they are "tainted" by the world. He himself remains an-

chored in a black world. He is on the board of a black-
owned bank. His best friends are black. He takes family
vacations to Africa. (Correspondents of the *New York
Times*, 2001:259)

Similar to the gay clone lifestylers that Martin Levine (1998) interviewed (see chapter 2), Smith likes to allow his marked identity to blossom free of the diluting and tainting influences of the
outside world. And similar to the gay commuters I interviewed
(see chapter 3), who traveled to Fire Island, San Francisco, and
other gay-specific spaces, Smith chooses his vacation plans based
on his identity membership. For Smith the salience of race is both
high-density and high-duration.

While Smith comes close to being a lifestyler in his retreat to
an all-black world, Richard Castañeda shuffles between two
worlds as a commuter to his Hispanic identity (Correspondents of
the *New York Times*, 2001:261):

[Castañeda] reared his son and daughter in the mostly
Anglo environment of Katy [Texas], where he and his wife,
Christina, fifty-three, an accounting assistant with Exxon-
Mobil Chemical, moved twenty-five years earlier. Yet he
has always regarded San Antonio as home. That is where
his mother's homemade tortillas await. That is where
Spanish is spoken. It is also where the Castañedas go
on many holidays and weekends. . . . Unlike Smith,
Castañeda was determined that his son and daughter
would live in the Anglo mainstream. They could have a
sense of their Mexican heritage, he said, but first they were
American. He did not want them to be harassed for speaking Spanish. "I thought the opportunities were better if my
kids were raised *completely* American," he said [emphasis
added].

Note that consistent with the commuter worldview, being "completely" American requires living in an Anglo neighborhood and

speaking English. To do otherwise is to adulterate, modify, and dilute an "American identity" with too much Mexican flavoring.
Likewise to be completely Mexican it is necessary to return to San
Antonio, to speak Spanish, and to enjoy Mexican cuisine. Castañeda lives two identities (American and Mexican) in relatively
pure forms rather than live one integrated Mexican-American
identity that combines both cultures. He commutes to ethnicity;
his ethnicity is situational and contextual.[1] He is existentially
American in Katy and Mexican in San Antonio. Smith and Castañeda clearly differ in the *duration* of doing their racially marked
identity; Smith is more of a racial identity lifestyler, anchoring his
social self in black social networks, while Castañeda commutes
to be Hispanic and generally limits his Hispanic social networks
to the weekend and holidays. Nonetheless, both maintain a relatively pure and distinct racial self by associating with social
networks comprised exclusively of their own race on either a full-
time (lifestyler) or part-time (commuter) basis. This is very different from an integrator philosophy, which assumes one can be
Hispanic or black and still be simultaneously authentically American, and where the boundaries between an authentic racial-
ethnic self and an authentic American lose their sharpness.

Density and the Social Construction of Authenticity

When sociologist Kathleen Blee was attending a West Coast racist
gathering as part of her research, a Texas skinhead told her he was
disgusted by the event because it was "so mild it was 'something
you could see on the family channel'"; as he explained to Blee,
"he made the long trip to 'get his juices going,' not to be part of
something concocted by 'wimps'" (Blee, 2002:1). Although this

---

1. See Ichiyama, McQuarrie, and Ching (1996) for a discussion of situational
ethnicity as it applies to Hawaiian students in the mainland United States.
They found that Hawaiians' ethnic identity declined in intensity while in
the United States, but that they compensated for this decline by traveling to
affirming Hawaiian-specific social situations.

commuter's[2] identity *content* is unusual, his complaint echoes that of commuters for a broad range of identities. The commuter travels to identity-specific spaces to "get fired up" and to revel in the high-density immersion of the full-identity experience. Upon finding mundane, unmarked elements of everyday life integrated into the marked identity space, the commuter is likely to react against the lack of clear separation between the ordinary world and the extraordinary space. He wants the pure immersion of the identity without any diluting influences and feels that he has been robbed of the authentic experience of the identity if the experience is watered down with nonauxiliary elements. In this case, "women hauling boxes of hamburger buns over to a large grill" made the event too similar to just another middle-American picnic to some of the commuting attendees who had expected a more unadulterated and higher-volume display of racism.[3]

The commuter goes into a setting hoping to capture the experience in its purest and most concentrated form. He seeks identity enclaves, where he can immerse himself into a subcultural identity at its very core. The purer the experience is, the better. The commuter does not want to be a mere bystander but a full-scale participant in the social worlds he visits. Like a tourist who desires the full and authentic experience of the different cultures he travels through, the commuter takes on the setting as completely as possible. When in Rome he does the authentically Roman thing. Indeed, when he performs the identity effectively, he is of-

---

2. I refer to this identity traveler as a commuter because he made a long identity-specific trip to play up his identity and "get his juices going." Given that a skinhead haircut is hard to hide he might more accurately be described as partway on the continuum between a commuter and a lifestyler. Since both lifestylers and commuters favor high density, it should be clear that regardless, he is opposed to what he perceives as the dilution and moderation of the integrator's performance of a racist identity.

3. See Blee (2002:1). Although the display seemed too diluted and tame to some of the attendees, Blee as a nonracist outsider had a quite different reaction; she was horrified by the event and its banal elements did very little to wash out the heavy flavor of racism for her.

ten mistaken by outsiders, and even some insiders, for a native rather than a commuting traveler to the subculture. This, indeed, may be his goal.

The integrator, in contrast to the commuter, wants to remain true to the self he manifests everywhere else. The integrator does not wish to stop living any part of the rest of the self to make room for the extra density required for a 100 percent pure display of any one attribute. Thus, while the commuter immerses himself completely into the setting, the integrator holds back from becoming completely immersed or involved in any particular setting. The integrator may incorporate small elements of the setting, but his main loyalties are to a context-independent self that varies little from one setting to the next. It is this unwillingness to commit full-scale to a specific collective identity or setting that causes both lifestylers and commuters to see integrators as watered down and thus less authentic representatives of a group.

The context independence of the integrator is in stark contrast to the context dependence of the commuter. The integrator maintains a steady and tranquil low-density display, while the commuter moves between an identity that is turned off, or at least very much on the back burner, and one that is on center stage in all its glory. This contrast can be demonstrated with respect to a patriotic American identity. Reflecting the integrator view, Adlai Stevenson saw "patriotic American" as an identity attribute that should remain a low-volume but permanent aspect of the self:

> What do we mean by patriotism in the context of our times? I venture to suggest that what we mean is a sense of national responsibility . . . a patriotism which is not short, frenzied outbursts of emotion, but the tranquil and steady dedication of a lifetime.[4]

Stevenson makes a distinction between integrators and commuters; he attacks patriot commuters on both the duration and

---

4. Stevenson (1953:39).

the density fronts. Arguing that the attribute should not be "short" but rather "steady" and permanent, Stevenson favors quiet consistency over a lifetime to the dramatic intensity of superpatriotic display in select marked times of crisis. His use of the term "tranquil" as a contrast to "frenzied outbursts" also captures the integrator's opposition to high volume.

In comparison to Stevenson's call for a quiet but high-duration integration of the patriotic self, many Americans, in the wake of the terrorist attacks of September 11, 2001, placed their patriotic self on the front burner and turned it all the way up. After 9/11, the *Boston Globe* asked its readers, "What is the most original and inspiring display of patriotism you witnessed over the past week?";[5] a high number of responses mentioned extremely colorful and visible displays including entire roofs, houses, or automobiles painted as American flags. For example, "One of my neighbors painted their car entirely in 3 large stripes; red, white, and blue. American flags were flying from all corners of the car." Similar to the way that the Fourth of July evokes a commute to one's patriot self for a day, 9/11 created an identity-amplifying space for commuters' high-volume displays of a patriotic American identity that are usually more submerged. Army recruiter Glenn DeShields captured the shifting densities in the displays of the commuter: "We want to jump on whatever the hot topic is and then, when it gets pushed to page 3, all we want to focus on is what's on page 1" (Moore, 2002).

For the commuter, like the lifestyler, being authentic to the identity means doing a particular identity in a concentrated manner. In their view, one can't simply put forth a halfhearted effort at doing "vegetarian," "punk," "Asian," "Jewish," or "African American" and be considered genuine authentic; one must do it all the way. Moreover, to do an identity all the way one must do it in conformity to a set of auxiliary attributes that have been cul-

---

5. See http://www.boston.com/news/packages/underattack/message_boards/patriotism/messages9.shtml, retrieved December 28, 2002.

turally or subculturally defined as the requisite ones to the identity. For example, an African American who listens to rap or blues and votes Democratic is generally regarded within the popular culture as more authentically African American than one who listens to country-western music and who votes Libertarian. Similarly, an Orthodox Jew in Skokie is often perceived as more authentically Jewish than a Reform Jew in Rockford.

Just as the gay identity disputes revealed in my data often centered on the distinction between gay purity/authenticity and gay moderation, similar debates play out along ethnicity and other axes of identity. In a study of ethnic identity, for instance, Nagel found that cultural and legal debates arose over how to distinguish ethnic authenticity from ethnic fraud. Nagel (1994:160) asserts that "even when ancestry can be proven, questions arise about the cultural depth of the individual's ethnicity (Was he or she raised on a reservation or in a city? Does he or she speak Spanish?), or the individual's social class (Was he or she raised in the inner-city or the suburbs?)." These concerns about cultural depth are, in fact, density and purity questions about the concentration of identity-specific social networks and the performance of auxiliary characteristics to an identity. In these discussions, ethnicity is implicitly regarded as a quantitative variable that one can have more of or less of. Life experience on a reservation is seen as "more Indian" and thus "more authentically Indian," for instance, than life in the city, because the reservation involves more densely concentrated identity-specific social networks than the city.

Attempts to represent identity authenticity through auxiliary characteristics can sometimes take unusual twists, as when the producers of a TV sitcom starring Korean American Margaret Cho encouraged her to appear more "authentically" Asian American by losing weight and taking on a straitlaced wholesome girl-next-door image instead of her usual live wire rowdy persona (see Savage, 2002:80). Ironically, audiences considered the portrayal "too stereotypical" and the show flopped. This points to the contested definitions of identity authenticity that occur on the axis of density. Lifestylers and commuters see identity authenticity as conforming to a well-defined collective identity with its associated auxiliary characteristics, while integrators see authenticity in maintaining significant elements of their own distinctive flavoring that is distinct from the collective flavor. In essence, lifestylers and commuters see authenticity as a social and sociological issue tied to the subcultural norms of the group, while integrators see it as a personal and psychological issue tied to nuances of the self.

Collective definitions of identity authenticity more clearly separate the marked from the unmarked than individual manifestations of personalized authenticity. These collective definitions weigh heavily in exoticizing minority cultures, but they also allow oppositional cultures to form their own unique communities and lifestyle enclaves and to create an "authentic" identity space that lifestylers can inhabit and commuters can visit. These high-density identity enclaves become the centers of subcultural fashion, identity politics, and artistic expression where lifestylers live and work and commuters visit; integrators sometimes adopt innovations from the enclaves and look to them for consumption cues.

The integrator, unlike the lifestyler or commuter, finds himself at the periphery of a wide range of identity commitments; he partakes of identity in many social realms, but never indulges fully in any specific attribute or realm. The commuter is likely to venture into a smaller number of environments and identity commitments but is more likely to delve deeper into the fewer realms and commitments that he does enter. The lifestyler commits to only one core identity and indulges in it deeply and completely.

Debates over authenticity can be found regularly in identity-specific publications. In the magazine *Vegetarian Times*, letters to the editor from vegetarian lifestylers complaining that the magazine isn't purely vegetarian enough often appear alongside letters praising the magazine for its breadth in appealing beyond a "narrow range" of "real" or "authentic" vegetarians. Two letters from the July 2002 issue reflect the high-density view of vegetarian lifestylers:

I've been a subscriber to *Vegetarian Times,* for several years now. As a vegan, I must say I am growing ever more disappointed with your magazine. You are fooling yourself if you think many of your readers are not vegan. You are delusional to think a vast number of non-vegetarians read your magazine. It is called *Vegetarian Times* for crying out loud. Just who do you think your readers are? (p. 10)

And

I have been a faithful reader of *VT* for over 20 years. Each month, reading my issue has been a way to feel a sense of harmony and purpose with a very special segment of the population, the vegetarian people. . . . It seems to me that *VT* has started compromising its integrity for the sake of money (reaching a wider readership by catering to non-vegetarians), and it saddens me. (p. 10)

In the high-density vegetarian's view, the depth and therefore the authenticity of *Vegetarian Times*'s commitment to "the vegetarian people" is called into question because the magazine is, in their view, compromising its principles by sacrificing depth and purity for breadth and marketability in catering to less concentrated, more diluted vegetarians and even nonvegetarians. The magazine responded by emphasizing that its readership was diverse and wanted a broader range of choices and stating that very few subscribers were vegans. A letter from another reader—"I've been a subscriber for some time and although I am not a real vegetarian, I love the magazine. Keep up the good work"—was used to back up the editors' claim that a broad range of people beyond vegetarian lifestylers are integrating a plant-based diet into their lives.

In contrast to the depth and purity of lifestylers and commuters, the integrator's primary value is moderation. The integrator sees herself as multifaceted with a stable essence that cannot be defined by any one trait. She has both moderation and breadth. This contrasts with the identity politics model advanced by lifestylers and commuters that plays up the potency and density of a single "monist" (King, 1988) identity attribute. The monist identity politics model implies mutually exclusive and polarized identity categories; those within each community have a common standpoint, which is clearly distinct from those of the others. The emphasis in the identity politics model is on difference rather than sameness between identity categories. Adherents of the monist identity politics model play up the potency of their identities as a liberating political act and believe that integrators are too willing to let their "core selves" get diluted by and assimilated into other attributes. Lifestylers worry, for instance, that if the purity of an identity is not defended in its most highly concentrated form, the noun will erode into a mere adjective and eventually wash away altogether. Carmichael and Hamilton (1967:55) express the lifestyler view with respect to black racial identity in arguing that integration requires a black person to deny one's self and ultimately threatens to erode the black community entirely: "Integration also means that a black person must give up their identity, deny their heritage. . . . The fact is that integration, as traditionally articulated, would abolish the black community." For lifestylers and commuters, integrating is the biggest threat to maintaining clear and distinct identities.

Integrators, by contrast, worry that too much articulation and emphasis on one attribute will erode the rest of their self. They are concerned that the adjective will monopolize and consume all of their other attributes and reduce their self to a one-dimensional noun. The integrator stresses moderation in part because she wants to get along with and not offend others. Moreover, she does not want to be judged by the extremes of her category. The integrator displays few if any auxiliary characteristics and wants to be judged as a complex individual rather than as a representative of a social category. The integrator often resents the lifestyler because she believes that she is unfairly judged by the lifestyler's conduct. The integrator's dislike of high-density displays is related to the ways in which auxiliary characteristics are used to reinforce stereotypes and prejudice. Stereotyping entails the ascribing of auxiliary characteristics to all members of a category. It involves ascribing auxiliary characteristics not only to lifestylers but also to commuters when they are off time and to integrators, when in fact those characteristics are not present. The integrator thus blames not only the prejudiced outsider but also the high-density insider for presenting the outsider with auxiliary characteristics to observe. For integrators, getting along with and understanding the basics of many subcultures and sharing experiences with many types of people is important. It is so important that integrators will regulate their own flavor to make sure no ingredient becomes too potent.

For lifestylers and commuters, however, the integrator's moderation is a weak representation of an identity attribute important to them. In their view the integrator is to the identity what weak beer is to fine liquor; the integrator is so watered down she poorly represents the category. Christian lifestylers, for instance, will often accuse integrators of not being true Christians because their Christianity is so watered down with secular flavors that their Christianity has no potency left. Some fundamentalist Christians will, in fact, use the term "Christian" only in reference to other fundamentalists. Similarly, some vegans will use the term "vegetarian" only to refer to other vegans. Lifestylers and commuters believe an identity attribute should be foregrounded in a salient and potent manner. The integrator's display of identity is too diluted to be genuine. "Mixing" is a negative thing to lifestylers and commuters because it threatens the purity and distinctiveness of an identity. Just as some members of ethnic groups fear that mixed marriages will lead to the dilution and eventual elimination of their ethnicity, lifestylers in general fear that mixing nonauxiliary characteristics with an identity will ultimately weaken if not eliminate it.

Whereas the lifestyler and the commuter view high-density displays as the most authentic, the integrator views such displays as counterproductive. To the integrator, the lifestyler and commuter are too concerned with the politics of personal style and visibility and not concerned enough with the difficult task of slowly changing hearts and minds in the larger culture through a milder and less oppositional presentation of self. Integrators associate high-density displays with the immaturity of youth and suggest that integration is the natural endpoint of the identity trajectory once one has aged out of higher-density displays. Their view is in opposition to identity scholarship that sees the cultural visibility of the lifestyler as the logical endpoint to identity acceptance.[6] This battle between those concerned with identity density and those concerned with identity moderation is played out in a number of identity categories.

In a familiar context where the term "moderation" is used, one might think of the person who has one daily drink with dinner as a sort of drinker integrator who integrates rather than brackets his identity as an alcohol drinker. This drinker contrasts himself with such drinker commuters as weekend party animals and binge drinkers, and with drinker lifestylers who organize the core of their identity around their attribute as an alcohol drinker. I should note that while in the context of vice there is clearly a negative connotation associated with density, it is the intensity of the identity and not the content that the integrator objects to. The Christian who has integrated elements of modern psychology and sociology that he learned in college or other secular reading into his sermons will find the old-time fire-and-brimstone preacher whose sermons remain unadulterated by such elements of secular life embarrassingly overdone and out of touch whether or not the fire-and-brimstone preacher commutes to other identities. For the integrator no attribute should become a singular way of life

---

6. See for instance, Troiden (1989), who sees the stages of sexual identity formation as a move from marginality and rejection to an endpoint of acceptance of one's "true self" and a commitment to the identity that involves "adopting homosexuality as a way of life" (1989:63). Although Troiden's definition of homosexuality as a way of life does not necessarily imply that one must be a lifestyler, it does assume both high density and high duration as the logical endpoints in the formation of an identity.

that supercedes and shapes other attributes, nor should it become the intense burst of salient identity that commuters make it when they binge on identity. That is, the moderation value of integrators that is articulated in the example of alcohol drinker integrators underlies other categories of identity integrators. Fingarette (1988:100) highlights the distinction between high-density activities and low-density thread activities in discussing heavy drinking as a salient component of identity for some drinkers:

> The broad interpretation that best fits the evidence is that heavy drinkers are people for whom drinking has become a central activity in their way of life. By "central activity" I mean any hub of activity (job, religious practice, serious hobby, family or community role) that in part defines and inspires a person's identity, values, conduct and life choices. For example in some people's lives religion is a central activity, a main thread around which life is woven, while for others religion is [a routine, integrated into but not central to one's lifestyle], an incidental decoration, as it were. For some people food or gambling are valued pleasures and recreational activities, but their role is circumscribed; whereas for others life comes to revolve around food or gambling. Just so, for some people having a drink or two is a pleasant occasional practice, but for the long-term heavy drinker life has come to center on drinking—life is pervaded by a preoccupation with drinking, shaped and driven by the quest for drink, drinking situations and drinking friends.

Note that in this analysis, the heavy drinker has something in common with high-density members of other identity categories such as cult members, intense hobbyists, workaholics, and heavy gamblers, who also organize a single attribute as a "way of life" (noun) or as a "central activity" (verb). When Fingarette refers to those who *seek out* "drinking situations and friends"—those he considers heavy drinkers—he implicitly includes commuters as well as lifestylers. Fingarette's observation reflects an integrator's (adjective) isosceles triangle (chapter 5) perspective wherein both lifestylers (nouns) and commuters (verbs) are seen as similar to one another because of the high-density salience they give an identity. For Fingarette, the key to heavy drinking is that the individual comes to organize his or her social situations and social networks around that facet of self. From this perspective whether one does so on a full-time or part-time basis is somewhat less important than that one feels the need to create identity- and activity-specific situations and friendship networks. The act of forming a distinct social network around a specific facet of self is also an act of accentuating the identity's density and significance.

The Densely Concentrated Purist and the Hyphenated Hybrid: Identity by Subtraction and Identity by Addition

While the integrator values moderation, lifestylers and commuters value purity. The concept of purity implies an either-or, binary view of identity (Zerubavel, 1991:34). Committed to clear distinctions between identities, lifestylers and commuters view blending attributes, mixing social networks, combining auxiliary traits from different identity attributes, and other hybridizing activities as threatening to the distinctiveness of identity. Unlike integrators, these identity purists prefer not to live with the contamination of disparate and seemingly incompatible attributes.

Lifestylers and commuters seek to concentrate an identity through subtraction, exclusion, and segregation of nonauxiliary ingredients, while integrators seek to dilute an identity through addition of nonauxiliary ingredients. The integrator, for instance, will say "I am a guy who just happens to be blind" or "I am an accountant who also happens to be Korean" as a way of reminding others that he has other attributes and that his marked attribute is only one adjective in a larger whole. By contrast, the lifestyler will isolate the attribute by saying "I am blind" or "I am a Korean" to accentuate rather than dilute the attribute. This is also reflected in social networks. Both the lifestyler and the commuter maintain identity-specific social networks that will help nurture and accentuate the identity. Their social networks are densely clustered around a specific identity rather than diffusely spread across a range of identity categories. Thus, the density of one's identity becomes observable in part by looking at the relative spread or concentration of an identity attribute in one's social networks. By contrast, the integrator's networks are as mixed as his own constellation of self.

The difference between identity by removing unwanted ingredients and identity by adding wanted ingredients can be illustrated by the distinction between commuters and integrators. Commuters manifest a presentation of self that is carefully crafted to momentarily subtract all facets of their identity that are inappropriate or unwanted in a particular social environment and to leave those facets behind, segregated to a more suitable setting. They then bring to the fore a dormant self that is toned down in other settings. One can argue, of course, that they are adding this dormant attribute (and the auxiliary characteristics that come with it) to the setting, but their primary activity is one of subtracting other facets to make room for this one facet to stand alone. By contrast, integrators present a self that includes an extensive list of disparate ingredients in the hope that no one flavor will stand out and define them.

The integrator articulates the additive strategy in terms like "broadening my horizons" and "expanding my circle of friends," while the lifestyler and commuter use metaphors of "winnowing out" impure elements from their identity-specific environments or "separating the men from the boys" (note also the imputation of maturity to successful lifestyling). They see identity as a zero-sum game where broadening one's horizons weakens one's core, and adding interests and ingredients waters down existing ones. Many identity-specific lifestyler enclaves maintain strict rules about who can and cannot enter in order to maintain the intensity and purity of the group. They also encourage the weakening, if not severing, of ties between the identity insider and outsiders to the identity category.

Disputes between purity and moderation are not necessarily limited to marked social categories. Although organizing unmarked attributes such as "white" or "native" differs from managing marked ones such as "black" or "immigrant" in that integration is more clearly the default strategy, some people do attempt to accentuate and isolate their unmarked attributes. What white lifestylers and white commuters, for instance, have in common is that they are both unhappy with the taken-for-granted unmarked character of whiteness and are attempting to mark it. They want to be judged by auxiliary characteristics of whiteness and demand that white integrators also regard their racial identity as more central. Their strategy is completely opposite the strategy of those in marked categories who want to unmark their identity. Whereas African American integrators attempt to *add* other ingredients of their self to dilute the salience and significance of their racial category and thus unmark it, white lifestylers and commuters attempt to *subtract* attributes other than race in order to concentrate the salience of their racial identity and thus mark it. Integrators seek to dilute an identity through addition, while lifestylers and commuters seek to accentuate an identity by concentrating it and eliminating all other flavors except complementary auxiliary characteristics.

A particularly interesting and salient version of creating a high-density identity through subtraction is the case of individuals who base their core identity on "not doings."[7] Such identities are explicitly defined by subtraction or absence of a behavior or attribute. For example, members of the voluntary simplicity movement base the core facet of their identity and their lifestyle on their lack of consumption.[8] Similarly, some ex-alcoholics, ex-convicts, ex–gang members, and ex–cult members explicitly organize their lifestyle and their social networks around their

---

7. For an excellent analysis of identity based on "not doings" and on forming identities around acts one has never done see Mullaney (2001).
8. For a study of identity within the voluntary simplicity movement, see Grigsby (2000).

opposition to their previous identity and thus still make alcohol, crime, gangs, cults, or consumption (in the case of voluntary simplicity) central to their identity and to their social networks but in a negative rather than an affirmative capacity.

Accentuating Markedness and Washing Out Markedness: Two Competing Density Strategies

As shown in the debates over gay identity described earlier, one strategy (used full-time by lifestylers and part-time by commuters) for organizing a marked identity is to make visible one's markedness and the distinctiveness of one's category, and to use such visibility to fight for collective rights. Another strategy (used full-time by integrators) is to emphasize unmarked ingredients in an attempt to minimize or wash out the flavor of the mark. Intense debates arise over volume between those who wish to accentuate the identity through presentation (commuters when "on" the identity and lifestylers) and those who wish to "tone down" their presentation (commuters when "off" the identity and integrators). Integrators are strongly opposed to high-volume displays and maintain that such displays hurt the image of the collective identity category, while lifestylers and even many commuters see the integrator as hurting the collective identity by compromising its principles and assimilating the identity away. While the integrator sees washing out the flavor of markedness as a positive, the lifestyler sees it as an erosion of identity and principle. The integrator complains that the lifestyler is too rigid and confrontational, while the lifestyler complains that the integrator is too impure and too willing to sell out for acceptance from the majority.

In "What Does It Mean to Be a Jew Today?" (2001), Alvin Snider highlights an integrator answer to the question when he borrows from Midwest-raised Jewish comedian Sandra Bernhard in stating that the "typical Jewish-American experience combines Hanukkah lamps and Hebrew school with lunches consisting of 'a big bowl of Campbell's bean-with-bacon soup and a bologna sandwich with Miracle Whip.'" Snider suggests that small-town Middle American values and Jewishness are a "forced marriage" of identities that works pretty well and that portends the future of Jewish identity as a "hybrid" identity rather than a "pure" and Orthodox one. For Snider a combination of ethnic flavoring and bland Middle American flavoring is not a contradiction. He suggests that while lifestylers perceive bland Midwestern hybrids as dissolving the Jewish community, he celebrates the transformation of Jewish identity from a unified set of auxiliary characteristics to one where the autonomous individual self is not too tightly bound to a collective vision of what it means to be Jewish.

This conflict parallels what social theorist Jeffrey Alexander considers two of the three separate modes of incorporation for minority groups. Alexander (2001:245–46) argues that "hyphenation (neutralizing negative qualities by symbolic association with the core)" and "multiculturalism (purifying subaltern qualities and pluralizing the civil sphere)," are two modes of incorporation. From this perspective the integrator opts for hyphenation and the use of Miracle Whip and other mundane everyday cultural artifacts (part of his ensemble of averageness) to emphasize a bland sameness with the core, while the lifestyler plays up his difference from the core and maintains a gap between himself and the mainstream everyday world by following dietary rules that inhibit eating with non-Jews at mealtimes and thus help enforce social segregation. The commuter, by comparison, plays high density on both sides, alternating between a strategy of multiculturalism that plays up markedness and a strategy of assimilation[9] that plays up unmarkedness. The commuter accentuates markedness in identity-specific spaces and plays up unmarkedness in generic public space. Alexander's description of assimilation captures the commuter's role in performing unmarkedness in the public sphere:

---

9. This is Alexander's other category besides hyphenation and multiculturalism. With assimilation, according to Alexander (2001:243), persons are separated from the qualities of the collective.

Insofar as assimilative processes occur, therefore, persons whose identities are polluted in the private sphere actually are learning how to exhibit new and different primordial qualities in the public sphere. What they are learning is not civil competence per se but how to express civil competence in a different kind of primordial way, as Protestants rather than as Catholics or Jews, as Anglos rather than as Mexicans, as whites rather than as blacks, as northwest Europeans rather than as southern or central Europeans, as middle class rather than working class persons. . . . *In assimilative incorporation the* qualities *that define "foreign" and "different" do not change; rather, the* persons *who are members of foreign and different outgroups are, as it were, allowed to shed these qualities in their public lives.* They can change from being "different" and "foreigners" to being "normal" and "one of us" (Alexander, 2001:244; emphasis in original).

The identity commuter sheds his marked skin in public life and takes on an intentionally generic civic identity. In ordinary, unmarked, everyday public space the commuter presents an ensemble of averageness that allows him to accentuate his unmarked self and fit into the ordinariness of the setting. Only in private spaces and in the relative privacy from the larger culture provided by identity-specific enclaves does the commuter switch skins and play up his markedness. Identity density is something that one can play up or play down, but it is primarily the commuter who uses this to her advantage.

Unlike the commuter, the lifestyler and the integrator are so committed to a coherent self that the thought of an inconsistent identity volume that expands and contracts to match one's setting is unappealing and threatening to their self-consistency. While together in their opposition to the commuter on the dimension of duration, the lifestyler and the integrator are pitted against each other on the dimension of density. Both see the other as threatening the integrity of the identity category. The lifestyler views category coherence as necessary to the integrity of the identity and sees the integrator as damaging this coherence because the integrator adopts attributes that are not generally considered to be auxiliary to the category. The integrator values interdependence among categories and sees the lifestyler's commitment to auxiliary characteristics as stifling to individual variation and to the identity's ability to coexist with other identities. Each sees the other as threatening the integrity of identity largely because they differ on whether identity is mostly a collective or an individual matter. The lifestyler views identity as a collective agreement, while the integrator is more likely to see identity as an idiosyncratic personal decision. The lifestyler claims that the integrator's low density prevents the integrator from living up to her full potential as a member of the category, while the integrator claims that the lifestyler's high density prevents the lifestyler from living up to her full potential as a complete human being.

For the integrator, catering to a general audience rather than to the identity-specialized audiences that lifestylers and commuters merge with is important. Indeed, the debates over potential are largely based on which of these audiences one intends to impress. The lifestyler and the commuter (when on high-density to an identity) are attempting to compete among an audience of identity specialists (e.g., African American specialists, Christian specialists, blues specialists, sports fan specialists) that requires subculturally specific insider knowledge, role models, and argot. The low-density integrator, by comparison, adapts to and interacts among an audience of identity generalists that requires breadth rather than depth in both knowledge and role models.

In communities that are explicitly oppositional in character, such as political activist groups, density disputes are very closely tied with differing conceptions of the group's goals with respect to the unmarked community at large. In Columbia, Missouri, for instance, some political activists choose to problematize the taken-for-granted quality of mainstream life and mark their oppositional stance with high-intensity displays of counterculture identity in hairstyle and T-shirts bearing feminist, antiwar, or anticonsumerist messages. Other activists hold equally oppositional political views but choose to emphasize their conventionality in personal appearance and thus gain more opportunities to befriend and persuade, rather than shock, potential allies among the less politically visible. In the summer of 2002 a conflict occurred over one activist's insistence on carrying a very large Palestinian flag during the weekly street-corner peace protests out of loyalty to a friend who had lost family in Israeli violence. Some of his more integrator-tending colleagues, playing to the larger unmarked community, felt that the flag was not only inappropriate to the particular protest situation, but also so big and "loud" that it overshadowed the smaller protest signs and reduced the protesters' chance of appearing as reasonable neighbors to the rest of the town. Underlying this conflict is the kind of density dispute that often occurs among activists. The activist lifestyler and the activist commuter both want to clearly distinguish themselves from the morally apathetic general society and to jolt the general society into recognition of their values, while the activist integrator wants to convince the general society that he or she is in many ways just like them and thus deserving of having his or her values considered for incorporation within the framework of mainstream ideas.

This distinction is likewise evident in disputes over academic, author, and artist identities. The lifestyler prides himself on being judged favorably among the most concentrated members of his category and on catering to an audience of the most specialized critics, while the integrator prides himself on broad popular appeal and on reaching beyond specialists to a general audience. What is in dispute between lifestylers and integrators is not duration (both put in a full-time commitment to their identity as scholars) but density. Whereas the scholar lifestyler, for instance, sees a brilliant intellectual teaching four classes a semester at a small college and writing books for introductory classroom instruction that reach a large audience as diluting his potential as a scholar, the scholar integrator is equally likely to see the lifestyler who buys out of classroom time with grants and publishes only in highly specialized journals as wasting his full potential as a contributor to the larger community beyond his small esoteric specialization in the academy. In the scholarly spaces of national academic conferences, for instance, there is a hierarchy between those scholars who do research at large universities and those who teach at small colleges and community colleges. Although the community college teacher and textbook writer puts in as much durational commitment to his scholarly identity, he lacks the auxiliary characteristics that specialists in his field value and define as authentic to being a "true scholar." From the lifestyler's perspective the small college textbook writer dilutes the purity of his scholar identity by writing for undergraduates rather than for research specialists. Meanwhile the community college teacher and textbook writer criticizes the "Ivory Tower" insularity and density of scholarly specialists at major research universities as lacking appeal beyond a select group of scholarly insiders. He sees the full-time researcher as too narrowly concentrating his scholar identity within a small academic ghetto of specialists.

Similarly among college athletes, the more integrating student-athlete will lament that the athlete lifestyler isn't living up to his potential as a complete student because his whole identity is wrapped up in athletics at the expense of other characteristics, while the lifestyler athlete will criticize teammates who see themselves as students who are athletes for not living up to their potential as complete athletes.

These debates between purity and moderation, between accentuation and dilution, and between specialization and generalization, center on the issue of density. In the next chapter, I look more closely at another facet of identity that further separates lifestylers from integrators but that also separates lifestylers from commuters—the facet of dominance.

»10«

Dominance Disputes
Identity Singularity vs. Identity Balance

Lifestylers value identity singularity and dominance while commuters and integrators value identity plurality and balance. If we think of one's identity as a diet of self, the lifestyler is an identity univore and the commuter and the integrator are identity omnivores.[1]

---

1. Peterson (1992) presented the idea of cultural "univores" and "omnivores" to distinguish between the insular and genre-specific cultural tastes of those in lower-status occupations and the differentiated and multidimensional cultural tastes of those in high-status occupations. Although Peterson uses the labels only in the context of cultural tastes, his concepts can be expanded to include identity more broadly (both achieved and ascribed identities).

Sociologists Richard Peterson (1992) and Bethany Bryson (1996, 1997) have noted a distinction between univores and omnivores with regard to musical tastes. We can extend these concepts beyond tastes to identity generally. Another way to look at their data is to see that it reflects the dominance/balance split between lifestylers of an aesthetic taste and integrators and commuters. Bryson (1996) shows, for instance, that many music fans have an omnivore's sensibility, enjoying a broad range of musical tastes but lacking intense commitments to any one genre. According to Bryson these people also tend to possess more diverse social networks generally. By contrast, she found musical taste exclusiveness to be highest in the four genres of heavy metal, country, rap, and gospel. Among the fans of these genres are a disproportionate number of univores who are deeply committed to a single musical idiom and who show little interest in the more widely distributed musical tastes of omnivores. Bryson further shows that these are the four genres that omnivores are most likely to exclude from their otherwise inclusive musical tastes (hence "multivore" might be the more precise term). Fans of these four genres are not only more exclusive with their music, but more likely to have exclusive social networks with respect to race, ethnicity, religion, class, and geographic region and to organize their musical tastes around such demographic attributes (see Bryson 1997:141). Moreover, music itself often takes a more central role in the overall identity and central activities of fans of these genres[2] than it does for fans of other genres.

Much of the debate between dominance (or singularity) and balance (or plurality) centers on how much of one's overall self a single identity attribute can and should determine. Some attributes are greedier and define or take up more of the self than others. Marked identities, especially those conferring low status, are more likely to produce larger percentages of univores who orga-

---

2. See, for example, the centrality of heavy metal to the overall lifestyle of its listeners in Gaines (1990). See also Weinstein (2000).

nize their self and their social networks around a single attribute, while unmarked identities allow the individual more freedom to simply regard the identity attribute as one of many and thus confer it no special consideration in determining one's living arrangement, self-definition or social networks.

For the univore, a single characteristic is a greedy identity, while for the omnivore multiple characteristics occupy the self and complement one another. The univore has a hierarchical identity structure where one attribute reigns and the others serve as auxiliary characteristics, while the omnivore has a flattened identity structure where a number of attributes share the same existential rank, with no clear lead attribute. Thus, for example, the artist univore will be defined by her art and will generally only allow auxiliary characteristics that contribute to her artist identity (bohemian, liberal, etc.) to occupy the rest of her self. Or a gun owner lifestyler will consider his hobby central to the self and will thus ensure as much as possible that other attributes such as political orientation (e.g., conservative), regional and rural/urban identification (e.g., Western and rural), organizational affiliation (e.g., the NRA) and gender presentation (e.g., masculine) will generally align with his gun owner identity. By contrast the omnivore artist or gun owner will experience these elements as only a small percentage of his or her self and will not necessarily share the expected auxiliary characteristics. A gun owner integrator or commuter, for instance, might vote Green, live in a northeastern city, and be feminine.

The recent debate over whether or not the Catholic church should lift its requirement of celibacy for priests is centered on the issue of dominance. Many see priest as a greedy occupational identity that requires a hierarchical identity structure where one attribute reigns and the others assist the lead attribute. From this perspective a celibate identity flows down hierarchically as the necessary and only auxiliary sexual identity available to serve a priest identity. From the lifestyler perspective, the priesthood should be a greedy and monogamous identity that necessarily eliminates the possibility of other strong commitments such as a spouse or children that would distract from his singular focus. As priest James Stack explains, celibacy frees the priest from competing commitments and spiritually focuses his energy ("Celibate and Loving It," 2002, C01). Moreover, lifestylers see celibacy as a useful requirement to weed out integrators and commuters who might lack a 100 percent commitment 100 percent of the time. As the Reverend Bill Parent, director of priestly vocations for the Archdiocese of Washington, states the case, "Celibacy is a tremendous help in testing one's seriousness about the commitment. . . . It raises the quality of the candidates who come forth because it provides a natural screen for those who are not as motivated" ("Celibate and Loving It," 2002, C01). For the lifestyler, *focus* is the all-important quality and "balance" is just a euphemism for lack of focus and commitment. In their univorous view, marriage is incompatible with the deep and undivided commitment required of a priest. For the identity omnivore, however, marriage may be a way to expand one's horizons and add breadth to one's self. Opponents of the celibacy requirement[3] see priest as an identity that can coexist with other significant identities such as spouse. They argue that while both identities are important, that it is possible to make space for each attribute in one's overall self and lifestyle. Maintaining that marriage and the priesthood are not incompatible and that the two can be integrated, they suggest that integrating is a sign of maturity and that they are not less authentic for wanting to marry ("Celibate and Loving It," 2002).

---

3. Interestingly, the *Washington Post* article on priests and celibacy ("Celibate and Loving It," 2002) notes that one of the leading proponents of lifting the celibacy ban is "as likely to be clad in his golf shirt as his priestly collar," for this proponent's style of dress further signifies his multidimensional view of the priest identity as something that can be balanced with other elements of self (for more on the importance of clothing as a symbolic cue for how one organizes an identity see Nippert-Eng [1996:50–57]). Wearing a golf shirt is not an auxiliary characteristic of a priest identity, but the identity omnivore sees no problem with wearing a presentation of self that is not directly and exclusively related to the priest persona.

Deep Commitments or Broad Horizons:
Identity Depth vs. Identity Breadth

The Catholic church's refusal to allow priests to expand their horizons by marrying is best understood from a lifestyler's perspective. From their view the priesthood is necessarily a greedy identity that requires a deep commitment, and each new ingredient that is added to the priest's recipe of self threatens to siphon depth from his commitment to be 100 percent priest 100 percent of the time. Classical sociological theorist Georg Simmel (1955:151) captured the dilemma of allowing breadth, in describing the opposition organizations have to their members expanding their diet to include other affiliations:

> The individual may add affiliations with new groups to the single affiliation which has hitherto influenced him in a pervasive and one-sided manner. The mere fact that he does so is sufficient quite apart from the nature of the groups involved, to give him a stronger awareness of individuality in general, and at least to counteract the tendency of taking his initial group's affiliations for granted. For this reason, representatives of the groups with which an individual is affiliated, are already opposed to the mere formality of a new affiliation, even if the purpose of the latter does not involve any competition with the previous group affiliations.

Unless the new affiliation is an auxiliary to the old, its very addition to one's life threatens to shrink the depth of the initial affiliation. This trade-off between depth and breadth is central to many identity disputes. Many organizations related to identity will, in an attempt to preserve the singularity of commitment of their members, attempt to limit their members' outside commitments. Identity lifestylers will often attempt to persuade other members of the category to limit their commitments outside of the identity category.

For the lifestyler, deepening one's commitment to a central attribute enhances self-identity. As a univore, the lifestyler is concerned with depth of commitment rather than breadth of commitments. For the omnivore, by contrast, broadening commitments and expanding horizons to include more attributes enhances one's self-identity. The trade-off between depth and breadth has advantages on both sides. Omnivores have a broader range of social networks and can successfully negotiate more social environments. Univores have an advantage in achieving excellence and in rising to the top of their social environments such as the profession, hobby, or ascribed attribute[4] that they lifestyle. The univore's singularity of focus and commitment allows him or her to devote the undivided attention, and to establish the focused social networks, necessary to specialize and excel in a particular area.

Studies of success, for instance, can be interpreted in terms of the distinction between identity univores and omnivores. Chambliss's (1989) sociological study of competitive swimmers, for example, can be analyzed and reinterpreted using the idea of identity univores and omnivores. Chambliss found that different levels of competitive swimming were not just quantitatively different but that they were qualitatively distinct in revolving around different sets of values, goals, and social networks. At lower levels participants were mostly into competitive swimming as a contributory activity to their recreational and social diet. Some did it to be well-rounded.[5] They enjoyed swimming and their friendships in swimming but it was not the focal point of their lives.

---

4. Becoming a spokesperson for an identity or rising to a leadership position in an identity politics organization are examples of rising to the top of an ascribed attribute.

5. Chambliss (1989:76) lists having well-rounded children as one of the goals of entering kids into competitive swimming among those with lower levels of swimming identity. This value is in sharp contrast to the singularity of Olympic swimmers, who prefer an intense focus on competitive swimming to being well rounded.

These swimmers appear to be swimmer integrators and commuters. By contrast, at the highest levels, such as Olympic swimming, the swimmers' social networks and everyday routines were organized around swimming, they shared elite coaches with other world-class swimmers, and they even trained and lived in swimmer enclaves such as Mission Viejo, California.[6] They are for all intents and purposes swimmer lifestylers.

Chambliss goes on to point out that it is not a unique inner talent or inner calling that makes some swimmers world class and other swimmers only good, but rather mundane things such as reorganizing their routines and their social networks. Although both lifestylers and their critics will often perceive the lifestyler as born that way and possessing an essential quality, Chambliss argues that there is no essential inner talent of world-class athletes. Nor, Chambliss points out, is duration of swimming the key variable (recall that both lifestylers and integrators are high duration). Many ordinary swimmers swim every day and yet never move into elite status. This is largely because they have no real desire to be among the world's elite swimmers; as Chambliss points out, many competitive swimmers consider swimming a fun social activity or good exercise and aren't really intent on becoming Olympic class. For them, swimming is a supplementary dish that broadens their horizons, not the entrée.

I mention the Chambliss study to illustrate that excellence may often correlate with the unidimensional focus of lifestylers. Whereas the integrator is a jack of all trades, the lifestyler is a master of one domain. The chess integrator, for instance, plays chess to sharpen his analytic intelligence or to socialize with others who find the discipline of chess stimulating, but the lifestyling chess player (such as a career grand master) is more interested in a narrow and focused commitment solely to chess. For the former,

---

6. Chambliss (1989:78) cites geographical location, "particularly . . . southern California where . . . everybody swims" as one of several factors that predict excellence as a competitive swimmer.

chess player is merely a part of a larger whole; for the latter it is more of a greedy consumer of the whole.

Focus and Balance:
Undivided and Divided Identity Commitments

For lifestylers, authenticity to the category as measured by a singular focused commitment to one attribute is most important. Integrators and commuters, by contrast, value balance among categories more than authenticity within a single category. They prefer a multidimensional, balanced identity diet to a full-time undivided commitment to one main identity course.

An example of the identity omnivore's objection to singularity of focus can be seen in one Oregon pastor's objection to another local church letting social activism dominate its entire agenda; in this pastor's view if you are involved only in activism you "have only one string on your banjo and you play it all the time" (Stein, 2001:30). This pastor's complaint is not that the other church brought an inappropriate content (politics) into church, but that the other church lacked balance in its high-density, high-duration approach to religiously driven social activism. On the other hand, it is likely that the pastor of the socially active church sees the first pastor's limited social activism as a diluted practicing of the social message of the Gospel that lacked intensity and duration and thus lacked authenticity.

In a debate over identity balance on a listserv for graduate students in sociology, one camp (the academic lifestylers) argued that any graduate student who wants to survive and complete graduate school must be committed to their dissertation twenty-four hours a day, seven days a week. Students in this camp argued that all other facets of one's life must be put on hold until the dissertation is complete. A graduate student's identity diet must consist of being a full-fledged graduate student and nothing else. Those with other things in their diets were not "serious graduate students" or "real academics." Academic commuters and integrators argued for a more balanced identity diet. Academic commuters argued that one should complete a dissertation by simply setting aside a few hours every day to spend *exclusively* on writing the dissertation and avoiding *all* outside distractions. Often they recommended finding a special place to do this. Thus, in the academic commuter's view, one need only bracket a small amount of time and space where they will be 100 percent academic to complete the dissertation. The rest of the time, they can commute to other selves for balance, while allowing their academic batteries to recharge. One academic commuter advised dissertation writers to

> get a life. Find a boyfriend or girlfriend. Care for a pet or animal and some plants. Take a drive out of town (or a bus ride or train ride) and explore your world. Do a hobby — piano, photography, whatever. Volunteer to teach poor children. If your whole world is in the department and you don't have something worthwhile to come home to, you'll never be happy. You need some *balance* and some outside friends. (emphasis added)

The phrase "get a life" often means "get some balance in your life." Identity omnivores direct this phrase at people who they think are letting one thing consume too much of their lives. Note, in the quote above, that the commuter suggests the lifestyler needs to *travel* out of town to other realms of the world and needs *outside friends* to ensure balance. The commuter suggests balance by traveling to other selves and different social networks, while the integrator argues for balance through mixing social networks. In the view of identity omnivores, finding a partner, getting a hobby, or doing volunteer work will add a new dimension to one's identity and thus help to balance it. Lifestylers, on the other hand, are wary of adding dimensions to their life that might dilute their purity and divide their full-time commitment to an identity.

The idea of balance appears frequently in the writings of identity omnivores. Given the greedy nature of academic identities, some academics have found it necessary to argue that it is still possible to maintain some balance to avoid being consumed by one's career. In an article on academic satisfaction, Gary Marx (2002:117) advises, "don't make your career your life" and lists "a one-dimensional life in which work overwhelmed everything else" first in the things he least admired among some of his role models. It is also worth noting that the second thing he mentioned was "one trick theory or methods ponies," suggesting that his dislike of singularity extends into other areas as well. Marx most closely approximates an integrator in his approach to academic life. He argues that academic work should reach the educated public and not just fellow scholars and complains that many academics consider work that reaches a broader audience as "too diluted" and "scholarly impure" to be considered authentically academic. As he puts it, "In trying to reach for (or at least not exclude) a general audience, one runs the risk of *dilution* and being labeled a popularizer or even a journalist. Books that are accessible are often suspect in the halls of academe [emphasis added]" (Marx, 2002:119). Specialists in other domains, such as the arts, make similar critiques of those who have general appeal. Such broad and diluted appeal is, from the lifestyler's perspective, selling out.

Zerubavel (1999:7), in a guide to writing theses, dissertations, and books, also takes an identity omnivore's approach to managing a scholar's life, arguing that we can become accomplished authors without letting our identity as an author "take over the rest of our life"; it is possible to "lead more well-rounded, balanced lives." He takes a commuter's rather than an integrator's approach to balance. He suggests organizing time into "A-time" for writing, "B-time" for other academic work, and "C-time" for household chores (Zerubavel, 1999:33–35), essentially allowing us to bracket our life into temporally distinct selves as an author, an academic, and a homemaker.

Another debate between identity univores and omnivores can be seen in the controversy over Sylvia Hewlett's *Creating a Life: Professional Women and the Quest for Children* (2002). Hewlett takes an omnivore's stance arguing that one can—and indeed *should*—combine career and childhood and have a multidimensional life. She uses the term "balance" multiple times to discuss the competing demands of workplace and family and argues that women are happiest when they are able to balance both (Hewlett, 2002:294). Critics point out, however, that she asks women to dilute their career aspirations in order to make room for children and thus to sacrifice excellence for balance. Hewlett argues that rather than forgoing children to excel at one's career, women will be happier if they combine a modest career in a family-friendly corporation with marriage and children. In her view, women should not become one-dimensionally defined by their careers at the expense of balancing career with family. As she explains it, focusing on a career "with a laser beam and postponing all else will work for men but not for women" (see Peterson, 2002:1D). She argues against a singularity of purpose characteristic of those who pursue and achieve a high degree of occupational success. Like the graduate student quoted earlier in this chapter, she believes that if one is completely absorbed in an occupation and has nothing to come home to one will lack balance and be unhappy. Reviewers who praise Hewlett emphasize this issue of balance, while critics see Hewlett as asking women to sacrifice too much of their professional aspirations and identity to make room for motherhood. Critics argue that the singular focus of Hewlett's "high-altitude achievers" is responsible for their success and that she is asking them to sacrifice their best quality. From their perspective Hewlett is asking women to sell themselves short by diluting their career focus, while from Hewlett's perspective high-altitude career women are not living up to their full potential because they don't have the right balance of family and work in their lives. Indeed, although Hewlett advocates integration and balance in women's lives, many readers view her as being a stealth "reproduction lifestyler" by implying that *all* women would be more fulfilled by choosing to favor their biological roles from the start and to only integrate career identities at low density.

Balance is presented from a slightly different perspective in Lisa Belkin's *Life's Work: Confessions of an Unbalanced Mom* (2002). Belkin combines the sensibilities of a commuter and an integrator. She argues for a commuter's kind of balance when she says that all of one's roles matter but they don't matter all of the time. She also recognizes the phenomenon of serial lifestylers when she observes that her mother's generation did it all but they did it serially, being first 100 percent committed to the mother identity and later to the career identity. She argues that one cannot give 100 percent each to career, kids, and personal needs at the same time and that this makes it hard, if not impossible, to find a balance between competing demands and identities. One can travel between the mother identity and the career identity to some degree (commuting) and one can combine them to some degree (integrating); Belkin argues that ultimately it's OK to not be 100 percent mother all the time and to make time and space for other activities.

Although a working mother, an academic, or a priest are all achieved identities, the univore/omnivore distinction applies equally to ascribed identities. For the lifestyler, being a bona fide member of an ascribed category is still something one must achieve by demonstrating authenticity and commitment through the manifestation of auxiliary characteristics and through the exclusion of attributes that are seen as inconsistent with the dominant attribute. To the racial lifestyler, for instance, being a true member of the category requires that one maintain a focus on race and demonstrate racial authenticity through actions and life choices. Those who do not focus sufficiently on their racial identity are seen among lifestylers as outsiders to the identity even though they have the requisite ascribed characteristics. Thus, for instance, some black lifestylers will define blacks who "act white" as de facto white or as "oreos" (black on the outside, white on the inside) and white lifestylers will define whites who don't place enough emphasis on their whiteness as lacking a true white racial identity. White racial identity lifestylers, for instance, claim that one's *true* racial identity was on the inside and thus the surface attribute of white skin color is not sufficient to merit the privileges and membership of white racial identity (Blee, 2002:63). According to lifestylers, for true membership in a category one must display the requisite auxiliary characteristics.

Master Status Revisited

The tension between depth and breadth of identity attributes is further reflected in the travel and lifestyle choices of lifestylers, commuters, and integrators. The commuter and the integrator travel to broaden their horizons, while the lifestyler is more inclined to stay in one place and absorb a culture fully at the exclusion of other uncomplementary cultures. Lifestylers tend to move to a marked identity space that accommodates their lifestyle and to stay there for an extended period of time, or in some cases they have lived most of their lives in the same place and have fully adopted the regional culture at the level of an identity lifestyle. Commuters, by contrast, travel among identity spaces. Integrators likewise have mixed social networks that expose them to travel through different social environments.

Travel can, however, sometimes decrease breadth and increase identity singularity and dominance when one travels from a place where one is a member of the unmarked majority group to an area where one is clearly marked as a minority. Some Americans who consider themselves quite multifaceted, for instance, will find that their identity as Americans becomes their central defining attribute when they experience the culture shock of traveling to a third-world country. This is especially apparent in some vacation places like parts of the Bahamas, where gated communities keep American vacationers in an American ghetto where they maintain a safe space separate from the alternative social networks available in the native culture. Similarly, I have talked to African Americans who considered their race and African heritage central in the United States, but who upon traveling to Africa found that their American identity suddenly became central.

In addition to travel, the breadth/depth distinction is played out in social networks. Lifestylers have deep, focused networks within their identity category while integrators have a balance of social networks that extend across a broader range of identity categories but that penetrate only thinly into the various category subcultures. Commuters occupy the middle ground, having some networks that extend with some depth into a subculture, but being involved in too many subcultures to have the lifestyler's depth.

Because the lifestyler is strongly anchored in one community, stays rooted in one space, and has a unidimensional social network, she is likely to have more strong ties and fewer weak ties than commuters or integrators. At the other end of the dominance divide, the multidimensional integrator is likely to have more, but weaker and less concentrated, social ties. Social network theorists (see Granovetter, 1973) have shown that weak ties give an individual access to jobs and other resources because of their broad reach and breadth. Although no one weak tie is predictably advantageous, their sheer breadth and number allow the individual a foot in the door to a wide array of arenas. Metaphorically, the integrator has a foot in many doors, while the lifestyler's entire self penetrates deeply into a single room.

The world of popular junior high school girls provides an extreme example of the integrator's multidimensional world of many weak ties:

> In the race for popularity, girls take on as many friends
> as they can, trying to balance them like so many saucers
> stacked and swaying on a tray. America Online hit the
> jackpot with its Instant Messenger technology, which
> allows girls to exchange cybermessages with their peers
> in real time—actually, about as many online buddies as
> can fit on a single screen. Girls can have a hundred people
> or more on their buddy lists. They can exchange messages
> with five people at once, have someone over at the house,
> and still be on the phone, thus managing multiple relation-
> ships at once. "It's like being able to be on the phone with

six individual conversations!" crowed eighth grader
Selley McCullough. "It's a way to extend your friendships."
(Simmons, 2002:158)

The language of extending rather than deepening commitments is
that of an integrator. The integrator attempts to balance multiple
relationships. Although this example points to multiple individual relationships, the process is similar for collective identity and
organizational relationships. The integrator attempts to balance
multiple affiliations and collective identities at the same time.
Just as her ties to individuals are broad but weak, her ties to different facets of identity are multiple but diluted. Integrators are
particularly appealing to marketers because of their extended social networks and numerous weak social ties. They are important
popularizers who spread elements of an identity beyond the enclaves and into the general culture.

Dominance disputes force us to reexamine the popular sociological concept of the "master status." A long-held belief in both
sociological and popular circles is that highly stigmatized identities constitute a master status that determines one's auxiliary
characteristics and dominates one's worldview, tastes, and self-
definition. A premise behind the master status concept is that
multidimensionality becomes impossible with some identities because the dominance of the master status washes out other attributes. Although this may be a useful heuristic in pointing out that
marked identities often saturate one's self more than unmarked
identities and thus make multidimensionality harder to manage
and balance, many commuters and integrators do balance their
marked and unmarked attributes to form a multidimensional definition and presentation of self.

Commuters and integrators challenge the unidimensional
master status model of self in different ways. For the commuter,
marked attributes are still extremely salient when focused on but
they are not always the focus of attention; there are too many
other attributes that sometimes act as the main course in their
diet of self. *The commuter challenges the permanence of the mas-*

ter status. For the integrator, marked attributes are background at-tributes rather than salient ones; there are too many simultane-ously competing ingredients for the flavor of the marked one to stand alone. *The integrator challenges the hierarchical dominance of the master status.* If we think of prejudice as the ascribing of auxiliary characteristics to all members of an identity category, then one error of prejudice is that it ascribes auxiliary characteris-tics to commuters and integrators and robs them of their right to individual nuance and multidimensionality. Analysts err, how-ever, in assuming that this robbery of marked members' right to individual nuance apart from their collective necessarily limits them to adopting the master status. Although it is true that life-stylers adopt the master status and attempt to battle oppression by redefining the value of the marked status as positive rather than negative, others find strategies to counterattack markedness and to stake a claim, even if only temporary (as in the case of commuters) or partial (as in the case of integrators), to be indi-viduals freed from the trappings of markedness.

»11«

Conclusion

This analysis has shown that there is considerable variation within social categories around how best to express category membership and identity. I have used the ideal types of lifestylers, commuters, and integrators to illustrate the diversity of ways in which individuals can organize an identity attribute. Lifestylers organize their identity as a noun and value dominance. Commuters organize their identity as a series of verbs and value mobility. And integrators organize their identity as a conglomeration of adjectives and value moderation. Each of these strategies has unique benefits and challenges.

Having laid out the ideal types of identity lifestylers (peacocks), commuters (chameleons), and integrators (centaurs) and their disputes over duration, density, and dominance both in a gay-specific and a generic context, I now want to conclude with a few notes about the structural conditions that will create variations in our identity triangle and about the coexisting and competing attributes within individuals that affect strategy choices and that can lead to different grammars to manage different parts of the selves. For theoretical clarity I have emphasized the similarities rather than the differences among different contents of identity that these strategies demarcate. I will now examine more closely structural factors, and factors of interacting identity attributes, that affect and constrain strategy choices to varying degrees. I start with factors that can metaphorically truncate some corners of the lifestyler-commuter-integrator triangle while leaving other corners intact. These are the structural conditions that are likely to distort the lifestyler-commuter-integrator triangle.

Structural Conditions

Oppression Truncates against Integrating and in Favor of Commuting

Had I conducted my empirical study in the 1940s instead of the 1990s, gay men openly integrating into suburban space would have been difficult, if not impossible, to find. Similarly, in some conservative, rural areas it might be hard to find gay integrators even today. Integration is an identity strategy associated with a degree of social acceptance within the larger culture. In order for one to live a marked attribute as only an adjective and not a big deal, other social actors must to some degree collaborate in that definition. The greater the stigma an identity attribute carries, the less possible it is to include that attribute openly in one's public self, experience it phenomenologically as just one part of the self, and integrate oneself fully into social networks that don't include the attribute. Where oppression is severe, the triangle is likely to shrink greatly at the integrator corner and to shrink somewhat at the lifestyler corner leaving most of the room for clustering at the commuter end.

Oppression serves a double function of marginalization. Not only does it render invisible the members of a marked identity in most spaces, but it magnifies their appearance of separateness and difference by making it appear as though all are high-density outsiders in marked spaces and times rather than low-density insiders among the rest of us. Where social stigma is coded at the level of law and practiced at the level of social mores rather than as less rigid social customs, one is likely to find the integrator point of the triangle especially sparsely populated. We see very few crack user and heroin user integrators, for instance, in a society where these substances are regarded as especially hard drugs and those using them are marked as criminals. The Nazi policy of coding Jewish stigma into law and eventually forcibly ghettoizing them and systematically shutting them out of German-integrating space is an extreme example of the way oppression can eat away the integrator corner on the triangle.

Visible Minority Status Truncates against Commuting and in Favor of Lifestyling

Some marked identities are easier to remove from view than others. The physically handicapped, the elderly, racial minorities, and the terminally ill generally cannot easily hide their marked attributes, making commuting very difficult. While they can commute from higher to lower density by altering their presentation of auxiliary characteristics, they can never commute to a zero percent presentational density. They can dim the brightness of markedness but never turn it off entirely since some of their auxiliary characteristics (e.g., skin color for racial identity) cannot easily be turned off. As a consequence they are robbed of the ability to do an identity on low duration. Visible minority status thus truncates against commuting. This creates interesting problems for the oppressed visible minority since in the absence of visibility, oppression would normally truncate in favor of commuting.

Many visible minorities do integrate; how effectively they are able to integrate depends in part on how much their auxiliary characteristics can be diluted. Although some cultural auxiliary characteristics can be diluted, physical ones often cannot. In cases where an identity is highly visible and very stigmatized and much of the stigma is associated with the physical rather than the cultural, even integrating is limited as an option. Where most auxiliary characteristics cannot be dimmed and where duration cannot be minimized and the identity attribute is highly stigmatized, the individual is virtually forced to lifestyle their attribute as a master status. If we think of prejudice as the ascribing of auxiliary characteristics to all members of an identity category, then one error of prejudice is that it casts the net of auxiliary characteristics far too wide and ascribes behavioral auxiliary characteristics to commuters when they are off time and to integrators even when those characteristics are not visible or present. It assumes all members of a category resemble lifestylers and makes no room for nuances within the category. This problem leads the visible minority to be painted into a lifestyler corner when the prejudiced person does not separate physical attributes from assumed auxiliary characteristics.

The fact that visibility pushes away from commuting in the direction of lifestyling is sometimes used by groups otherwise not possessing strong visibility to facilitate solidarity and to strengthen commitment to an identity. Some lifestyler religious sects, for instance, will encourage their members to radically alter their physical appearance so that they cannot easily commute to or integrate back into the rest of the society. Some tattoo collectors who place body art on their face or entire body voluntarily strengthen the permanence of their commitment to an identity by making it an indelible auxiliary characteristic. The spiky, dyed, or supershort haircuts and body piercing of punks is a less extreme (because less permanent) move in this direction.

Low-Cost Attributes Truncate against Lifestyling and in Favor of Integrating

Some identity attributes carry low social costs because they are over axes of identity (such as hobby or cultural taste) that are not viewed as directly tied to political power or because they represent the unmarked pole on a politically or socially charged axis (such as heterosexual identity or white racial identity). As noted in chapter 10, identities not considered greedy because of their unmarked social value or lack of connection to salient disputes are less likely to be lifestyled than socially greedy ones. In an ideal world where there is absolutely no social cost to an identity it is probably the case that most people would choose to be integrators to most of their identities. Commuting and lifestyling, while by no means caused solely by oppression, do tend to be higher for anyone identifying where there are social costs to living an identity openly and around others who don't share in the identity. When an identity carries low social costs it is especially likely to carry a low degree of dominance in one's overall self-identity. Very few stamp collectors, jazz fans, or cooks, for instance, live their identity as a master status. Similarly, fewer Swedish Americans experience their ethnic identity as a master status than Italian Americans or Chinese Americans, and fewer northerners organize a significant portion of their self-identity around their regional identity attribute than southerners.

Yet in the real world there is almost no identity that carries absolutely zero cost. Even such mundane identities as being a sports fan, a role game player, a Democrat, a vegetarian, or a mystery novel fan are likely to carry at least minor costs of social disapproval in certain settings and thus create sufficient costs that some people will prefer the alternate costs of commuting to the identity. Similarly, even unmarked attributes such as being white, heterosexual, male, and Christian carry costs in some contexts and cause people to play down the attribute in some settings or to avoid such settings.

Although the lifestyler point is greatly depopulated, or chopped back with respect to low-cost identities, there are still some people who live an identity content near 100 percent volume and duration, that most people feel can be integrated at extremely low cost, or even with privilege. Society at large often looks askance upon those who take a hobby like antique collecting or raising pets to a high-duration, high-density extreme or who choose to make an unmarked attribute, such as white race or Christianity in the United States, so pervasive to their definition of self and so exclusive to their social networks that they winnow out all influence from outsiders. In the latter cases (those who mark their low-cost pole of a politicized axis and thus increase its cost), lifestyling is often a preemptive response to an eroding privilege, based on the mere fear of becoming marked on the new terms of a secular society that marks religion (as is the case with some Christian lifestylers) or on the new terms of a multiracial society that will mark all races including whites (as in the case of white lifestylers).

Other Factors that Influence Grammar Strategies

Both commuting and lifestyling appear to be more traditionally associated with youth, while integrating often comes with the expanded set of life experiences that commonly accompany age. One frequent lifecourse pattern is for individuals to first commute to and experiment with a marked identity, then to make a clean and complete break from the mainstream or parent culture and to commit to an oppositional subculture as a lifestyler. After that, the accumulation of social capital and its accompanying commitment to stability over mobility or singularity as they age allows them to slowly reintegrate the parent culture with the oppositional culture in a nonhierarchical collage of self. In this model of identity, the move from parent culture to oppositional culture to integrating parallels the way many individuals move from childhood to adolescence to adulthood; they are born into a parent culture, they eventually commute to become more independent, and in the peak of their new identification they may break completely free from and want nothing to do with their parent culture. As they age they begin to reintegrate the two. This sequence of events as it relates to any given identity may be part of an individual's actual growing up, or it may simply follow the same pattern, but later in life. As we have seen, lifecourse-scale movement between identity grammars does not always follow the same path, however, because it is life experience and not age itself that affects people's identity strategies. Therefore, although this pattern of oppression-commuting-lifestyling-integrating may be more common than others, those whose lives have worked out in other patterns show us that this is not the only possible trajectory.

Different geographic contexts also lend themselves to differing degrees of lifestyling, commuting, and integrating. Lifestylers tend to cluster at the urban or rural extremes (albeit very different contents of identity at the two extremes) where group-specific social networks are easier to maintain. Commuting is common in homogeneous environments where some presentations of self are tacitly prescribed and others are proscribed as well as an adaptation that occurs in border areas between different subcultures. An ideal commuter habitat is located in an area where there are many different homogeneous enclaves in close association or where there is a homogeneous identity space located near an oasis of heterogeneity. Integrating is a strategy that is common in a wide variety of environmental settings, but most often in environments that are somewhat heterogeneous and tolerant of a moderate range of variability among identities. Lifestylers and commuters use space to carve out an identity and to give it a distinct subcultural location. It is not only that lifestylers and commuters create identity-specific spaces, but such spaces also help produce more lifestylers and commuters. Likewise, just as integrators and commuters help create unmarked spaces by toning down or submerging their markedness, these spaces in turn produce more integrators and commuters. Geography is both effect and cause of identity strategies. Not only do lifestylers self-select to live in and commuters to spend leisure time in identity-expressive spaces, but over time the spaces themselves have a rubbing-off effect on individual inhabitants. The poignant feeling that you can't go home again is an artifact of the bidirectional interaction between place and self.

The effect of sex and gender on identity grammar is interesting. Sociolinguist James Milroy (1992:86) found that female English speakers in Belfast are more likely than males to conform their speech to the pronunciation norms of the larger language community, though they do not suppress their local dialect entirely. This low-density presentation of a social identity marked in the larger society is characteristic of an integrator's identity strategy. The hypothesis that women are more likely to act as integrators, and thus as conduits for social (including linguistic) mixing and change, I find at least tenable based on informal observation and worthy of further investigation.

A complicating factor in identity grammar strategies is when two highly marked identity attributes interact. In the United States, for instance, black women, lesbians and gays of color, and other members of two politically marked categories have found that the lifestyler model usually requires them to hierarchize their oppressions, reduce dominance, and thus integrate or commute one of their attributes to make room for the other one.[1] For those who experience each identity as an important part of themselves, being asked to submerge one and foreground the other is not an attractive option. Consequently, many members of multiply marked statuses are left with integration. They cannot escape all social oppression in identity enclaves, since those inhabiting them may still oppress them as members of the other marked identity; their only complete escape is an unattractive retreat from social life altogether.[2] They are thus often forced into the integra-

---

1. See, for instance, King (1988) on the role that multiple jeopardies play and on the ways that black women, for example, object to requirements to choose to become either a black lifestyler or a woman lifestyler.
2. The formation of lifestyler enclaves for the dual identity is in theory another option but an increasingly difficult one, since the more oppressions one adds to the mix the smaller the circle of available inhabitants.

tor's compromise of finding reasonably tolerant space where the inhabitants leave one alone or treat markedness as relatively incidental.

Coexisting Identity Grammars in the Self

Having started this chapter at the general level, I now want to address the individual level. For heuristic purposes I have previously separated lifestyling, commuting, and integrating as though they were always mutually exclusive strategies. Although as ideal types they are mutually exclusive, no one in the real world is located *precisely* at any one corner of the triangle. Thus, in the real world an individual can practice a combination of identity strategies. To illustrate this point, I return to Charles, our integrator from the epigraph to chapter 4:

> [My partner and I have] lives that are very typical, typical in every way. We don't fit the gay stereotypes. There's this image that if you're gay you screw around, you do drugs, you get crazy, etc. And that's not necessarily the case. It's not the case at all. We're not screwing everyone in sight. We're not wearing dresses. And on Saturday night you know what I'll be doing? I'll be watching the Yankees in the World Series and screaming and yelling and swearing at the top of my lungs in boxer shorts just like everyone else. (Charles, Yankee fan, October 1996)

At first, Charles sounds like a gay integrator. He talks about his low-volume persona and his lack of gay auxiliary characteristics. Yet at the end of the quote we see on Saturday night a short-duration burst of high-volume behavior around a Yankee fan identity. It appears that Charles is an *integrator* of gay identity, but also a *commuter* to a Yankee fan identity. During the World Series games of 1996, this low-cost variable would be a greater predictor of Charles's behavior (screaming, yelling, and swearing at the top of his lungs), the spaces he inhabits (a local sports bar), and the social networks he associates with (other Yankee fans) than any other attribute. In fact, during a World Series game Yankee fan would be a momentary master status for Charles just as it is for many other baseball fans in the New York area. His primary tribal identification of outsiders and insiders during the game would center almost exclusively around who is and who is not a Yankee fan. Most of the time his Yankee fan self remains dormant (even if not consciously hidden),[3] but in the context of an autumn World Series run he turns his Yankee fan identity on high volume. It goes from an identity in remission to a momentary master status.

How can Charles integrate one identity and commute another? In this case, the two identities can coexist because the density of his Yankee fan identity, while high, has a very low duration as well as a low social cost and thus little dominance in his overall ordering of self. Even among integrators, in the real world no one's life is so balanced and their attributes kept so even all of the time that they never commute to play up or play down facets of their selves when the situational setting strongly encourages it— it's just that the threshold for encouragement needed to elevate one and suppress other aspects of identity is higher. Similarly, even the most segmenting commuter brings some attributes of himself along for the ride across settings, and even the most singularly defined lifestyler still has some characteristics that are not merely derivative from what she experiences as her main "core self."

Yet even though identity grammars are more complicated and variable in actual practice than in theory, these types do resemble reality enough that people can recognize and find uses for them in understanding their own lives. We can see, for instance, that Charles appears to live for the most part as an integrator of his gay and suburban selves or that Mark's preference (p. 119) for mixed

3. It should be noted that even among gay commuters very few consciously intend to be 100 percent hidden to everyone outside gay space and that often the dormancy of their gay self was maintained through a combination of active attempts to mask the identity and passively not presenting the identity or bringing the issue up; the decision depended on the context.

social networks with black, Jewish, and heterosexual integrators is related to the larger strategies by which he organizes his own identity as an integrator of male, gay, suburban, and student identity attributes. Likewise, we can see that Randy's bifurcated straight and gay worlds (chapter 3) reflect a very different way of handling social networks and managing a marked identity.

I invite the reader to play around with these identity strategies in two ways. First, I encourage you to use these categories to examine your own constellation of identity attributes and to think about what aspects of yourself might come closest to the lifestyler (peacock), the commuter (chameleon), and the integrator (centaur). By way of example I describe instances of each of the categories from my graduate student days when I considered myself a graduate student lifestyler, a heavy metal commuter, and a heterosexual integrator. I was in many ways a sociology graduate student lifestyler living in a graduate dorm (a lifestyler ghetto) that was only fifty yards from the sociology department and spending most of my time and investing most of my social networks in the department. Nonetheless, I occasionally commuted to a live heavy metal club where I fully immersed myself in the experience entering the mosh pit and wearing the completely black garb of the most committed metal followers.[4] In order to maintain my reputation as a serious graduate student, I kept this characteristic that is nonauxiliary for academics hidden from my professors and also, for that matter, did not reveal my Ph.D. student identity inside the club. Finally I was a heterosexual integrator, recognizing my sexual identity as a part of my self but preferring mixed straight and gay social networks. Like gay integrators, as a heterosexual integrator I rarely consciously hid my sexual identity nor did I foreground it. Also like many gay integrators, when I was in a space that did not match my sexual identity, I found that people usually assumed my sexual identity to match the space I

---

4. The integrator writer won out over the commuter metal fan in my internal battle over whether or not to include this example in the book.

was in. Thus, when I was in gay space doing research my sexual identity was often masked by default even though my intent was to neither deliberately mask it nor consciously foreground it.

To show how understanding one's preferred dominant form of identity management can be of practical value, I offer one more personal example. My wife realized after reading a draft of this manuscript that what few conflicts we had in our relationship mostly resulted from the fact that I tend to be more of a commuter with a few very intense commitments and she more nearly approximates an integrator with a much broader range of commitments. Prior to reading the draft she had wondered why I was sometimes reluctant to engage in new activities that would expand my horizons, while I was trying to convince her to become more intensely involved in activities we already enjoyed together. My view as a commuter was that we should delve even more deeply into the things we were already interested in and accomplished at. Her view as an integrator was that we had some good interests in common and that we should find more and become exposed to a broader range of human experience together. She wanted to see how we as a couple would react to new situations and people we would encounter. I saw this as spreading our interests too thin and taking time away from our more advanced commitments.[5] Our conflicts were in essence grammar disputes resulting from the different ways commuters and integrators view the world and organize their lives. Once we recognized this dispute, we were able to come up with a reasonable compromise that accommodates both styles of identity grammar. She has become more intense in those areas where we both have interests

---

5. For instance, on vacations we both enjoy going to nature areas to practice our passionate hobby of observing wildlife. When I put on my vacationer hat I become a 100 percent full-time high-density wildlife watcher and perceive all other activities as intrusions. My wife, as more of an integrator, enjoys wildlife watching but also likes the quirky small-town attractions and the cultural offerings of the cities along the way. She prefers a less one-dimensional vacationer identity.

and I have allowed more "side trips" than I would normally make. Having done so, we both feel that we have gained something from deviating from our usual identity strategies.

In addition to practical value in everyday life, these identity grammars provide a general analytic lens onto larger political, social, and cultural debates over collective identity. Thus, I also invite you to go beyond your own personal self-identity to analyze grammar strategies and disputes among the collective identity groups that you are affiliated with or interested in. Among members of a collective you consider important are there some who organize their identity as a noun, others as an adjective, and still others as a verb? Are there disputes over durational and density commitments to the collective identity? Do some people value category authenticity while others value mobility and still others moderation in their category?

Each identity management strategy—living an identity as a noun, doing it as a verb, incorporating it as an adjective—represents a way to organize one's identity, and each grammar standpoint makes its own unique contribution to debates over personal and collective social identity. By analyzing the lifestyler-commuter-integrator triangle from each vantage point to see the competing benefits of commitment, mobility, and moderation we can better understand and address contrasting definitions of and conflicts over social identity. These ideal types remind us that the contested terrain of social identity is complex, dynamic, and multifaceted.

Appendix

Grounded Theory and Analytic Fieldwork

The approach I adopted in my field research combined the perspectives of "grounded theory" (Glaser and Strauss, 1967) and "analytic fieldwork" (Zerubavel, 1980). The grounded theory approach requires that theory emerge from data rather than a priori hypotheses and research questions shaping what data is gathered. Glaser (1992) suggests that grounded theory questions should be formal, neutral questions without a preconceived agenda such as what the main concern of ethnographic subjects in the substantive area under study is and what class of phenomena this issue belongs to. The analytic fieldwork approach requires that one's theoretical concerns drive one's empirical foci. Central to the analytic fieldwork approach is that one abstracts generic patterns rather than factual peculiarities from one's research (Zerubavel, 1980).

When I began interviewing gay men in the suburbs during spring 1992, I employed the types of open-ended questions that grounded theory requires so that my interviewees would largely dictate the substantive topics of the interview. The one question I asked all informants was "If you were writing about gay life in the suburbs, what would you focus on?" I expected that informants might discuss levels of oppression, the climate for gay and lesbian rights, responses to AIDS, and a host of other gay issues that were in the news in 1992. But these issues arose only rarely. Instead, informants consistently answered by defining themselves against the kinds of gays they were not. The following is a typical response:

> I would focus on how were not like the flamboyant gay guys you always see on TV. We're just pretty ordinary guys who happen to be gay. We don't act feminine, but we're not body builders either. Most of us have never marched in a pride parade. You know, we're just ordinary people who go to work during the week, go to church some Sundays, and do pretty much what everyone else is doing. It's not very exciting, but that's the way it is and I would want more people to know that.

Given the frequency of such responses, it became clear to me that a central issue among informants was how much they disassociated from the public image of gay life presented by the more visible members of the gay ghettos of San Francisco and New York. In line with Glaser's two orienting questions, I determined that the main concern of subjects was the cultural representation of gay individuals by their urban extremes and that this class of phenomena belonged to the issue of identity. In addition to interviewees distancing themselves from urban gay culture, several talked about adopting a different identity on weekends, or leading double lives. How individuals organize their identity across time and space thus also emerged as a significant issue to pursue further. An advantage of this open-ended approach is that the issues emerged from respondents themselves; before I had even begun to focus on the topic in my own analytic framework, I was able to determine that identity distinctions were important to informants. Having determined that identity was the issue that best captured the class of events emerging from the interviews, I returned to the field with an explicit analytic sensitivity to how individuals manage their identity. Gay identity in the suburbs appeared to be the ideal empirical site from which to further observe this phenomenon.

Although grounded theory is a good starting point for theory construction, I believe that theory-oriented ethnographers benefit from gradually shifting to the more focused theoretical approach of analytic fieldwork. In practice, too much grounded theory has been developed with far more emphasis on groundedness than on theory. Much ethnographic grounded theory has stayed close to the data throughout the research process and eschewed broad theoretical questions for narrower substantive questions. Although many ethnographers' pursuit of specific knowledge about unique subcultures is valuable in its own right, they do not provide the kind of general contribution to social theory and to broad substantive sociological questions that I wanted to pursue. Ethnographers need not forgo exploring the broad general questions that interest theorists, however. Specific substantive phenomena can be effectively used as case studies to highlight broader general theoretical issues.[1] In the tradition of sociologist Erving Goffman, this book attempts to develop a general theory from a specific ethnographic case.

In 1995, I reentered the field using the methodological strategy that Eviatar Zerubavel (1980:25) introduced as "analytical field research." Analytical field research develops a selected focus on empirical issues that will best achieve broader theoretical or epistemological concerns. Thus, it requires focusing on specific conceptual elements and issues rather than capturing all of a subculture in its entirety. I began, therefore, to focus my conversations and interviews on the spatial and temporal organization of identity. I asked more questions about what people did in different places and at different times and how they acted in different contexts. In analyzing my notes I began to bracket off information that was not specifically related to identity. As I began to limit my focus to identity, new patterns emerged. For instance, what I had initially seen as a binary dispute between suburban gays and visible urban gays began to take shape as a three-way dispute among "gay lifestylers," "gay commuters," and "gay integrators." Moreover, parallel disputes could be found in other identity categories such as African Americans, feminists, immigrants, and punk rockers. Similarly, what had looked like a simple divide between "closeted

---

1. See, for instance, Chambliss's (1989) use of a case study of Olympic swimmers to develop a general theory on the stratification of excellence.

gays" and "out gays" suddenly became clear as a conflict among people who treat their identity as a verb, a noun, or an adjective.

Ultimately, the empirical case of gay men (a marked category) in the suburbs (an unmarked setting) provided a theoretically ideal setting from which to examine how individuals spatially and temporally organize and present a marked identity attribute. A generic analytic lens allowed me to see patterns that transcended the specific factual content and context that I was studying. This case is helpful for its illumination of different types of identity strategies and their inner dynamics, and so to me, the key merit of the sample derives from its *theoretical utility* even though learning more about the "everyday gay" may itself also be empirically interesting.

The Informants and the Interviews

The interview data come from formal interviews conducted from 1995 through 1997 with thirty primary informants living in the outer suburbs of New York, and supplementary data come from a hundred short, informal conversations with additional gay men in the area from 1992 through 1998. In the initial grounded theory phase of my research, I found my informants at a suburban bar. As I began to focus on the spatial and temporal dimensions of identity, however, I branched out into different social networks of gay men such as those who commute to urban centers and those who do not go to bars. I met my commuters primarily through research and bar connections with gay men, while I tended to meet integrators as often through my predominantly heterosexual social networks as through my gay ones. Primary informants ranged in age from the early twenties to the late forties. About half were single and half were in relationships ranging from a few months to eighteen years in length. The vast majority were white (twenty-eight primary informants were white, one was Asian, and one was Hispanic). Although most were middle-class or upper middle-class professionals, a few were wealthy, and a few were working class. Formal interviews ranged from one to five hours with a median length of ninety minutes. Some additional interview data from the earlier initial study among eight primary informants (four of whom were also included in the newer list of informants) from 1992 through 1994 is also included in a few cases where it best represents a point that also came out in later interviews. Most interviews took place privately at the homes of the informants. Two-thirds of the formal interviews were transcribed word for word and are reported as transcribed, omitting nonverbal speech sounds (like "um"). In cases where an informant refused to be taped, I took extensive notes with the informant's permission and reconstructed responses as accurately as possible immediately after the interview.

References

Adam, Barry D. 1987. *The Rise of a Gay and Lesbian Movement.*
Boston: Twayne.

Adler, Sy, and Johanna Brenner. 1992. "Gender and Space: Lesbians and
Gay Men in the City." *International Journal of Urban and Regional
Research* 16:24–34.

Alexander, Jeffrey C. 2001. "Theorizing the 'Modes of Incorporation':
Assimilation, Hyphenation, and Multiculturalism as Varieties of
Civil Participation." *Sociological Theory* 19:237–49.

Anderson, Elijah. 1978. *A Place on the Corner.* Chicago: University of
Chicago Press.

Auld, M. Christopher. 2002. "Smoking, Drinking, and Income." Unpub-
lished manuscript, Department of Economics, University of Calgary.

Barker, Roger G., and Herbert F. Wright. [1955] 1971. *Midwest and Its Children.* Hamden, CT: Archon.

Baumgartner, M. P. 1988. *The Moral Order of a Suburb.* New York: Oxford University Press.

Bawer, Bruce. 1993. *A Place at the Table: The Gay Individual in American Society.* New York: Simon and Schuster.

———. 1996. *Beyond Queer: Challenging Gay Left Orthodoxy.* New York: Free Press.

Belkin, Lisa. 2002. *Life's Work: Confessions of an Unbalanced Mom.* New York: Simon and Schuster.

Bell, David. 1991. "Insignificant Others: Lesbian and Gay Geographies." *Area* 23:323–29.

Bell, Jarrett. 1999. "Underwood to Visit Dolphins as 'a Courtesy.'" *USA Today,* August 23, 14C.

Bernstein, Mary. 1997. "Celebration and Suppression: The Strategic Uses of Identity by the Lesbian and Gay Movement." *American Journal of Sociology* 103:531–65.

Black, Donald. 1976. *The Behavior of Law.* New York: Academic Press.

———. 1995. "The Epistemology of Pure Sociology." *Law and Social Inquiry* 20:829–70.

Blee, Kathleen M. 2002. *Inside Organized Racism: Women in the Hate Movement.* Berkeley and Los Angeles: University of California Press.

Brekhus, Wayne. 1996. "Social Marking and the Mental Coloring of Identity: Sexual Identity Construction and Maintenance in the United States." *Sociological Forum* 11:497–522.

———. 1998. "A Sociology of the Unmarked: Redirecting Our Focus." *Sociological Theory* 16:34–51.

———. 2000. "A Mundane Manifesto." *Journal of Mundane Behavior* 1(1):89–106.

Bronski, Michael. 1984. *Culture Clash: The Making of Gay Sensibility.* Boston: South End.

Brunsma, David L., and Kerry Ann Rockquemore. 2000. "Socially Embedded Identities: Theories, Typologies, and Processes of Racial Identity among Biracials." Paper presented at the Annual Meeting of the American Sociological Association, Washington.

Bryson, Bethany. 1996. "Anything but Heavy Metal: Symbolic Excusion and Mutual Dislikes." *American Sociological Review* 61:881–96.

———. 1997. "What about the Univores?: Musical Dislikes and Group

Based Identity Construction among Americans with Low Levels of Education." *Poetics* 25:141–56.

Butler, Judith. 1990. *Gender Trouble: Feminism and the Subversion of Identity.* New York: Routledge.

Carmichael, Stokely, and Charles V. Hamilton. 1967. *Black Power: The Politics of Liberation in America.* New York: Random House.

Castells, Manuel. 1983. *The City and the Grassroots: A Cross-Cultural Theory of Urban Social Movements.* Berkeley and Los Angeles: University of California Press.

"Celibate and Loving It: For Many Priests, True Happiness Lies in the Joining of Self and Church." 2002. *Washington Post,* June 6, C01.

Chambliss, Daniel. 1989. "The Mundanity of Excellence: An Ethnographic Report on Stratification and Olympic Swimmers." *Sociological Theory* 7:70–86.

Chauncey, George. 1994. *Gay New York: Gender, Urban Culture, and the Making of the Gay Male World.* New York: Basic.

Chouinard, Vera, and Ali Grant. 1996. "On Being Not Even Anywhere Near the Project: Ways of Putting Ourselves in the Picture." *Bodyspace: Destabilizing Geographies of Gender and Sexuality,* edited by Nancy Duncan, 170–93. New York: Routledge.

Connell, R. W. 1987. *Gender and Power: Society, the Person, and Sexual Politics.* Stanford: Stanford University Press.

———. 1992. "A Very Straight Gay: Masculinity, Homosexual Experience, and the Dynamics of Gender." *American Sociological Review* 57:735–51.

———. 1995. *Masculinities.* Berkeley and Los Angeles: University of California Press.

Correspondents of the *New York Times.* 2001. *How Race Is Lived in America: Pulling Together, Pulling Apart.* New York: Times Books.

Coser, Lewis. 1974. *Greedy Institutions: Patterns of Undivided Commitment.* New York: Free Press.

Crow, Dennis. 1994. "My Friends in Low Places: Building Identity for Place and Community." *Environment and Planning D: Society and Space* 12:403–19.

D'Emilio, John. 1983. *Sexual Politics, Sexual Communities: The Making of a Homosexual Minority in the United States, 1940–1970.* Chicago: University of Chicago Press.

Davis, Mike. 1998. *The Ecology of Fear: Los Angeles and the Imagination of Disaster.* New York: Holt.

Davis, Murray S. 1983. *Smut: Erotic Reality/Obscene Ideology.* Chicago: University of Chicago Press.

———. 2001. *Aphoristics: How "Interesting Ideas" Turn the World Inside Out.* Indian Lake, NY: Superior Books.

Davis, Tim. 1995. "The Diversity of Queer Politics and the Redefinition of Sexual Identity and Community in Urban Spaces." In *Mapping Desire: Geographies of Sexuality,* edited by David Bell and Gill Valentine, 284–303. New York: Routledge.

Dilallo, Kevin, and Jack Krumholtz. 1994. *The Unofficial Gay Manual: Living the Lifestyle (or at Least Appearing to).* New York: Main Street.

Douglas, Mary. 1966. *Purity and Danger: An Analysis of Concepts of Pollution and Taboo.* New York: Praeger.

Durkheim, Emile. 1982. *The Rules of Sociological Method.* Edited by Steven Lukes. New York: Free Press.

Durkheim, Emile, and Marcel Mauss. [1903] 1963. *Primitive Classification.* Translated and edited by Rodney Needham. Chicago: University of Chicago Press.

Epstein, Steven. 1987. "Gay Politics, Ethnic Identity: The Limits of Social Constructionism." *Socialist Review* 43/44:9–54.

Erikson, Kai T. 1966. *Wayward Puritans: A Study in the Sociology of Deviance.* New York: Wiley.

Esterberg, Kristin G. 1996. "A Certain Swagger When I Walk: Performing Lesbian Identity." In *Queer Theory/Sociology,* edited by Steven Seidman, 259–79. Cambridge, MA: Blackwell.

Ezekiel, Raphael. 1995. *The Racist Mind: Portraits of American Neo-Nazis and Klansmen.* New York: Viking.

Feagin, Joe. 1991. "The Continuing Significance of Race: Antiblack Discrimination in Public Places." *American Sociological Review* 56:101–16.

Fingarette, Herbert. 1988. *Heavy Drinking: The Myth of Alcoholism as a Disease.* Berkeley and Los Angeles: University of California Press.

Fischer, Claude S. 1975. "Toward a Subcultural Theory of Urbanism." *American Journal of Sociology* 80:1319–30, 1337–41.

Flanagan, Owen. 2002. *The Problem of the Soul: Two Visions of Mind and How to Reconcile Them.* New York: Basic.

Fleck, Ludwik. [1935] 1979. *Genesis and Development of a Scientific Fact.* Chicago: University of Chicago Press.

Forest, Benjamin. 1995. "West Hollywood as Symbol: The Significance of Place in the Construction of Gay Identity." *Environment and Planning D: Society and Space* 13:133–57.

Fox, Kathryn J. 1997. "Real Punks and Pretenders: The Social Organization of a Counterculture." In *Constructions of Deviance: Social Power, Context, and Interaction,* 2d ed., edited by Patricia A. Adler and Peter Adler, 343–58. Belmont, CA: Wadsworth.

Gaines, Donna. 1990. *Teenage Wasteland: Suburbia's Dead End Kids.* New York: Pantheon.

Gardner, Carol Brooks. 1994. "A Family among Strangers: Kinship Claims among Gay Men in Public Places." In *The Community of the Streets,* edited by Dan Chekki, 95–118. Greenwich, CT: JAI Press.

Garfinkel, Harold. 1967. *Studies in Ethnomethodology.* Englewood Cliffs, NJ: Prentice-Hall.

Geertz, Clifford. 1973. "Thick Description: Toward an Interpretive Theory of Culture." In *The Interpretation of Cultures,* 3–30. New York: Basic.

Gergen, Kenneth. 1991. *The Saturated Self.* New York: Basic.

Glaser, Barney G. 1992. *Basics of Grounded Theory Analysis: Emergence vs. Forcing.* Mill Valley, CA: Sociology Press.

Glaser, Barney G., and Anselm Strauss. 1967. *The Discovery of Grounded Theory.* Chicago: Aldine.

Goffman, Erving. 1959. *The Presentation of Self in Everyday Life.* Garden City, NY: Doubleday Anchor.

———. 1963a. *Behavior in Public Places: Notes on the Social Organization of Gatherings.* New York: Free Press.

———. 1963b. *Stigma: Notes on the Management of Spoiled Identity.* New York: Simon and Schuster.

Granovetter, Mark. 1973. "Strength of Weak Ties." *American Journal of Sociology* 78:1360–80.

Grazian, David. 2000. "The Fashion of Their Dreams: Nocturnal Identities in a Chicago Blues Club." Paper presented at the Annual Meetings of the American Sociological Association, Washington.

Greenberg, Joseph. 1966. *Language Universals.* The Hague: Mouton.

Grigsby, Mary Elizabeth. 2000. "Buying Time and Getting By: The Voluntary Simplicity Movement." Ph.D. diss., University of Missouri at Columbia.

Gross, John J. 2002. *A Double Thread: Growing Up English and Jewish in London.* Chicago: Dee.

Gupta, Akhil, and James Ferguson. 1992. "Beyond 'Culture': Space, Identity, and the Politics of Difference." *Cultural Anthropology* 7:6–23.

Hayden, Tom. 2001. *Irish on the Inside: In Search of the Soul of Irish America*. Verso: London.

Hequembourg, Amy, and Jorge Arditi. 1999. "Fractured Resistances: The Debate over Assimilationism among Gays and Lesbians in the United States." *Sociological Quarterly* 40:663–80.

Herrell, Richard K. 1992. "The Symbolic Strategies of Chicago's Gay and Lesbian Pride Day Parade." In *Gay Culture in America: Essays from the Field,* edited by Gilbert Herdt, 225–52. Boston: Beacon.

Hewlett, Sylvia Ann. 2002. *Creating a Life: Professional Women and the Quest for Children*. New York: Talk Miramax Books.

Hoffman, Kathy Barks. 1999. "Football a Way of Life for Underwood, but Pressure Caused Problems." Associated Press State and Local Wire (Lansing, MI, October 2).

Hughes, Everett. 1945. "Dilemmas and Contradictions of Status." *American Journal of Sociology* 50:353–59.

Humphreys, Laud. 1970. *Tearoom Trade: Impersonal Sex in Public Places*. Chicago: Aldine.

Ichiyama, M., E. McQuarrie, and K. Ching. 1996. "Contextual Influences on Ethnic Identity among Hawaiian Students in the Mainland United States." *Journal of Cross-Cultural Psychology* 27:458–75.

Jenkins, Richard. 1996. *Social Identity*. London: Routledge.

Jones, Katharine W. 2001. *Accent on Privilege: English Identities and Anglophilia in the U.S.* Philadelphia: Temple University Press.

King, Deborah. 1988. "Multiple Jeopardies, Multiple Consciousness: The Context of a Black Feminist Ideology." *Signs* 4:42–72.

Knopp, Laura. 1992. "Sexuality and the Spatial Dynamics of Capitalism." *Environment and Planning D: Society and Space* 10:651–69.

Koffka, Kurt. 1935. *Principles of Gestalt Psychology*. New York: Harbinger.

Kohler, Wolfgang. 1947. *Gestalt Psychology: An Introduction to New Concepts in Modern Psychology*. New York: Liverright.

Lang, Robert E., and Karen A. Danielsen. 1997. "Gated Communities in America: Walling the World Out?" *Housing Policy Debate* 8:740–75.

Lee, J. A. 1977. "Going Public: A Study in the Sociology of Homosexual Liberation." *Journal of Homosexuality* 3:49–78.

Lesser, Elisabeth. 2001. "The Adventure of Spirituality: Letters from the Heart." *Spirituality and Health Magazine,* spring, 32–39.

LeVay, Simon, and Elisabeth Nonas. 1995. *City of Friends: A Portrait of the Gay and Lesbian Community in America.* Cambridge: MIT Press.

Levine, Martin P. 1979. "Gay Ghetto." In *Gay Men: The Sociology of Male Homosexuality,* edited by Martin P. Levine, 182–204. Boston: Beacon.

———. 1990. "Gay Macho: Ethnography of the Homosexual Clone." Ph.D. diss., New York University.

———. 1998. *Gay Macho: The Life and Death of the Homosexual Clone.* New York: New York University Press.

LRP Publications. 2002. *Workplace Substance Abuse Advisor* 16, no. 14 (June 13).

Martin, Patricia Yancey, and Robert A. Hummer. 1989. "Fraternities and Rape on Campus." *Gender and Society* 3:457–73.

Marx, Gary T. 2002. "Looking for Meaning in All the Right Places: The Search for Academic Satisfaction." In *The Lessons of Criminology,* edited by Gilbert Geis and Mary Dodge, 109–35. Cincinnati: Anderson.

McAdam, Doug. 1986. "Recruitment for High-Risk Activism: The Case of Freedom Summer." *American Journal of Sociology* 92:64–90.

McDowell, Linda. 1995. "Body Work: Heterosexual Gender Performances in City Workplaces." In *Mapping Desire: Geographies of Sexuality,* edited by David Bell and Gill Valentine, 76–95. New York: Routledge.

Melbin, Murray. 1987. *Night as Frontier: Colonizing the World after Dark.* New York: Free Press.

Merton, Robert K. 1968. *Social Theory and Social Structure.* Enlarged ed. New York: Free Press.

Milroy, James. 1992. *Linguistic Variation and Change: On the Historical Sociolinguistics of English.* Oxford: Blackwell.

Minnich, Elizabeth Kamarck. 1990. *Transforming Knowledge.* Philadelphia: Temple University Press.

Moore, Lyford M. "Experts Say Fading of Overt Patriotism Is Normal." *Courier-Post,* March 10 (http://www.southjerseynews.com/terrorswake/m031002d.htm).

Mullaney, Jamie L. 1999. "Making It 'Count': Mental Weighing and Identity Attribution." *Symbolic Interaction* 22:269–83.

———. 2001. "Like a Virgin: Temptation, Resistance, and the Construction of Identities Based on 'Not Doing.'" *Qualitative Sociology* 24:3–24.

Murphy, Sheila, Dan Waldorf, and Craig Reinarman. 1993. "Drifting into

Dealing: Becoming a Cocaine Seller." In *Deviant Behavior: A Text-Reader in the Sociology of Deviance,* edited by Delos H. Kelly, 451–72. New York: St. Martin's.

Murray, Stephen O. 1996. *American Gay.* Chicago: University of Chicago Press.

Nagel, Joane. 1994. "Constructing Identity: Creating and Recreating Ethnic Identity and Culture." *Social Problems* 41:152–76.

Nippert-Eng, Christena. 1996. *Home and Work: Negotiating Boundaries through Everyday Life.* Chicago: University of Chicago Press.

Obol, Sadat. 1994. "When in Rome: Do Your Own Thing." Ph.D. qualifying paper, Rutgers University.

Peake, Linda. 1993. "Race and Sexuality: Challenging the Patriarchal Structuring of Urban Social Space." *Environment and Planning D: Society and Space* 11:415–32.

Peterson, Karen S. 2002. "Having It All—Except Children." *USA Today,* April 7, 1D.

Peterson, Richard A. 1992. "Understanding Audience Segmentation: From Elite and Mass to Omnivore and Univore." *Poetics* 21:243–58.

Pike, Kenneth L. [1954] 1967. *Language in Relation to a Unified Theory of the Structure of Human Behavior.* The Hague: Mouton.

Plummer, Kenneth. 1981. *The Making of the Modern Homosexual.* Totowa, NJ: Barnes and Noble.

Rockquemore, Kerry Ann. 1999. "Between Black and White: Exploring the Biracial Experience." *Race and Society* 1:197–212.

Savage, Dan. 2002. "Margaret Cho Gets a Dose of Savage Love" (interview). *Mother Jones,* May/June, 80–81.

Schwalbe, Michael L., and D. Mason-Shrock. 1996. "Identity Work as Group Process." *Advances in Group Processes* 13:113–47.

Schwartz, Barry. 1981. *Vertical Classification.* Chicago: University of Chicago Press.

Scott, Kody (aka Sanyika Shakur). 1993. *Monster: The Autobiography of an L.A. Gang Member.* New York: Atlantic Monthly Press.

Seidman, Steven. 1996. Introduction to *Queer Theory/Sociology,* edited by Steven Seidman, 1–29. Cambridge, MA: Blackwell.

Seidman, Steven, Chet Meeks, and Frannie Traschen. 1999. "Beyond the Closet? The Changing Social Meaning of Homosexuality in the United States." *Sexualities* 2:9–34.

Signorile, Michelangelo. 1993. *Queer in America.* New York: Random House.

Simmel, Georg. 1955. *Conflict and the Web of Group Affiliations*. Translated by Kurt H. Wolff and Reinhard Bendix. New York: Free Press.

Simmons, Rachel. 2002. *Odd Girl Out: The Hidden Culture of Aggression in Girls*. New York: Harcourt.

Simpson, Ruth. 1996. "Neither Clear Nor Present: The Social Construction of Safety and Danger." *Sociological Forum* 11:549–62.

Snider, Alvin. 2001. "What Does It Mean to Be a Jew Today?" *Chronicle of Higher Education*, November 23, 10.

Stein, Arlene. 1997. *Sex and Sensibility: Stories of a Lesbian Generation*. Berkeley and Los Angeles: University of California Press.

———. 2001. *The Stranger Next Door: The Story of a Small Community's Battle over Sex, Faith, and Civil Rights*. Boston: Beacon.

Stevenson, Adlai E. 1953."The Nature of Patriotism" (speech August 27, 1952, to American Legion Convention, New York City). 39. In *Speeches* (with an introduction by Stevenson), 39. London: Andre Deutch.

Taylor, Verta, and Nicole C. Raeburn. 1995. "Identity Politics as High-Risk Activism: Career Consequences for Lesbian, Gay, and Bisexual Sociologists." *Social Problems* 42:252–73.

Till, Karen. 1993. "Neotraditional Town and Urban Villages: The Cultural Production of a Geography of 'Otherness.'" *Environment and Planning D: Society and Space* 11:709–32.

Toby, Jackson. 1957. "Social Disorganization and Stake in Conformity: Complementary Factors in the Predatory Behavior of Young Hoodlums." *Journal of Criminal Law, Criminology, and Political Science* 48 (May–June):12–17.

Troiden, Richard R. 1979. "Becoming Homosexual: A Model for Gay Identity Acquisition." *Psychiatry* 42:362–73.

———. 1989. "The Formation of Homosexual Identities." *Journal of Homosexuality* 17:43–74.

Trubetzkoy, Nikolaj. 1975. *Letters and Notes*. Edited by Roman Jakobson. The Hague: Mouton.

Tuan, Yi-Fu. 1984. "In Place, out of Place." *Geoscience and Man* 24:3–10.

Vaid, Urvashi. 1996. *Virtual Equality*. New York: Doubleday.

Valentine, Gill. 1993. "(Hetero)sexing Space: Lesbian Perceptions and Experiences of Everyday Spaces." *Society and Space* 11:395–413.

Van Gennep, Arnold. [1908] 1960. *The Rites of Passage*. Chicago: University of Chicago Press.

Vinitzky-Seroussi, Vered. 1998. *After Pomp and Circumstance: High*

School Reunion as an Autobiographical Occasion. Chicago: University of Chicago Press.

Waldrop, M. Mitchell. 1992. *Complexity: The Emerging Science at the Edge of Order and Chaos.* New York: Simon and Schuster.

Walters, Suzanna Danuta. 2001. *All the Rage: The Story of Gay Visibility in America.* Chicago: University of Chicago Press.

Waters, Mary. 1990. *Ethnic Options: Choosing Identities in America.* Berkeley and Los Angeles: University of California Press.

Watson, Tracey. 1987. "Women Athletes and Athletic Women: The Dilemmas and Contradictions of Managing Incongruent Identities." *Sociological Inquiry* 57:431–46.

Waugh, Linda. 1982. "Marked and Unmarked: A Choice between Unequals in Semiotic Structure." *Semiotica* 38:299–318.

Weber, Max. [1925] 1978. *Economy and Society.* Berkeley and Los Angeles: University of California Press.

Weeks, Jeffrey. 1985. *Sexuality and Its Discontents: Meanings, Myths, and Modern Sexualities.* London: Routledge and Kegan Paul.

Weightman, Barbara A. 1980. "Gay Bars as Private Places." *Landscape* 24:9–16.

Weinstein, Deena. 2000. *Heavy Metal: The Music and Its Culture.* Rev. ed. New York: Da Capo.

West, Candace, and Sarah Fenstermaker. 1995. "Doing Difference." *Gender and Society* 9:8–37.

West, Candace, and Don H. Zimmerman. 1987. "Doing Gender." *Gender and Society* 1:125–51.

Williams, Richard. 1990. *Hierarchical Structures and Social Value: The Creation of Black and Irish Identities in the United States.* Cambridge: Cambridge University Press.

———. 1995. "Introduction: Challenges to the Homogenization of 'African-American.'" *Sociological Forum* 10:535–46.

Winnick, C. 1962. "Maturing out of Narcotic Addiction." *United Nations Bulletin on Narcotics* 14:1–7.

Woods, James D. 1993. *The Corporate Closet: The Professional Lives of Gay Men in America.* New York: Free Press.

Zerubavel, Eviatar. 1980. "If Simmel Were a Fieldworker: On Formal Sociological Theory and Analytical Field Research." *Symbolic Interaction* 3:25–33.

———. 1981. *Hidden Rhythms: Schedules and Calendars in Social Life.* Chicago: University of Chicago Press.

———. 1982. "Personal Information and Social Life." *Symbolic Interaction* 5:97–109.

———. 1991. *The Fine Line: Making Distinctions in Everyday Life.* New York: Free Press.

———. 1996. "Lumping and Splitting: Notes on Social Classification." *Sociological Forum* 11:421–33.

———. 1997. *Social Mindscapes: An Invitation to Cognitive Sociology.* Cambridge: Harvard University Press.

———. 1999. *The Clockwork Muse: A Practical Guide to Writing Theses, Dissertations, and Books.* Cambridge: Harvard University Press.

Subject Index

Author Index